ALICE WALKER

ALICE WALKER

A Critical Companion

Gerri Bates

CRITICAL COMPANIONS TO POPULAR CONTEMPORARY WRITERS
Kathleen Gregory Klein, Series Editor

Greenwood Press
Westport, Connecticut • London

Library of Congress Cataloging-in-Publication Data

Bates, Gerri.
    Alice Walker: a critical companion / Gerri Bates.
      p. cm. — (Critical companions to popular contemporary writers, ISSN 1082–4979)
    Includes bibliographical references (p.) and index.
    ISBN 0–313–32024–1 (alk. paper)
    1. Walker, Alice, 1944—Criticism and interpretation—Handbooks, manuals, etc.
2. Women and literature—United States—History—20th century—Handbooks,
manuals, etc. 3. African Americans in literature—Handbooks, manuals, etc.
I. Title. II. Series.
  PS3573.A425Z57 2005
  813′.54—dc22   2005020066

British Library Cataloguing in Publication Data is available.

Library of Congress Catalog Card Number: 2005020066
ISBN: 0–313–32024–1
ISSN: 1082–4979

First published in 2005

Greenwood Press, 88 Post Road West, Westport, CT 06881
An imprint of Greenwood Publishing Group, Inc.
www.greenwood.com

Printed in the United States of America

The paper used in this book complies with the
Permanent Paper Standard issued by the National
Information Standards Organization (Z39.48–1984).

10 9 8 7 6 5 4 3 2 1

For My Professors

Dr. Jean Fisher Turpin
1910–99
Professor Emerita, Morgan State University

Dr. Harry L. Jones
1924–97
Professor Emeritus, Morgan State University

Dr. Mary Jane Lupton
1938–
Professor Emerita, Morgan State University

Contents

Series Foreword

The authors who appear in the series Critical Companions to Popular Contemporary Writers are all best-selling writers. They do not simply have one successful novel, but a string of them. Fans, critics, and specialist readers eagerly anticipate their next book. For some, high cash advances and breakthrough sales figures are automatic; movie deals often follow. Some writers become household names, recognized by almost everyone.

But, their novels are read one by one. Each reader chooses to start and, more importantly, to finish a book because of what she or he finds there. The real test of a novel is in the satisfaction its readers experience. This series acknowledges the extraordinary involvement of readers and writers in creating a best seller.

The authors included in this series were chosen by an Advisory Board composed of high school English teachers and high school and public librarians. They ranked a list of best-selling writers according to their popularity among different groups of readers. For the first series, writers in the top-ranked group who had received no book-length, academic, literary analysis (or none in at least the past 10 years) were chosen. Because of this selection method, Critical Companions to Popular Contemporary Writers meets a need that is being addressed nowhere else. The success of these volumes as reported by reviewers, librarians, and teachers led to an expansion of the series mandate to include some writers with wide critical attention—Toni Morrison, John Irving, and Maya Angelou, for example—to extend the usefulness of the series.

The volumes in the series are written by scholars with particular expertise in analyzing popular fiction. These specialists add an academic focus to the popular success that these writers already enjoy.

The series is designed to appeal to a wide range of readers. The general reading public will find explanations for the appeal of these well-known writers. Fans will find biographical and fictional questions answered. Students will find literary analysis, discussions of fictional genres, carefully organized introductions to new ways of reading the novels, and bibliographies for additional research. Whether browsing through the book for pleasure or using it for an assignment, readers will find that the most recent novels of the authors are included.

Each volume begins with a biographical chapter drawing on published information, autobiographies or memoirs, prior interviews, and, in some cases, interviews given especially for this series. A chapter on literary history and genres describes how the author's work fits into a larger literary context. The following chapters analyze the writer's most important, most popular, and most recent novels in detail. Each chapter focuses on one or more novels. This approach, suggested by the Advisory Board as the most useful to student research, allows for an in-depth analysis of the writer's fiction. Close and careful readings with numerous examples show readers exactly how the novels work. These chapters are organized around three central elements: plot development (how the story line moves forward), character development (what the reader knows of the important figures), and theme (the significant ideas of the novel). Chapters may also include sections on generic conventions (how the novel is similar or different from others in its same category of science fiction, fantasy, thriller, etc.), narrative point of view (who tells the story and how), symbols and literary language, and historical or social context. Each chapter ends with an "alternative reading" of the novel. The volume concludes with a primary and secondary bibliography, including reviews.

The alternative readings are a unique feature of this series. By demonstrating a particular way of reading each novel, they provide a clear example of how a specific perspective can reveal important aspects of the book. In the alternative reading sections, one contemporary literary theory—way of reading, such as feminist criticism, Marxism, new historicism, deconstruction, or Jungian psychological critique—is defined in brief, easily comprehensible language. That definition is then applied to the novel to highlight specific features that might go unnoticed or be understood differently in a more general reading. Each volume defines two or three specific theories, making them part of the reader's understanding of how diverse meanings may be constructed from a single novel.

Taken collectively, the volumes in the Critical Companions to Popular Contemporary Writers series provide a wide-ranging investigation of the complexities of current best-selling fiction. By treating these novels seriously as both literary works and publishing successes, the series demonstrates the potential of popular literature in contemporary culture.

Kathleen Gregory Klein
Southern Connecticut State University

Acknowledgments

Thank you
Roddie Anne Blackwell
Eatonton-Putnam Chamber of Commerce
Eatonton, Georgia

Thank you
Judy Kicinski
Sarah Lawrence College Library

Thank you
Kathy Kline, Debra Adams, and Apex Publishing

Thank you
Alice Walker
For a moment of your time at your book signing
Washington, D.C.

Thank you
"King of Hearts"

1

The Life of Alice Walker

A godsend arose in Detroit, Michigan, in 1965 in the person of Dudley Randall (1914–2000). The deaths of four innocent little girls in a Birmingham, Alabama, bombed church in 1963 moved Randall to compose "The Ballad of Birmingham," which he published as a broadside sheet and called a Broadside Press publication. His vision was to establish a publishing house that would reach unknown writers, create a sense of community, and build relationships. With $12 and an unused bedroom where he set up printing equipment, Randall started Broadside Press, an alternative to mainstream publishing houses that denied access to people of African heritage. He became the inspiration for an extraordinary group of poets and writers who would leave their mark on the Black Arts movement and the turbulent Civil Rights era. Among the many whom he mentored, nurtured, and inspired were the then not-yet-famous Amiri Baraka (LeRoi Jones), Gwendolyn Brooks (1917–2000), Nikki Giovanni (Yolande Cornelia Giovanni), Haki Mahabuti (Don L. Lee), Ron Milner, Sonia Sanchez, and Alice Walker. Randall published Walker's second poetry collection, giving her exposure to African American academics who introduced her poetry to their students. From there she went on to greater literary accomplishments.

The birthplace of Alice (Malsenior) Tallulah-Kate Walker is Eatonton, Georgia, a rural farming town of Putnam County, north of Macon,

Georgia, between Monticello and Sparta. She was born February 9, 1944, a Wednesday. If the line "Wednesday's child is full of woe" from the much-loved juvenile verse has any validity, it may apply to Walker, for she would become a woman of deep sensitivity, taking on causes and expressing through her art form all manner of things gone awry in the world. She is the eighth and last child and third daughter born to Minnie (Lou) Tallulah Grant Walker and Willie Lee Walker, who spent their married years eking out a living primarily as sharecroppers and laborers in a dairy. To compensate for financial shortages, Walker's mother worked in domestic service and as a seamstress. By the time Walker entered the world, her parents were older, had less vitality, less patience, and failing health. Thus, Walker often longed for the robust parental attentiveness that her older siblings had received. The absence of energetic parents sometimes caused her much internal struggle and pain.

Walker's brothers, Willie Fred (b. 1930), William Henry (b. 1934 d. 1996), James Thomas (b. 1935 d. 2002), Robert Louis (b. 1940), and Curtis Ulysses (b. 1942), and her sisters Mamie Lee (b. 1932) and Annie Ruth (b. 1937) assisted their parents in the fields planting, weeding, and picking the cotton and corn that they grew. Baby Alice, too young to be a farmhand and of little help, played gaily among her mother's morning glory vines, initiating herself to the wonders of Mother Nature. Later in life she reflected on the beauty of her mother's flower gardens, which she referred to as her mother's art, culminating in the essay "In Search of Our Mothers' Gardens" and the collection of womanist prose of the same title.

Walker had little contact with people on a day-to-day basis outside of her immediate family, except her parents' employers. This limited contact with strangers contributed to her escape into worlds of fantasy where she engaged in her favorite pastime, "people watching," intensely observing people's facial expressions and watching their actions. As a little girl she looked forward to the highlight of weekly trips into town on Saturdays with her parents and siblings to shop or attend the Saturday night picture shows to watch westerns, for she got to see and observe all the towns-people. She welcomed these trips also because they were an escape from the crowded, inferior housing in which her family lived. Walker loved the outdoors, spending time climbing trees and romping through the fields. Walker believes that her writing is rooted in the need to be surrounded by space and that the best writing topics come to her when she is taking a nature walk (*A Conversation with Alice Walker*).

One of Walker's fondest and most valuable memories from her childhood was the sense of community she felt from her family's membership in the Wards Chapel African Methodist Episcopal Church where she was baptized. This edifice was the sacred space for Christian rituals, prayers, and songs, and the place where the congregation welcomed the first Easter speech of an outgoing little girl who loved to recite before audiences as if her performance were a rite of passage or an initiation into a world of literary and creative forces. Walker, who sensed that members of the congregation believed that she was a pretty little darling, felt secure and affirmed in this church community (*My Life As Myself*). She lost her father, Willie Lee Walker, in 1973 from complications of diabetes, emphysema, and pneumonia and her mother, Minnie Tallulah Grant Walker, whom Walker called her most significant influence, to cardiac arrest in 1993. Their remains lie in Wards Chapel Cemetery along with other ancestors who inspired Walker through their storytelling and encouragement.

Willie Lee Walker, one of the first African American men to vote in Eatonton, wanted his children educated and was an instrumental force in the construction of Putnam County's first school for African American children, although racist white men burned it down. Walker's parents enrolled her in school at the age of four to circumvent the hard labor of the fields. School officials quickly advanced this precocious child to the first grade. Four years after settling into academic life in the little country school, Walker experienced a tragic accident that interrupted her daily routine.

At the age of eight in 1952 tomboy Walker and her brothers played a game of cowboys and Indians—she was the Indian, complete with bow and arrow. Her brother Curtis, using a BB gun that had been a Christmas gift, accidentally shot her with a pellet in the right eye. The injury caused blindness and the development of a white film and the formation of a glob of scar tissue over the sightless eye. The disfigurement was quite distinguishable, and Walker viewed the eye as a deformity, which had a great impact on her life. Her grades suffered and she developed a sad countenance, often feeling ashamed and suicidal. The victim of constant teasing from classmates because of the unsightly eye, her confidence and her belief that she was pretty vanished. Believing that her eye was permanently disfigured, Walker retreated inward, no longer wanting to explore the wide-open spaces of nature, but instead focusing more on reading and writing than on her surroundings. She dreamed of death and ways to accomplish it, considering falling on swords or slashing her wrists. For hours on end she sat reading, undisturbed. People gave her gifts of books. She discovered the European classical authors, reading them over and over again. Her mother felt that reading and writing were medicinal for Walker. This single event, the mishap with the BB gun, more than any other, established her future endeavor. More than 30 years later Walker writes about the life changing injury in "Beauty: When the Other Dancer Is the Self."

Walker's parents neither sternly reprimanded her brother Curtis for his carelessness with the BB gun nor blamed themselves for purchasing it. To her dismay, they instead sent her away to live with her grandparents, since she was the victim of constant ridicule from the neighboring children where the family had moved. A year would pass before she rejoined her family as a member of the household. This parental decision stirred up anger within Walker, for she felt that she had not been the one to err and, therefore, was unjustly punished as the innocent victim. Prior to this incident she imagined herself a scientist, pianist, or painter, but these aspirations were replaced with feelings of alienation. She used to scrape together the weekly cost of piano lessons, 50 cents, by selling eggs given to her by her mother until there were no more eggs to sell and she had to forego the lessons. However, the BB gun occurrence became the impetus for Walker to focus on reading and writing, a pastime that was cheaper than piano lessons. To lift herself out of the slump she began to keep a journal. As she scribbled her emotions on paper, her feelings of sadness, alienation, and suicide lifted from her over time, causing her to feel healed, eventually renewing her zest for life. The journal became a pivotal instrument in her life because she could analyze her feelings from day to day and ascertain the extent of her emotional recovery. Miraculously, keeping the journal helped her to feel whole, a feeling that would later become a very important aspect of her creative art. She still adheres all these years later to the practice of journal writing.

Although the problem causing the disfigurement and deformity, a cataract, was corrected by Massachusetts General Hospital physician Dr. Morris M. Henry (Dr. O. Henry in Walker's "Beauty") on a visit to her brother Bill in Boston—she was his children's babysitter during summer vacations—when Walker was 14, she never regained vision in her right eye.

Walker loved her father, "a fat funny man with beautiful eyes and a subversive wit," but viewed him as a man with shortcomings, namely, sexism. Her father acknowledged the systemic entanglement of racism that trapped him and his family, but he was blind to his own web of sexism. Walker saw him as someone indoctrinated into the patriarchal culture of sexism, incapable of fighting it, refusing to release it. This all-encompassing sexism caused him to treat his wife and his daughters differently from the way he treated his sons. Her father believed that the role of a wife was to cook, clean, and care for children; male children never washed dishes or swept floors; the wife and female children did that. Why? The answer was simply that boys did not do household chores because they were boys. Girls, however, performed house labor and adhered to certain restrictions. They had to be enclosed, shielded, and kept from doing active things. Needless to say, Walker challenged the wisdom of her father.

Walker's reunification with the family after having lived with her grandparents for a year manifested within her a newly emboldened spirit. She challenged her father's system of values and beliefs. The two clashed for years until she left home to attend college. Walker later acknowledged that she had to reexamine herself for long periods in order to reconcile herself with her father. She had to realize that her father could not fathom the injustice of his attitudes. To him his actions were normal everyday life actions, not to be opposed. Walker decided to focus on his other qualities that she loved about him, those things that were difficult to see when her attention was on his not seeing her as a person, not seeing her for who she was, seeing her only as a girl. When she focused on his good qualities and reached out to him as daughter to father, she embraced him warmly (*My Life As Myself*). Because Walker felt that she was always in search of a father figure, she spent a few adult years reuniting and reconciling with him, affirming the father that she loved and admired. However, she understood him better after his death in 1973 than she ever did while he was alive. Her own home was Walker's introduction to patriarchal power. Her relationship with her father and her disdain of sexism appear thematically in her art and her political activism.

Minnie (Lou) Tallulah Grant Walker, whom Walker described as "a large, soft, loving-eyed woman," was her greatest support system, her storytelling inspiration. She loved her mother dearly. Two specific events, cherished memories of her mother, caused Walker to see her in greater depth. The first event took place at her father's funeral in 1973. Her mother looked at him for the final time, her husband for a lifetime now silenced by death, and spoke with civility—no smiles, no tears, no regrets—as if he were standing next to her, "Goodnight Willie Lee, I'll see you in the morning." Hearing her mother's words made Walker realize that the secret to the healing of emotional wounds was forgiveness (*A Conversation with Alice Walker*).

The second event took place at the bedside of Walker's dying mother approximately 20 years later. Walker felt complimented when her mother looked at her and told her daughter that she was "a little mess, ain't you."

Walker took this to mean that her mother acknowledged and sanctioned her rebellious and subversive nature, that the polite, respectful, good girl image that she displayed in the presence of family was just a mask. Walker, believing that her mother approved of the unmasked Walker, the one who had been there all the time, thanked her mother for letting her know that she approved before she made her transition from life to death (Gussow). In honor of her mother, Walker published a collection of poetry entitled *Goodnight Willie Lee, I'll See You in the Morning* (1979). Further testament to the love, honor, and respect that Walker had for her mother is the fact that forgiveness became a central point of Walker's life, fiction, and poetry.

Walker's brothers treated her with cruel, somewhat typical male sibling jesting. She grew up with four of them but played mostly with the two who were two and four years older than she, Curtis and Robert. Her oldest brother, Fred, who showered her with lots of hugs and kisses when she was a toddler, left home when Walker was three years old. When Curtis caused the injury to her eye, he and Robert were more concerned about themselves than they were about going to their parents for help. Dreading physical discipline they pleaded with Walker not to reveal all the facts to their parents. Since they played on a tin roof of a makeshift garage, they asked her to say a protruding wire pierced her eye; she, in severe pain, agreed to the fabrication. Her final vision out of her right eye was a tree growing under the porch that she saw through the slats, its branches climbing beyond the porch's railings reaching to the rooftop. Not knowing the actual events that led to the accident, the parents treated the eye injury homeopathically. Placing lily leaves around her head, her father worked to bring down the fever she developed. Her mother nourished her with soup to no avail, for her appetite was gone. When the eye became infected, Walker's parents made an appointment with the physician, only to be told that they were too late. The bad news was that she would have permanent loss of sight in her right eye, and that the sympathetic eye would deteriorate as well. Fortunately, she retained sight in her left eye. Curtis, guilty because he was responsible for the eye injury, became her protector against the incessant teasing from other children. He came to her defense often, so often that he began to boast about his heroism. Glad to have his support initially, Walker soon tired of his bragging. Today, one of Walker's brothers, Fred, retains a home base in Eatonton for himself and all family members, Grant Plantation, the ancestral home of Minnie (Lou) Tallulah Grant Walker. This home is the gathering place of all the siblings and their descendants whenever they visit Eatonton.

Walker struggled to become close to her two older sisters Molly and Ruth. As a child she felt that Ruth suffered needlessly because of their father's short-tempered negative verbiage toward her, causing Ruth to escape the family home at the first opportunity—marriage. Walker thought Ruth too man-centered, although her behavior most likely resulted from their father's not treating the boys and the girls equally. Molly, a scholarship recipient and world traveler, shared her experiences with the family, telling them about the things she learned at school and the places she visited during her trips to various places. An excellent cook, she often prepared meals for the family that were a change from the usual sharecroppers' food. However, Walker again felt a surge of emotional pain when she learned that Molly was ashamed of the family, felt disdain for their provincial mores, and thought them unworthy of meeting her acquaintances.

What Walker learned was that her sisterhood with them required her comprehension of the oppression of women. Once she understood the limits and the extremes of sisterhood, she moved forward in her relationships with her sisters. The life experiences of Molly and Ruth affected them; those experiences shaped the women that they blossomed into. Therefore, once Walker realized that oppression molds lives, she accepted the frame of sisterhood that she had with them. Walker wrote "For My Sister Molly Who in the Fifties" in honor of her sister. Walker's other sister Ruth heads Walker's The Color Purple Foundation, an educational charity. Moreover, she paid homage to her sister Ruth for the stories she told, for storytelling is a lifeline for Walker. Because Ruth told the stories and Walker wrote them, another component to their sisterhood evolved. Walker used her experiences from these relationships to explore female oppression in her writing.

"Metaphorical richness" is the term Walker uses to describe the storytelling abilities of her parents (Mitgang). Similarly, her grandparents were master storytellers too and often entertained Walker and her siblings with tales from their oral culture. Mary Poole, her father's great-great-great-grandmother, walked from Virginia to Georgia carrying a baby on each hip, an action forced on her by the slave owner. Walker's mother's grandmother Tallulah was Cherokee. Because the Walker family kept stories about their relatives alive, Walker mastered the art form that she grew up hearing.

Walker's best friend from the time when was two until she turned six was Cassie Mae Terrell, affectionately called Sister Terrell. The two loved laughter. They were inseparable, having sleepovers at each of their houses, until Cassie's family moved to New Jersey. Walker saw Cassie again 20 years later, after life and a brutal husband defeated her. The husband denied her the basic necessity of life—food—resulting in Cassie's malnourishment, an end to her attractive features, and silence to her laughter. This turn of events in Cassie's life was one occurrence that led to Walker's interest in women's liberation ideology.

Walker learned valuable lessons of self-sufficiency and independence while growing up in the South, understanding the importance of knowing how to work and how to grow food. The necessity of having a house also was a valuable lesson that she carried into adulthood. Equally valuable was the great respect she developed for elders, which she retained. She never ceased listening to elders, paying attention to them, and really hearing them. Walker expects to receive the same healthy respect from the younger generation that she extends to elders when she assumes her place as an elder. Another advantage of growing up in the South was the kind of adherence to order that was imposed on the African American community, for disorder could so easily lead to humiliation or death. Therefore, a sense of community unity was mandatory.

The part of growing up in the South that Walker disliked was her feeling of having lived through slavery because she was born to share-croppers on a plantation. To her the sharecropping system was worse than slavery because the disenfranchisement of former slaves after the Civil War created a system under Reconstruction that took exploitation to a new level. Under slavery people worked and were never paid. Under the sharecropping system former slaves worked and were rarely paid and ended up in debt. Under slavery owners had to make some meager provisions for the slaves, supplying them with annual rations of inferior food and clothing. Under the sharecropping system former slaves received nothing. People like Walker's parents labored hard but were never out of debt to the employers whose land they worked and lived on. Walker's father's income was approximately $300 a year. This system of exploitation is the legacy of Walker's birth. It robbed her of her early life, which to her was a lifetime (*My Life As Myself*). Walker explores the sharecropping system and what it does to family relationships in *The Third Life of Grange Copeland* (1970). Eventually becoming an activist, Walker worked to overturn an unfair economic system.

Walker graduated from the predominately African American Butler-Baker High School in 1961. Her peers voted her most popular student and crowned her queen of the prom; she had regained her self-confidence following her successful eye surgery. Her valedictorian status won her a "rehabilitation" scholarship from the state of Georgia, which she used to enroll in the prestigious Spelman College in Atlanta, Georgia, the oldest African American college for women in the United States. Her small rural community also contributed $75 to help launch the college career of one of its own. In addition, her sister Ruth wrote a check for $100, a graduation present for being at the top of her class; Walker never cashed the check for fear it would bounce. While Walker was in high school, she loved a handsome young African American man, Porter Sanford III, whom she dated until she left for college. Away from home she entered into other romantic relationships with other people, one of which resulted in a pregnancy that led to an abortion.

When Walker left home for Spelman College, her mother surprised her with three gifts that she purchased with her wages of less than $20 per week. Walker cherished them because her mother never owned such luxuries. One was a sewing machine to make clothes for herself. This symbolized independence and self-sufficiency, two important survival skills for Walker. Later in life, after researching the life of writer Zora Neale Hurston, Walker concluded that Hurston was too dependent on others, thus her slump into financial ruin. Hurston, Walker thought, had too little knowledge of survival and too few survival skills. In *The Color Purple* (1982) Walker gives the character Celie the wherewithal to earn a living using her sewing machine after she transforms herself from an abused dependent to a free spirit. The second gift was a well-made suitcase to travel, one better constructed than any Walker had seen used by any Eatonton residents. She had her mother's blessing to see the world and return to Eatonton only when she needed to connect with her family. Walker traveled the roads that eventually took her to Africa, Angola, China, Cuba, Europe, and Mexico, to name a few. She gave the character Celie the chance to travel after her liberation from a marriage of oppression. A typewriter was the third gift, sealing Walker's destiny and giving her permission to write her own stories and the stories of her foremothers.

Walker arrived on campus at a time when the Civil Rights movement and student participation in it were under way. She, too, found herself caught up in the spirit of protest, participating in demonstrations and rejoicing in the people en masse engaged in trying to change a repressive social, political, and economic apartheid system. Walker's freshman year culminated in 1962 with an invitation to the home of Coretta Scott King and Dr. Martin Luther King Jr. in Atlanta, Georgia in recognition of selected Spelman students' impending trip to the World Youth Peace

Festival in Helsinki, Finland. The students' advisor, a California white peace activist, arranged for Mrs. King to address the group. Walker neither met Dr. King nor the King children on this visit to their home. Nearly 10 years later Walker returned to the King home to interview Mrs. King, this time meeting Mrs. Christine Farris, Dr. King's sister, and discussing among many things Obidiah Scott, Mrs. King's father, an activist and political candidate in Marion, Alabama. After her Finland trip she traveled to Europe throughout the summer, affording her opportunities to interact with other people and cultures.

Howard Zinn, historian, activist, and author, mentored Walker at Spelman. He writes about history from the viewpoint of the victims instead of the victors. His lessons in civil disobedience influenced Walker's approach to protest. Staughton Lynd, historian, activist, and author, also mentored Walker at Spelman, encouraging her to stay focused and pursue her academics. As a student at Sarah Lawrence, Walker met Professor Lynd's mother, Helen Merrell Lynd, who would also affect her life. Professor Staughton Lynd became an important part of Walker's academics and her politics. Because of the encouragement of these two men, Walker continued her academic studies, gleaning all she could from the college experience.

Whether she found Spelman too Victorian or puritanical, too concerned with quotas, or too lax in the development of the self among the co-eds, Walker did not graduate from the college (*My Life As Myself*). Instead, she transferred in 1964 to Sarah Lawrence College in suburban Bronxville, New York, another women's institution, receiving one of the few scholarships offered to African Americans. Here she graduated with her liberal arts B.A. in 1966. Attendance at both of these women's colleges, Walker later explained, involved her in an educational process that focused on job or life preparation, but not on the preparation of the self. The people responsible for her development, Walker thought, were too focused on the administrative requirement of filling quotas (*My Life As Myself*).

Walker's academic experience at Sarah Lawrence was a rewarding one. Helen Merrell Lynd, co-author with her husband of *Middletown in Transition: A Study in Cultural Conflicts*, an important sociological study, and a philosophy professor, made the subject of philosophy understandable for Walker. Professor Lynd introduced Walker to the works of Albert Camus (1913–60), whose writings would influence her creativity, showing her how life, suffering, and joy teach lessons. She also learned from Professor Lynd that loneliness is useful, and "sadness is positively the wellspring of creativity." To Walker Professor Lynd was strong, sturdy, and fragile in the same way that a red-orange tulip is both delicate and strong ("A Talk").

Jane Cooper also mentored Walker at Sarah Lawrence. Walker saw Professor Cooper as a peaceful person, always willing to listen, a pine tree, the kind of tree that a seven-year-old adopts as a best friend. Finding her "quiet, listening, and true," Walker adopted Professor Cooper as her friend (*In Search of Our Mother's Gardens*, 37–39). Because of Cooper's mentoring and influence, Walker adopted the practice of silence, listening to the self and letting the self lead, speak, and express.

At Sarah Lawrence the young collegiate Alice Walker navigated her way to the classroom of the privileged and popular Jewish professor of poetry Muriel Rukeyser (1913–80). Poet Anne Sexton (1928–74) referred to Rukeyser, a successful published poet, as "Muriel, mother of everyone" because Rukeyser relished honing the talents of the future women writers who were enamored of her as professor and critic during her 13-year-tenure at Sarah Lawrence. Walker referred to her as cosmic consciousness, neither afraid nor intimidated. She and Walker were kindred spirits, for Rukeyser was an earlier version of what Walker would blossom into, both successfully merging art and activism. As a journalist Rukeyser covered the trial of the Scottsboro Boys in Alabama, a cause célèbre for those who worked on behalf of African American justice. These were nine little boys who were arrested and accused of raping a white woman. The authorities arrested Rukeyser for her vehement verbal protests. She also reported on the Spanish civil war, traveled to Vietnam unofficially on a peace mission, and continued with a bold heart by showing up in South Korea to protest the government's imprisonment of writers. In addition, Rukeyser wrote passionately on the *Amistad* revolt about a group of enslaved Africans who seized the ship of their white kidnappers in an effort to return to Africa. They were unsuccessful in their journey and ended up on American shores where they were charged with the most heinous offenses and imprisoned. They challenged the very foundation of justice in America in an effort to win their freedom.

Walker saw in Rukeyser a dedication to social causes and a commitment to poetic art that garnered her admiration. Rukeyser saw in Walker raw talent that needed opportunity. Walker identified Rukeyser as the "original one-of-a-kind." She taught Walker that living in the world on your own terms is possible. Rukeyser submitted Walker's short story "To Hell with Dying" to various publishers and to Langston Hughes (1902–67), who published it in *The Best Short Stories by Negro Writers: 1899–1967*. Hughes followed up with a handwritten note of encouragement to Walker. The two became friends and established a bond that only his death could end. In addition, Rukeyser personally submitted Walker's first collection of poems to Monica McCall, her own literary agent at Harcourt Brace Jovanovich. Not until Walker graduated from Sarah Lawrence College in 1966 did Harcourt Brace Jovanovich editor Hiram Haydn, who received the manuscript from Monica McCall, accept the poems for publication (Mitgang). Thus, Harcourt Brace Jovanovich, the first mainstream press to publish Walker's poetry, published *Once: Poems*, which began a lengthy relationship between Walker and the publishing magnate. Rukeyser wrote of Walker's volume of poetry, "brief slashing poems—young, and in the sun," while Walker spoke of Rukeyser as an "amethyst, rich and deep, purple, full of mystical changes, moods, and spells." This introduction to a wide public earned Walker a place in the sun and a relationship with the public that has remained exemplary and edifying.

Walker's college experience at Sarah Lawrence afforded her an opportunity to travel in her senior year to Europe and to East Africa, where she resided among the Bugandans and the Kikuyus in Uganda and Kenya. These experiences are revealed in "African Images, Glimpses from a Tiger's Back" in *Once: Poems*. While her trip to the motherland was rewarding, she found too much famine, drought, and war there *(A Conversation with Alice Walker)*. In Kenya she learned about the misogynous practice of female circumcision or what she termed female genital mutilation. This experience had such an impact on her that it affected her physically, interrupting her sleeping and eating patterns. Restless and deprived of sleep, she wondered what she could do to bring this issue to the world's attention. The result was *Possessing the Secret of Joy*, a chilling account of a traditional practice cloaked in fiction, the first part of a trilogy. The second part is a documentary titled *Warrior Marks: Female Genital Mutilation and the Sexual Binding of Women* with filmmaker Pratibha Parmar. The third part is a companion book *Warrior Marks*, which chronicles her experiences. An advocate against the millennia-old practice of female circumcision and infibulations, Walker continues to lend her voice to this cause.

In Australia Walker met some aboriginal grandmothers, occupants of the land for 40,000 years, who introduced her to the art of the hunt. Their skill and adeptness of survival impressed Walker, who felt compassionately connected to them. She regretted that they have been marginalized and decimated by the colonial invasion, which will cause the inevitable annihilation of this cultural group *(My Life As Myself)*. Walker's experiences in Australia are disguised in *The Temple of My Familiar* as continent travel and life connections over a period of 500,000 years.

At Sarah Lawrence following her African and European ventures, Walker came to grips with the fact that she was pregnant by her white former boyfriend David DeMoss. She slumped into anxiety and depression. Since these were the days before *Roe v. Wade,* a woman's right to choose to abort legally was not an option. Thinking about what her predicament would do to her family in Eatonton—either disappoint or shame them—Walker for the second time in her life became suicidal, sleeping for weeks with a razor blade under her pillow. Knowing that her death would devastate her family, she underwent a safe but illegal abortion through the assistance of a college friend, Carole Darden. She wrote incessantly to come to terms with her emotional state. Her thoughts of suicide and death cover several poems, most completed in one week, in *Once: Poems* and the short story "The Abortion" in *You Can't Keep a Good Woman Down: Stories.*

After graduation from college in 1966, Walker worked for four months for the New York City Welfare Department, a job that provided the finances for her to write. She lived on the Lower East Side between Avenues A and B in a building without a front door. She then felt the lure of the South once again and the call to activism, moving to Mississippi in the summer of 1966 to be in the center of the Civil Rights movement. She stopped on the way in Georgia, participating in voter registration drives. While in Mississippi she assisted people who had been evicted from farms and removed from welfare roles as a consequence of registering to vote and taught history to Head Start teachers (Mitgang).

Also in Mississippi Walker re-met Jewish activist and former law student Melvyn Rosenman Leventhal. They met the summer of 1965 before she returned to live permanently, rekindled their romantic attraction, and married on March 17, 1967, although interracial marriage was illegal in Mississippi. She separated her love for him from the wicked things she witnessed whites doing in Mississippi. She admired his courage as he bravely entered restricted communities to have discussions with people who suffered injustices. The two of them went on a mission to make a difference, to make changes. The cases that Leventhal handled desegregated the public schools of Mississippi, a first-time occurrence in one hundred years. For Walker this event was a milestone, for the African American people of Mississippi so feared white people that they deliberately appeared dejected before them to avoid any hostile reactions from them. Some towns in Mississippi prohibited African Americans from walking on the sidewalks; therefore, when people took a stand and risked being killed to restore their pride and regenerate their crushed spirits, Walker and Leventhal felt very much a part of that blossoming. They were a team and a marriage, rebellious for the period in their thinking, politics, and love (*A Conversation with Alice Walker*).

The union of Walker and Leventhal produced one child, a daughter, Rebecca Grant Leventhal, born November 17, 1969, three days after Walker completed *The Third Life of Grange Copeland*. She wrote about becoming a mother in "One Child of One's Own: A Meaningful Digression within the Work(s)." Walker felt immediately connected to all women in the world and especially to her mother, who had given birth eight times without anesthesia. Walker finally understood the incredible pain women endured in peopling the world, that every occupant of the globe exits the body of a woman who accomplished delivery in agonizing pain. She realized the secret that patriarchal power withheld from the world: the heroic nature of giving birth and women's humility of keeping silent after the journey. Upon giving birth women are automatically connected to the future. Tillie Olson, one of Walker's favorite writers and the mother of four daughters, once told Walker that having a daughter Rebecca's age would help her to understand the culture. Having a daughter meant facing the stark realization that the culture shapes her and has a preconceived plan to mold her into a little doll machine. Walker's response to Olson's prediction was that the possibility of her very own daughter evolving into a cultural clone was a moot issue; after all, Rebecca's mother is not a cultural clone (*My Life As Myself*).

Mississippi was a habitual battleground, and the couple responded to the constant threats by packing up and moving to New York in 1974 where Leventhal had attended law school. Living in a one-bedroom apartment over Washington Square, Walker took a job as an editor at *Ms.* magazine, and Leventhal worked for the NAACP Legal Defense Fund (Mitgang). However, the strain on the marriage took its toll. The unresolved tensions from the dangerous work in civil rights, the fear that once made them cling to each other turned into space between them, and the exhaustion of the fight for equality transformed their wedded bliss into unbearable sorrow; these differences contributed to the break up. By 1976 they would be divorced, and Walker would be making plans to move to the opposite side of the country. Walker memorializes this time in her life in the essay "To My Young Husband" in *The Way Forward Is with a Broken Heart*.

INFLUENCE OF THE CIVIL RIGHTS MOVEMENT

The Civil Rights movement began in 1865, when the United States House of Representatives passed the 13th Amendment to the Constitution, previously adopted by the Senate in 1864, which abolished slavery. The enactment of the Black Codes by the former Confederate states prohibited the former slaves from enjoying basic rights accorded to other groups in the restored states, such as public assembly, ownership of firearms, jury service and testifying, and public school attendance with all people. African Americans endured and strove against these inequities individually and collectively for nearly one hundred years. There arose a generation whose intolerance to such injustices exploded into collective public action when an exhausted Rosa Parks refused to give up her public transportation seat to a white rider, prompting the Montgomery bus boycott of 1955–57 under the leadership of Dr. Martin Luther King Jr. and the courageous member churches of the Southern Christian Leadership Conference (SCLC). The boycott ended but the movement did not, resulting in the 1960s in the first sit-ins, building takeovers, and freedom rides. Alice Walker left Eatonton, Georgia for Spelman College in Atlanta in 1961, not realizing that she would become a participant in and an eyewitness to the historic Civil Rights movement that would impact her life in ways that she never imagined.

Walker's arrival on campus coincided with an already formed Student Nonviolent Coordinating Committee (SNCC), established at Shaw University in Raleigh, North Carolina in 1960. It was operating full force in Atlanta, a hotbed of student unrest by Clark, Morehouse, Morris Brown, and Spelman students, among the many who rallied to the cry of "jail over bail" to unite against oppressive forces that denied them life's privileges and joys. Walker, both witness and participant, was excited to be involved in protest and elated to bear witness to the historic actions of thousands of students who went to jail for the cause, many suffering indignities there. Walker recalled one young man who was forced to drink a bottle of ammonia by a white racist male; this resulted in the young man's hospitalization, but he was happy to have done his part for the movement. This protest was the first time Walker witnessed so many people involved in an effort to change the segregated social structure of apartheid in the United States (*A Conversation with Alice Walker*). Walker also traveled to Washington DC, to take part in the August 1963 March on Washington. Sitting high in a tree but unable to see the podium, Walker listened intently to Dr. Martin Luther King Jr.'s "I Have a Dream" oration. Five years later she would attend the funeral of Dr. King, walk in the processional following Dr. King's mule-cart drawn coffin, and suffer a miscarriage as a result of the stress and long walk.

As an activist at Spelman, Walker met individuals who would achieve national prominence as activists and leaders, such as Julian Bond and John Lewis. With them she participated in the sit-ins, demonstrated, and marched before moving on later to Mississippi where she would also work in civil rights. Walker reflects on her memories of the turbulent Civil Rights movement in *Once: Poems, Revolutionary Petunias and Other Poems,* "Advancing Luna—and Ida B. Wells" in *You Can't Keep a Good Woman Down: Stories,* and *The Way Forward Is with a Broken Heart.* In *Meridian* she explores the sexism within the movement itself, a side of the Civil Rights movement that received little exposure. She also wrote an essay entitled "The Civil Rights Movement: What Good Was It?" that won first place in the annual essay contest of *American Scholar* magazine in 1967.

ACADEMIC AND LITERARY CAREER

Jackson State College in Jackson, Mississippi offered Walker Writer-in-Residence in Black Studies in 1968–69, which she accepted. Several academic posts succeeded this one. She was Writer-in-Residence at Tougaloo College in Tougaloo, Mississippi in 1970–71 and Lecturer in Literature at both Wellesley College in Wellesley, Massachusetts and University of Massachusetts, Boston, in 1972–73. At Wellesley Walker created one of the first courses on African American women writers in the United States, which led to her discovery of writer Zora Neale Hurston. She later taught this course at the University of Massachusetts, Boston. She became an editor for *Ms.* magazine in 1974. She later moved to San Francisco, California in 1978 and then to Mendocino, California, one hundred miles north of San Francisco, where she has a cabin in the country. She resumed an academic career as Distinguished Writer in African American Studies at the University of California, Berkeley, and Fannie Hurst Professor of Literature at Brandeis University in Waltham, Massachusetts in 1982. A naturalist, Walker founded Wild Trees Press in Navarro, California in 1984 with a mission to publish the creative works of unknown writers. J. California Cooper's *A Piece of Mine,* nominated for the Book of the Year Award by the American Library Association, became the first publication of the new press in 1984. She serves as a member of the Board of Trustees of Sarah Lawrence College. Walker is currently a full-time writer.

When Walker made California her home, Robert Allen, editor of *Black Scholar,* became her romantic partner. He catered to her needs, driving her endlessly through the state in search of an idyllic area to compose *The Color Purple*. He drove her to Mendocino twice, waiting for her to make a decision. She settled there in the vicinity of San Francisco and called the new dwelling her country home. She made her decision after seeing a little African American boy walking down the road with an air of perfect peace. She reasoned that if an African American boy could feel at peace anywhere in the country, the area was probably a good place to settle. The relationship with Allen terminated after thirteen years.

Walker managed to build up a world of accomplishments for herself. She was Bread Loaf Writers' Conference Scholar in 1966. Walker became Merrill Writing Fellow in 1966–67 and McDowell Colony Fellow in 1967. That same year she won the *American Scholar* essay contest for her piece on the Civil Rights movement. In 1969 she received a National Endowment for the Arts grant. She addressed the Black Students' Association at Sarah Lawrence College in 1970, speaking on "The Unglamorous but Worthwhile Duties of the Black Revolutionary Artist, Or of the Black Writer Who Simply Works and Writes." Walker received a Radcliffe Institute Fellowship in 1971. She received an honorary PhD from Russell Sage College in Troy, New York in 1972. She also in 1972 delivered the convocation address at Sarah Lawrence College, "A Talk: Convocation 1972: How to Speak about Practically Everything, Briefly, from the Heart." She similarly spoke to a group in Jackson, Mississippi at a restaurant that had refused to admit people of color; her address was "Choice: A Tribute to Dr. Martin Luther King, Jr."

Walker gained double rewards in 1973 when she won the Southern Regional Council's Lillian Smith Award for poetry and the nomination for the National Book Award for *Revolutionary Petunias and Other Poems*. She received the Richard and Hinda Rosenthal Award from the National Institute of Arts and Letters in 1974 for *In Love and Trouble: Stories of Black Women*. The Guggenheim and MacDowell Colony Fellowships were awarded in 1977. She was also the recipient of the National Endowment for the Arts Grant and Fellowship. She was keynote speaker for Muriel Rukeyser Day at Sarah Lawrence College in 1979. In addition, she received the National Book Critics Circle Award nomination for *The Color Purple*, the American Book Award for *The Color Purple*, and the Pulitzer Prize for *The Color Purple* in 1983. Walker received as well the Doctor of Honorary Laws from the University of Massachusetts. She received a citation for Best Books for Young Adults from the American Library Association in 1984 for *In Search of Our Mother's Gardens: Womanist Prose*. She was honored with the O'Henry Award in 1986 for "Kindred Spirits."

In 1989 she received the Langston Hughes Award from New York City College and the Nora Astorga Leadership Award.

The next two decades were equally filled with recognition for Walker. The Bay Area Book Reviewers Association honored Walker with the Fred Cody Award for Lifetime Achievement in 1990. That same year she won the PEN West Freedom to Write Award. In 1994 Walker was given the California Governor's Arts Award. Another honor was the Alice Walker Literary Society chartered at Spelman College in 1997. The University of Oklahoma Center for Poets and Writers honored her with the Literary Ambassador Award in 1998. Walker received the Lifetime Literary Achievement Award from the Enoch Pratt Free Library in Baltimore, Maryland in October 2004. A noteworthy moment in Walker's life is the making of the controversial novel *The Color Purple* into an equally controversial cinematic production directed by Steven Spielberg. Proud of their native "son," the people of Eatonton, Georgia, held a parade and a Hollywood-type premiere of *The Color Purple* at the Pex Theater in Walker's hometown in 1986. *The Color Purple* was also adapted into a musical production in 2004 and made its world premiere at the Alliance Theatre in Atlanta, Georgia, in September-October 2004 and is scheduled to open on Broadway in New York City in the fall of 2005.

RECEPTION

Walker used to imagine an ideal reader, one not unlike herself but 50 years into the future. She wrote for this imagined audience, taking her cue from critics, believing that she was giving the public what it wanted. This strategy worked well for her until she realized while working in academic settings that students of various cultures and colors understood her creative work and wanted her to create more volumes. Then she made a decision to concentrate on expressing her views of life through art and to allow the end result to help others. This time she took her cue from the writings of Flannery O'Connor, who wrote that writers should write for themselves, and she decided to adopt Toni Morrison's statement that she writes books that she likes to read. No longer did Walker focus on an imaginary Alice Walker as reader (Bonnetti).

Many college and university professors help students grasp an understanding of creative works by homing in on their political contexts. Walker thrives on the difficult and the political. Her strong views increase in intensity with each subsequent publication, which is the reason some critics believe that her writings are propagandistic. California bureaucrats censored some of her stories because they believed that she advocated immorality and certain nutritional trends, for example, lesbianism and food grown without pesticides, hormones, or antibiotics.

Some African American males specifically find either Walker's novels or Walker herself too intimidating. Walker believes that African American male critics think that novelists who write about women's issues produce a lesser creation. A *New York Times* critic wrote that Toni Morrison's *Song of Solomon* was an important subject, one that pleased him. Walker interpreted his response to refer to the subject of African American men. But Walker believes that such subjects apply to all women writers, not just African American women writers (Bonnetti).

Certain African American men and African American male theorists and critics respond negatively to Walker's male characters—especially the older generation of African American males, not so much the younger generation. The older generation's concerns are with her representations of them, that they are mean or evil. They dislike her neorealistic portrayals of African American communities. Walker takes their attacks on her as outpourings of their bruised egos, concerned only with how the readers perceive them. Walker thinks that their reactions to this concern stymie any ability to comprehend what she is trying to accomplish in her novels. She believes that when some African American men read her novels, they ignore the women, seeing them only as decorative or bothersome. Walker feels that these men pay more attention to the male characters in her novels because they are trying either to learn from them or to emulate them. She feels that all men are void of the necessary analytical skills to read novels about women with deep "sensitivity and belief" (Bonnetti). Michael Thelwell, professor in the W.E.B. Du Bois Department of Afro-American Studies at the University of Massachusetts, sees Walker as not universally loved but just significant in the feminist movement because of her use of recycled clichés of feminist rhetoric (Vanessa).

Feminist readers admire Walker for her artistic ability, as well as other qualities. She has a devoted international following, lining up at book signings, filling the seats at lectures, making her novels best sellers. She establishes personal relationships with her readers; she becomes their friend. She writes as if she is speaking directly to the reader, sitting with the reader telling the story. Her literary trajectory is high. Academics make her novels assigned readings not only in Women's Studies and African American literature classes but also in core American literature classes and classes across the liberal arts, for she covers so many issues. She is one of the most highly respected and recognized authors in the

United States. The reading public loves her creative writings for the same reasons that many (not all) African American males dislike her art: the vivid portrayals and deep insights into aspects of American life generally and African American life specifically. Readers cannot sit comfortably in the chair when Walker's writings are the topics of discussion. Because she is the recipient of numerous literary prizes, readers continue to demand her insightful voice on the spiritual, the secular, the environmental, the human, and the personal.

During the course of her literary career the talented Alice Walker has invigorated the study of literature. She brings to the field remarkable energy and expertise in the telling of women's stories. Her special appeal stems from her ability to develop the stories of African American women, who are noticeably absent from American literature. These are women who find themselves exploited and victimized emotionally, physically, and psychologically, women who endure alienation and confinement, women who struggle to get from margin to center, whose only way out sometimes is insanity. But she is careful to balance the less stable with strong women who rise above their unfortunate circumstances to achieve wholeness and to contribute to others in their communities, restoring hope, laughter, and joy.

Moreover, Walker is adept at portraying individual relationships— parent and child, male and female, or female and female. She allows the reader to peep inside verbally and physically abusive marriages, inside the mindset of patriarchal racism and sexism, and inside a society that sustains patriarchal power and control. The reader grapples along with the characters to break free from tortured and entrapped souls to discover self-worth and mechanisms of survival. Walker is one of the few writers who examines the impact of poverty on relationships, how lack contributes to a negative dichotomy between men and women, and how it feeds illiteracy and scenarios of brooding and desolation.

The power to transform is another technique that appeals to Walker's audience. These transformations may be generated by the Civil Rights movement or women's roles in it, or by communities that transform themselves into more positive places. Walker is adept at getting her characters to see possibilities and collective potential. Renewal—whether individual, community, or spiritual—becomes an integral component in the telling of Walker's stories. In addition, ancestor worship, acknowledging the past and those who have disembodied themselves, has special appeal in her writing. Best of all, Walker weaves an exciting tale around womanist issues in the African American community. She tells stories about the complexities of life, and her stories are solidly honest.

Many experiences, events, and people influenced Walker to become the writer she is today. Good musicians are an entity that Walker feels operate with a certainty of freedom of expression, sinking into whatever they sing, leaving no line of demarcation between their feeling and their singing. One such musician whose musical talent Walker admired, among others, is the white French singer Edith Piaf (Edith Giovanna Gassion 1915–63). To reach a superb level of singing, Walker believes that the singer must have life experiences, must endure much, suffer much, and understand even more. These experiences distinguish the pure essence of a musical vocal talent like Edith Piaf, whom Walker believes understands the message of the song, from someone with a melodic voice who just sings. For instance, Walker listens to Bessie Smith (1894?–1937) and Janice Joplin (1943–70), who sings the songs that Bessie Smith recorded, but Walker feels that Joplin lacks the intensity required to make Smith's songs meaningful. Smith lived the life, endured and suffered, giving her that extra edge in infusing a message into her songs (Bonnetti). Therefore, Walker feels that had Janice Joplin lived longer and endured the rigors of life more, the extra edge needed to infuse her songs with message would have developed within her. Walker's fiction and poetry include songs and music and are poetically musical. She creates the character Shug Avery in *The Color Purple* as a bluesy "jook joint" singer who takes life to task, endures some troublesome times, and suffers monumental pain, earning her the right to sing the blues. Walker believes that she must experience, understand, and empathize with her characters and her subject in order to weave a good story, just as a vocalist must experience and understand the message of the song in order to sing it well.

Walker's life is constant change, always moving in the direction of highs and lows, valleys, plateaus, and peaks. She searches for ways to reinvent herself. A lifetime journey led her to embrace her completeness, the whole of everything that makes her who she is. The theory of double consciousness espoused by W.E.B. Du Bois holds no truth for her. She scorns the idea that African Americans are split into two opposing selves, one black and one American. She embraces her multiracial, multinational identity, seeing herself today as someone who is triracial, trispiritual, and bisexual (Gussow). She incorporates into her racial identity her African, Native American, and European heritages. She traces her ancestry back to Africa, the Cherokee nation, and Scotland and Ireland. She decided not to deny any part of herself, not to identify herself as solely African American. These three sides of her make her the American that she is. Similarly, her spirituality is threefold. She was baptized a Methodist, but she is now a practicing Buddhist. The third component is earth religion, or paganism, which simply means someone spiritually connected to the earth and to nature. She is a naturalist who respects all things of nature and is interested in its preservation. She is all of these. And she can fall in love with a woman as easily or with equal difficulty as she can fall in love with a man. She loves both women and men sexually.

Walker's daughter Rebecca published *Black, White, and Jewish: Autobiography of a Shifting Self* (2001) under the name Rebecca Walker. In it she portrays her mother as a freethinking parent who relinquished most of her parental control to her daughter, resulting in her daughter becoming her own unwise lawgiver and frequent mistake maker. This memoir reflects on interracial and interfaith relationships, the expectations of "movement children" who are the offspring of the merged races and cultures of the Civil Rights movement. Ironically, Rebecca as a 12th-grade senior made a decision to change her name, incorporating her mother's name into her own. Walker did the same in 1994 when she turned 50, incorporating her mother's grandmother's Cherokee name Tallulah, into her own. She took the name to the chief of the Cherokee nation to learn its meaning; the chief gave her the connotation basket maker, the best that he could decipher from his knowledge of his nation's language. Walker affirmed that definition because she saw herself as a weaver of stories. Her new name became Alice Tallulah-Kate Walker. For Rebecca the name-changing act privileges her blackness and downplays her whiteness, creating an infinite link between mother and daughter. Walker's *The Way Forward Is with a Broken Heart* explores dysfunctional familial relationships, a theme that also interests Rebecca Walker. A woman of conviction, Alice Walker is insightful, compassionate, and strong—a visionary. Historically connected to African American literature, her writings are the biographical personifications of herself. Much of her work centers on women, circumstances of oppression, and the twin evils of racism and sexism. She is a gifted writer, able to weave the stories coming from her oral and written background into a unified whole. Following the lead given to her by the late Dudley Randall, Broadside Press publisher—writing should not only be pretty but also have a purpose—she uses her gift to weave stories of the human experience. She is interested in the edification of her readership, leaving them with a feeling of catharsis, the essence of classical literature.

2

Literary Contexts

Alice (Malsenior) Tallulah-Kate Walker, American by nationality and African American, Cherokee, and Scottish-Irish by ethnicity, is a southern writer. She is a biographer, critic, editor, essayist, novelist, poet, theorist, and short story writer. She is also an educator, lecturer, and activist. She achieved recognition internationally as one of the major writers of the latter part of the twentieth century, with voluminous literary scholarship devoted to her work. Much of her renown is a result of the following she acquired as an editor at *Ms.* magazine. As of late 2005 she had to her credit five children's books, an edited collection of the literary achievements of Zora Neale Hurston, two essay collections, and four autobiographical collections. She also produced two works of nonfiction and one independent documentary film on female genital mutilation. Her literary oeuvre also includes eight volumes of poetry, three short story collections, over 60 articles, and eight novels. Although she has managed these accomplishments, her fame stems mostly from the controversy surrounding her Pulitzer Prize-winning epistolary novel *The Color Purple* and the film of the same title adapted from the book and directed by Steven Spielberg. In addition, she acquired recognition when she rescued from oblivion the writings of the literary foremother Zora Neale Hurston. Finally, her coinage of the theoretical term *womanist,* which she defines in the essay "In Search of Our Mothers' Gardens," gained her some prominence.

Alice Walker's literary heritage in the United States has eighteenth-
and nineteenth-century origins, beginning with the colonial and antebellum periods. Lucy Terry (1730–1821) penned "Bars Fight" (1746),
the first poem of record written by an African woman, although it
was not published until 1855 in Josiah Gilbert Holland's *History of
Western Massachusetts.* Terry's important historical verse documents the
Massachusetts Native American raid on the colonists, an event she witnessed. The literature of Terry's period reflected the national idealism
of the revolutionary period, that is, contempt for British nationals and
Native American people. Assuming a conservative Christian stance, Terry
wrote sympathetically about the fate of the colonists, echoing themes of
cultural and racial conflicts, ruling-class resistance, territorial disputes,
and violence against women. Similar themes more than two centuries
later appear in the poetic volumes of Alice Walker, for example, *Good
Night Willie Lee: I'll See You in the Morning* (1975), *Once: Poems* (1968), and
Revolutionary Petunias and Other Poems (1971).

Lucy Terry, however, is not the founder of the African American
women's poetic literary tradition. That honor goes to Phillis Wheatley
(1753?–84), whose *Poems on Various Subjects, Religious and Moral* (1773)
became the first published volume of poetry in the English language
by a woman of African heritage in the American colonies. Wheatley is
not only the founder of the African American women's poetic literary
tradition but also the African American literary tradition, the African
American women's literary tradition, and the African American literary
criticism tradition, resulting from the reception of Wheatley's poetry by
colonial critics. Wheatley's publication debuted during the slavery era,
a period marked by Christian religious dogma that Africans and African
Americans were intellectually inferior and void of souls. Therefore, a
"reform the heathen" propaganda campaign espoused by church fathers
encouraged the education of Africans in Christian doctrine, instructing
them that the Christian God ordained their caste and acceptance of their
enslaved state was equivalent to absolute obedience to God. Wheatley's
poetry, especially her religious poems such as "On Being Brought from
Africa to America," seemed to support this view, offering a Christian
apology for slavery and Christian justification for it as well, indicating
that Christianity refined and reformed Africans. Wheatley's acquiescence
to this Christian doctrine and strict adherence to it are tantamount to
exercising survival skills. Given her situation, she quietly and calmly
detoured her way into the patronizing acceptance of the Massachusetts
elite male-dominated society.

However, Wheatley was not without public scrutiny and fascination. So awestruck were members of the white male elite, such as Benjamin Franklin and George Washington, over Wheatley's precociousness, race, and gender that they granted her an audience, showing the white reading public and themselves that an African was capable of literary production. Wheatley later stood before a panel of 18 of Boston's affluent and influential genteel representatives to be interrogated in a trial to determine her intellectual acuity. This august tribunal subsequently attested to the literary capabilities of young Wheatley, despite her so-called uncultivated barbarianism. Regardless, the southern colonist Thomas Jefferson, remaining skeptical and unconvinced, held fast to his convictions that slaves were intellectually incapable of making contributions to literature, that is, religion could bring into existence a Phillis Wheatley but religion could not bring into existence a poet. Jefferson even left a legacy in his *Notes on the State of Virginia* that Africans were incapable of higher-level thinking ability and dismissed Wheatley's poetic accomplishments as an accident of nature or trivial pursuits. Unfortunately, many whites adopted Jefferson's condescending and recalcitrant ideology, believing stereotypically that people of African heritage were nonproductive in theory and in practice.

Nevertheless, Wheatley continued to produce poetry, subtly creating in defiance of the established norm, enslaved in her person but free in her mind. Her creative abilities and strength of mind eventually freed her from physical servitude but not from societal indoctrination about her race and caste. Her perseverance would become the impetus for her literary descendants to disprove Jefferson's ideology and build on the tradition that Wheatley founded. Twentieth-century African American critics often misunderstood Wheatley's raceless poetry, emphasizing that she neither excelled nor failed in poetic creativity but was an accomplished imitator. They expected her to lodge a great poetic challenge to the injustices of the institution of slavery. However, Alice Walker, a literary descendant of this tradition, suggested in "In Search of Our Mothers' Gardens" that Wheatley as creative spirit needs reexamination and reanalyzation. Scholars both male and female misunderstood her references to European imagery and icons. The critics failed to uncover Wheatley's divided loyalties and divided mind, which time and hindsight justify. Walker emphasized that Wheatley's literary aesthetics prospered in spite of her chattel existence, allowing her to leave a legacy of creativity—a book that influenced African American literature in general, as well as the African American women's literary tradition.

Wheatley is pivotal to the genre of poetry and to the African American women's literary tradition and the African American literary tradition for two reasons. First, she launched a successful defense of her intellectual capability, proving to the elite of white male citizens that her ability to read, write, speak, think critically, and reason analytically was authentic. Her performance before this awestruck audience gained her private audiences with some of Boston's and England's most important citizens. Wheatley met with or received correspondence from the Earl of Dartmouth, John Hancock, and Samuel Mather (brother of Cotton Mather), among others. Second, as founder of the tradition Wheatley established early on that African/African American intellect was on par with that of the learned citizens of the day, disputing somewhat the prevailing myth that Africans were intellectually inferior to whites. Although Wheatley's oral defense established the precedent of intellectual capability of Africans/African Americans, critical inquiry into the issue would endure through the centuries. Thus, the literary influence of Alice Walker becomes central to reassessments of the poetry of Phillis Wheatley, that Wheatley was "not an idiot or a traitor" but a woman with a gift who passed down the mind's garden of song. Walker exemplifies this same tenacity in the creation of the poetic art form that she values so much and shares with an international readership.

The essay, another literary genre preferred by Alice Walker, was also an outlet of expression for African American prose writers both slave and free. The first book of essays published by an African American woman was Ann Plato's (1820?–?) *Essays* (1841). Born free, Plato, an essayist, poet, and teacher, conveyed in her writings the connection between an educated mind and a liberated mind-set, exhorting African Americans to be steadfast in pursuit of their common goals. Plato encouraged pursuit of an education, but knowledge was just the first step on the road to freedom. An emancipated mind would ultimately manifest an emancipated body and spirit. Also, Frances E. W. Harper (1825–1911), a free African American activist, educator, essayist, lecturer, novelist, and poet, used the essay form to present themes of protest focusing on abolition of chattel slavery, economic and sociopolitical causes, intellectual advancement, temperance, and women's issues. Harper's book *Poems on Miscellaneous Subjects* (1854), an essay and poem compilation, and her poems "The Slave Auction" and "A Double Standard" in particular evinced these early protest themes. Thus, many scholars consider Harper the forerunner to the African American protest poetry tradition. Alice Walker, similarly to Plato and Harper, also uses the essay to articulate concerns about

African American sociopolitical issues and African American women's heritage and roles in American society.

Following the dominance of poems and essays in the eighteenth and early nineteenth centuries, the genre to come of age in the latter eighteenth century and most of the nineteenth century was the autobiographical slave narrative, or emancipatory narrative, a genre identification preference used by some African American scholars that is considered more definitive of the path from bondage to freedom. These slave or emancipatory narratives also are sometimes disguised as autobiographical novels. Initially, they appear as vehicles for those held in captivity to respond to their existence of enslavement. Narratives published by captured African males, such as John Marrant (1755–90?) and Gustavus Vassa (1745–97), were not attacks on the institution of slavery but were conservative accounts reflecting the acceptance of the social roles to which their owners assigned them. The later narratives, for example, those published by William Wells Brown (1814–84), Josiah Henson (1789–1883), Henry "Box" Brown (1815?–?), and Frederick Douglass (1818–95), to name but a few of the 30 narratives published prior to the Civil War, are strong protests against chattel slavery, indicative of the abolition movement and the temper of the times in the vivid descriptions of the horrors of slavery and the cultural interactions of slaves and enslavers.

Characteristically, autobiographical slave narratives are narrative, autobiography, and epic. Most importantly, their narrative formats have story lines that give historical accounts of oppressors and oppressed people and include as protagonists escaped slaves who emancipate themselves through the assistance of abolitionists and other sympathizers. Equally important, as autobiography the slave narratives center on the saga of the self in triumphing over existential, historical, and social hindrances. Above all, in these narratives as epics the protagonists are symbolic heroes who personify cultural archetypes that represent the desires of a people. These heroes are examples of African trickster figures that connive and scheme against the presumed mental superiority of slave owners to emerge victorious against overwhelming odds. Crucial to the legitimacy of autobiographical slave narratives is the fact that they are grounded in truth, providing actual details of a horrific institution and giving vivid accounts of births, parentage, deaths, whippings, hard labor, task masters, cruel owners, familial dissolutions, insufficient necessities, slave auctions, slave patrols, name changes, and escapes. The narratives provided white audiences with documentary material and social and political evidence that would propel abolitionists and sympathizers alike to take a pro-emancipation platform and work to abolish slavery in all territories where it existed.

Frederick Douglass's *Narrative of the Life of Frederick Douglass, An American Slave, Written by Himself* (1845) epitomizes the classic slave narrative in its episodic presentation of the realities of slavery and skilled incorporation of narrative, autobiography, and epic. James Olney in *The Slave's Narrative* outlines the established set of conventions for slave narratives and explains the intentional twofold purpose for these conventions: to structure the descriptive narrative content and to recount the realities of institutional slavery (147–75). The protagonist is both character and narrator, but the narrative voice must always remain the subject self of the narrative, never evolving emotionally, morally, or intellectually. The character, on the contrary, is the object self of the narrative and focuses solely on keeping the reader's attention on the cruel injustices of an inhumane system of which the character is an unwilling victim. Douglass successfully conforms to the prescriptive conventions, using the lives of the slaves in the narrative to illustrate real practices, causing the reader to ponder whether the barbarians are really barbaric and the civilized are really civil.

Douglass takes the slave narrative to another level by exceeding the basic requirements of slave narrative conventions. He merges objectivity and the antislavery argument, thus synthesizing the slave narrative prototype and the slavery critique; Douglass foregrounds the narrative and backgrounds the critique. He manages this cohesion by incorporating seven philosophical ideas within the narrative framework: the psychological, sociological, cultural-anthropological, historical, phenomenological, hermeneutical, Afrocentric, and feminist and womanist, methodologies used in modern schools of criticism. For example, Douglass subtly critiques his dilemma regarding human relationships and the societal separation of whites and people of African heritage, evincing a "double consciousness" (psychological). Furthermore, he critiques slave existence and the hierarchal roles of slaves within the institution, those who work the fields, the house, the boats, and the headquarters farm (sociological). He explores folk themes, oral traditions, cultural perceptions, cultural articulation, and reasons for songs or singing (cultural-anthropological). Douglass points to events pertaining to slaves as a cultural group and changes within the cultural group resulting from temporal and geographical settings (historical). Further, he illustrates rituals, sacrifices, and repetitive patterns (phenomenological). He even more shows examples of spiritual inclusion and interpretation (hermeneutical); African presence and influence in labor practices and agricultural development (Afrocentric); and patriarchal patterns—slave owners, slaves, and free men—in the sexual victimization and exploitation of women of African heritage (feminist and womanist). The result is the creation of a metatext that is reflexive, as well as effective. These sophisticated textual conventions of Douglass's slave narrative debunk the stereotypes held by some of Douglass's day that underestimate African and African American intelligence and undervalue such writers' contribution to belles lettres. With this novel approach in depicting the life of slaves and simultaneously inspiring action on the part of the reader, Douglass elevates himself and his cultural group from the dregs of intellectual alienation to the heights of creative genius. Douglass's narrative, slave narrative par excellence, would become a mandatory template for those writing slave narratives after him and a vital source for those writing twentieth-century slave narratives.

Another important slave narrative is Mary Prince's (1788–?) *The History of Mary Prince, A West Indian Slave, Related by Herself* (1831), the earliest slave narrative to chronicle the brutality that women endured in the slavery system. However, the slave narrative of (Isabella) Sojourner Truth (1797–1883) became a powerful addition to the African American women's autobiographical tradition. Lacking the tools of literacy, Sojourner Truth dictated her life's account in 1859 to white sympathizer Olive Gilbert, who empathetically captured the spirit of her voice and the power of her oratorical skills, publishing the *Narrative of Sojourner Truth.* The assistance of white friend Frances Titus resulted in the publication in 1878 of Truth's expanded autobiography supplemented with her *Book of Life*, documentary material from her life, and has been reprinted twice as *Narrative of Sojourner Truth; A Bondswoman of Olden Time, with a History of Her Labors and Correspondence Drawn from Her "Book of Life."* Truth's narrative contains a version of an extemporaneous speech entitled "Ar'n't I a Woman?" that she delivered at the Women's Rights Convention in Akron, Ohio in 1851, and that transformed the itinerant preacher and activist into a legend and a symbol of abolitionist and racial spirit and pride. The crux of the thematic argument presented in the speech regarding women's issues and their roles in the liberation struggle became more important than the claim made by some scholars that Truth never spoke the famous phrase "Ar'n't I a Woman?" Although two versions of the speech appear in print, one in the *Anti Slavery Bugle* of June 21, 1851 and the other in the "Book of Life," the legendary phrase attributed to her propelled her into African American literary history as an iconic advocate of African American and women's rights.

While Sojourner Truth's contribution to the slave narrative tradition is significant, Harriet Ann Jacobs's (1813–97) *Incidents in the Life of a Slave Girl, Written by Herself* (1861) is also a treasured volume in the slave narrative genre. Jacobs's account was rescued from literary obscurity by literary historian Jean Fagan Yellin, and it is thanks to her persistent inquiry and thorough research that literary scholars now appreciate its significance. Jacob's narrative is the single slave narrative by an African American woman that has a traceable genesis, a documented evidentiary trail. Fagan presented manuscripts and Jacobs's correspondences to her contemporaries as proof of authorship of the narrative. Amazingly, Jacobs corresponded with Lydia Maria Child, J. Sella Martin, Amy Post, and Anne Warren Weston and wrote to periodicals, such as the *New York Tribune* and *Liberator*. Scholars rejected the narrative as Jacobs's own composition because they believed instead that its editor, Lydia Maria Child, a white abolitionist, actually penned the narrative. Through Fagan's research, however, history and literary scholars now know that the narrative is not a fictionalized account of slave life.

Harriet Jacobs's narrative is significant because it records in lengthy details and specifics slavery's betrayal of women of African heritage, its betrayal to the "Cult of Womanhood." Using the pseudonym Linda Brent, Jacobs is novelist, narrator, subject, and object of her narrative. The story line disguises her reality of Edenton, North Carolina, where she lived with her parents and younger brother until her mother's death when she was 6 years old. Then the plantation's mistress Margaret Horniblow, a woman of some compassion, briefly reared her and instructed her in reading, writing, and sewing. After Horniblow's death Jacobs, 12 at the time, was willed to Mary Matilda Norcom, Horniblow's 3-year-old niece. Jacobs's life of sexual victimization and exploitation began at the Norcom plantation at the hands of Mary's father, Dr. Norcom, the prototype for Dr. Flint in the narrative. Because of Dr. Norcom's lascivious behavior, Jacobs learned to exploit her own sexuality in resistance to his unwanted sexual advances, flirtatiously ensnaring white attorney and neighbor Samuel Tredwell Sawyer (Mr. Sands in the narrative) in a clandestine relationship and bearing his son Joseph in 1829 and his daughter Louisa Matilda in 1833. This she did as a mechanism of retreat from Dr. Norcom and escape from the physical brutality of the system. She hoped that Dr. Norcom would sell the children to their father, which he eventually did. Jacobs does not mask the truth in this exposé of the southern patriarchal system. Frederick Douglass also warns in his narrative about a system that is both "profitable" and "pleasurable," creating a mulatto class of slaves in the South. Separating myth from reality, Jacobs lifts the veil from the circumstances of nineteenth-century slave women, their perils and their pain. Thus, *Incidents in the Life of a Slave Girl, Written by Herself* with its explanatory analysis of gender issues is a key rediscovery and contribution to African American women's slave narratives in the autobiographical novel tradition.

Equal in importance to Jacobs's narrative, Harriet E. Adams Wilson's (1828?–63?) *Our Nig; Or, Sketches from the Life of a Free Black, In a Two-Story White House, North, Showing That Slavery's Shadows Fall Even There* (1859) is the first published novel in English by an African American woman in the autobiographical novel tradition. As with Harriet Jacobs's narrative, literary scholars believed that Wilson's book had white authorship until Henry Louis Gates Jr. in the 1980s performed the necessary research to establish her identity. Her life began in Fredericksburg, Virginia where she was hired out in her young life to work under harsh conditions that ruined her health. She later moved to Milford, New Hampshire, as a young adult, married Thomas Wilson in 1851, delivered a son named George Mason Wilson in a "County House," or welfare home, in 1852 in Goffstown, New Hampshire and moved to Boston in 1855. The child lived about seven years, succumbing to death approximately seven months after the self-publication of Wilson's novel. Thomas Wilson neither supported adequately nor resided with his family for any lengthy period, preferring instead to be a seaman. Harriet Wilson's fragile health prevented her from ordinary or difficult employment, which resulted in a destitute economic status, forcing her to surrender her son to white foster parents following spousal abandonment. Wilson believed writing to be a gentler profession that would allow her to regain custody of her son and support him and her, but the tragedy of his untimely death took a personal toll and the Civil War interrupted any market demand for anticipated sales of her book.

Harriet Wilson's life is the impetus for the fictional *Our Nig*. The significance of this narrative is its theme, which centers on an African American woman of mixed racial heritage who is confined to indentured servitude in the household of a northern family. The heroine, Alfrado, is the love child of a white woman and African American man. She struggles to achieve empowerment, self-determination, and self-actualization. The novel is a critique replete with widespread race, class, and gender issues typical of antebellum America. These issues are not limited just to the southern aristocracy but are similarly found in northern two-story white houses. The narrative commentary reveals that slavery has diverse forms, literal chain-and-shackle bondage and figurative indentured servitude; both are forms of imprisonment and oppression. The novel's antagonists are northern women who have nothing in kind or in common with southerners. They are not antebellum enslavers, but they operate a system of usury toward the novel's mixed-race heroine that is as vicious as enslavement. *Our Nig* is not only important for its theme and critique but also significant for its plot structure. It is a reworking of plot styles developed by Wilson's contemporary white female novelists. Through this revisionist working of European plot styles, Wilson uses her innovative skills to contrive a plot structure that is uniquely her own formula. She weaves a narrative saga out of the sequence of events befalling her female mulatto protagonist. By concentrating on the heroine and not on Alfrado's parentage or mulatto status, Wilson draws attention away from the obvious and to the humanity of her character. Alfrado is a single woman on a quest to establish her independence from those who would attempt to suppress her elevation. She exemplifies Christian qualities and a determined will. She does not sink to the depths of despondency but rises to the heights of hope as she progresses to a brighter coming day.

Another borrowing of European women's novel-writing structure is Hannah Crafts's *The Bondwoman's Narrative* (2002), the first known novel written by an African American fugitive slave woman (around the 1850s) and possibly the first novel written by an African American woman. This narrative is the recent discovery of Henry Louis Gates Jr. His authoritative eye caught an auction description listing in a Swann Galleries catalog for "Printed and Manuscript African-Americana," a listing that intrigued him. The blurb referenced a possible original unpublished manuscript authored by a person intimately familiar with the institution of slavery. Ironically, the manuscript listed as lot 30 came from the private collection of Dorothy Burnett Porter Wesley (1905–95), librarian, bibliographer, and historian at Howard University's Moorland-Spingarn Research Center. Revelation of the manuscript's prior ownership excited Gates even further and led him to arrange for the successful acquisition of lot 30. After some meticulous investigative scrutiny and exhaustive research to verify authenticity, Gates published Hannah Crafts's novel. It is the latest addition to the canon of nineteenth-century African American literature by women, a valuable asset to the repertoire that is the African American historical literary tradition.

The Bondwoman's Narrative, entitled in the manuscript *The Bondwoman's Narrative By Hannah Crafts, A Fugitive Slave Recently Escaped From North Carolina,* is an autobiographical novel, a fictionalized version of the life of Hannah Crafts (a possible pseudonym; her identity remains unverified).

The novel follows slave narrative conventions, autobiographical accounts of slavery by the escapee, and aspects of the sentimental novel, that is, emotional overindulgence. Crafts's text indicates her familiarity with Frederick Douglass's *Narrative of the Life of Frederick Douglass, An American Slave, Written by Himself,* for her descriptions about parentage, tools of literacy, and self-teaching are similar to Douglass's. For example, she has no parents to speak of, a benevolent old white woman from the North instructs her in the alphabet, and she hones her literacy skills by browsing through old books and newspapers in the slave owner's library.

Furthermore, some scholars writing in *In Search of Hannah Crafts: The Bondwoman's Narrative* claim that Crafts sampled from contemporary writers of her day in constructing her manuscript. Catherine Keyser believes that Crafts must have done a critical reading of Charlotte Brontë's *Jane Eyre* (1847), pointing out similarities in wording, events, and structure, even the synopsis of the British novel. Additionally, Hollis Robbins claims that Craft's rain scene is from Charles Dickens's *Bleak House* (1852), as well as other content and diction. Robbins also asserts that Walter Scott's *Rob Roy* (1819) is a possible source of Craft's word choices, although to a lesser degree than Dickens. Jean Fagan Yellin thinks that Crafts borrowed her gothic style from Harriet Beecher Stowe's *Uncle Tom's Cabin* (1852) in addition to stock characters and reactions to slave cruelty. Similarly, Shelley Fisher Fishkin points out that Crafts's novel is an extraction of William Wells Brown's abolitionist play *The Escape, or, A Leap for Freedom* (1858), the first play published by an African American male; Brown read it publicly in various places beginning in 1857. One similarity with Brown's play is that it has a prominent character named Hannah who is urged to marry a slave whom she does not love, the plot that leads to escape in Crafts's novel. Another similarity is the arrogant, haughty, and selfish Mrs. Gaines, the equivalent of Crafts's Mrs. Wheeler. Because literary critics generally perceive the novel as purely a European imaginative construct, Hannah Crafts's *The Bondwoman's Narrative* tilts the scale on this common assumption. Crafts transforms components of British texts to tailor slave characters in her own novel. Researchers ponder the possibility that a rethinking or a rewriting of the canonical novel tradition in America may be due.

The significance of the slave narrative tradition is important to writers like Alice Walker and other twentieth-century African American novelists. They have access to an encyclopedic treasury of the time before the Civil War that they use to help readers jump over the hurdles of difficult times. Knowledge of the enslavement period—its psychological brainwashing of an entire group of people, its curses, downfalls, and defeatism—is mandatory for the writer to master in order to weave a story of liberation and the quest for personal freedom, the narrative's primary emphasis. The slave narrative continues to influence the crafting of contemporary works primarily because it is such a good edification medium. The narrative format may originate in slavery, but by the narrative's end freedom will be attained. Because contemporary slave narratives contain elements of an autobiographical voice, readers have an affinity with the character who is not limited by the system. Contemporary slave narratives include Ernest Gaines's *The Autobiography of Miss Jane Pittman* (1971), Toni Morrison's *Beloved* (1987), and Alice Walker's *The Color Purple* (1982).

Following the antebellum period and the emphasis on the slave narrative began the Reconstruction period and the passage of the 13th Amendment to the Constitution, which formally abolished the institution of chattel slavery in the United States forever. Although the struggle for equality would always be a pressing need for African Americans, post–Civil War individuals pursued literacy and education as personal goals. Many African American women were at the helm of new organizations geared toward self-help for the former slaves. One woman's voice was central in helping to address the needs of women early in the period. Anna Julia Cooper felt that the new period was the "woman's era," a time when women needed to make their voices heard in colored women's clubs and the suffrage movement. Cooper responded to the tradition of the dominant culture that formerly represented African American women in abolitionist work and literary production.

Cooper's *A Voice from the South, By a Black Woman of the South* (1892) focuses on women's issues and analyzes the race problem and its negative effects in American society. Cooper's book, moreover, addresses the human condition and how best to improve the status of those relegated to the lowly places in life. In Cooper's opinion America failed to provide mechanisms of uplift to all its citizens, for any society that dooms any of its members to a permanent low caste will never achieve the fullness of its possibilities. The period in which Cooper writes is an era in which women, African American and white, tore down barriers that prohibited them from becoming meaningful contributors to society. At that time society was more receptive to white women, although mass protests were the channels used to get them this attention. The 1890s also marked a backlash in African American progress, and it was a climate that tolerated an increase in lynchings.

Cooper's essays are women-centered and family-centered, making her the first African American woman to introduce in print theoretical ideas geared to women thinkers. Her theories differ from traditional European theories because they are not merely academic exercises to be discussed in academic circles. They are aesthetic and practical; they are for the masses, not just the cultural elite, although she does stress that an educated African American class with the capacity to lead must implement the theories. Cooper proposes tactics of survival in conflict resolution, a prototype that stresses never to give up the struggle against misconceptions regarding race, class, gender, politics, education, and economics. These ideas are her political platform to postulate her theory of social action and responsibility. Her theories are not just ideas of the imagination but something more fundamental, the incorporation of consciousness into what might be perceived as abstract thinking. She considers each and every thought and concludes that cognizance and consciousness are inseparable because the experiences of the new nation do not occur independently of the mind.

Cooper put forth a theory that for 250 years African Americans were virtually ignored by the artistic community. However, their lot offered something new and invigorating, unmatched and unparalleled, a gem of a discovery. In African Americans rested art, music, and poetry waiting for the pen of Shakespeare types. Cooper identifies these undiscovered and untapped artists as the "silent factor," what Alice Walker and Zora Neale Hurston would later call the "folk." Although oppressed and emasculated, these people endured in their new environment of America, becoming poetry in motion—silent poetry. Cooper believed that the African American people's "weird moanings," "fitful gleams of hope and trust," "strange and sad songs," and "half coherent ebullitions" were fertile ground for any half-awake researcher. Cooper saw artistic African Americans as an original laboratory, a talent pool indigenous to America, a group that would revolutionize literature in America.

Anna Julia Cooper is the cultural and theoretical forerunner to Alice Walker's womanist theory, which she articulates in her groundbreaking essay "In Search of Our Mothers' Gardens." Alice Walker believes that one of the weaknesses of most white feminist novelists is that they do not consider the entire culture. She believes that there are exceptions of course, such as Tillie Olsen and Grace Paley, who write with scope. Walker believes that the problem is that white feminists do not have connections with communities other than their own. They do not evince that they have Third World friends, associates, or contacts. They seem unable to write outside of the box. Walker believes that most white feminist writing is romance, which becomes obvious when feminist movies are made from feminist novels. Walker believes that these novelists' skills of observation are evident in their descriptions of white men, which are quite thorough, but they are stuck in this vein. Their popular novels define this relationship but go no further. Even when they examine social ills, they give their personal solutions without studying social problems, limiting solutions to their world. Walker believes that this problem needs addressing by white feminists: the personal as political has to be removed from the confines of the house (Bonnetti).

Joan Didion is a feminist writer whom Walker believes has no sense of the struggles of others, failing to widen her scope to see others. In Walker's opinion Katherine Mansfield (1888–1923) also can be categorized as not other-culture interactive in her writing. She feels that writings such as *Up the Sandbox* play into the hands of the ruling patriarchy by dehumanizing and feminizing leaders such as Fidel Castro. She believes that material such as this is financially successful but culturally distasteful. Likewise, when these writers do include others, she thinks that it is tragic for white feminist writers to repeat the mistakes of white male writers, such as, looking at another culture and finding it comic.

Walker is impressed, however, with the writing of Virginia Woolf (1882–1941), indicating that her material is lasting. She appreciates Woolf's inclusiveness, for example, in *Orlando,* when she brings in other cultural groups. On the opening pages of the novel, the English children are striking at the head of a Moor that has been brought back from the war. Walker feels that this very telling small scene draws readers into what is occurring in the culture, eliminating an encapsulated, isolated experience (Bonnetti). Walker feels that even with minimal contact, feminist writers could accomplish some inclusiveness in their writing. The absence of the acknowledgment of others is one of the experiences that prompted Walker to envision a theory that was more inclusive.

Walker thinks that the surest way to perish is to cut self off from experiences that are enlarging, to cut self off from self. The things that make people loving, expansive, thoughtful about human relationships, and thoughtful about nature need to be cherished. The ideal way to achieve this harmony is to avoid formalism and rigidity at all costs. Walker feels that people need to bloom; this flourishing ensures the happiness of the present generation and their descendants (Bonnetti). Her contemplations made a theory that was more inclusive even more significant.

Alice Walker articulates concerns about heritage and the role in American society of African American women and women of color. In her pivotal essay "In Search of Our Mothers' Gardens," she uncovers a matrilineage that is the wellspring from which all creativity flows. She unmasks this mother lode as a spiritual connectedness of female experiences that is the source of the continuation of contemporary creativity. Mothers' gardens are the taproot, the central source, that births into existence all manner of creative womanhood, but the challenge for African American women and women of color is to tap into the source in order to perfect or achieve fullness of outcome.

"In Search of Our Mothers' Gardens," too, is more than contemporary criticism. It is an investigation into the origin, history, and text geared primarily, but not exclusively, to African American women and women of color. It opens the door to a new theoretical approach called *womanist*, a term coined by Alice Walker in the epigraph to the volume *In Search of Our Mothers' Gardens: Womanist Prose*, which serves the purpose of exploring the reserves of literature and art by African American women and women of color. Walker returns to the historical past in order to comprehend the present, but the descent into the past takes place in the mind. "In Search of Our Mothers' Gardens" examines the mind's gardens, flowers, and inheritance.

Walker's term *womanist* is not the same as generic womanism or the *Africana Womanism* coined by Clenora Hudsom-Weems, who after testing and shaping her theory at various academic gatherings witnessed its fruition in her widely acclaimed book *Africana Womanism: Reclaiming Ourselves* (1994). Hudson-Weems's term is neither a derivative of nor an appendage to African feminism, black feminism, feminism, or Walker's popularly accepted womanist. One difference is that Africana Womanism rejects as foremost in women's struggle gender as an issue and the male as an enemy. It also focuses globally exclusively on women of Africana heritage, and it has no identification with any traditional feminist organizations.

Walker's term, however, has a connection to the established feminist movement in the United States. It identifies African American feminists and feminists of color without referring to their color while simultaneously liberating them from a group that has an attachment to oppressors. She offers an extensive unabridged denotative and connotative explanation of the newly coined term in which she refers to loving the "folk." These are people like those in Zora Neale Hurston's *Mules and Men* and those like Walker's own parents, individuals who are tied to the land, appreciate nature, have very little in materialism but are wealthy in love and kindness. Through womanist theory Walker explores the oppressions, insanities, loyalties, creativity, and triumphs of African American women and women of color.

"In Search of Our Mothers' Gardens" is an exploration of discovery into the aesthetics of African American creativity. Discovery for Walker in this essay begins with the words of the African American writer Jean Toomer (1894–1967), whose venture through the South in the 1920s led him to discover the unique spirituality of black southern women, a spirituality that was "intense," "deep," and "unconscious." To Toomer these women were the "mules of the world" entrapped in a lifetime of toil; they were "exquisite butterflies trapped in evil honey." Yet, they had the ability to separate the fatigued body from the freed mind. The capability of performing separation of body and mind allowed them to sow the seeds of their indomitable spirits into what appeared to be infertile red clay.

These women that Walker alludes to were the mothers and grandmothers of the current generation who produced from this seemingly nonproductive soil not an immediate harvest but a future horn of plenty. They were "Saints," their bodies "shrines," and their minds "temples." Walker suggests that this generation of African American women and women of color needs to reconnect to the temples that are their minds, the resting place of the spirituality of these sainted foremothers. To Walker they were "Artists" and "Creators" who endured abuses to preserve their gardens of spirituality, the basis of their art. Though the bodies of these sainted foremothers perished, their creative spirits did not.

Then Walker points to one such creative spirit, a foremother, Phillis Wheatley, a slave in America's revolutionary period. Walker alludes to the fact that Virginia Woolf, an Anglo foremother, did not have Phillis Wheatley in mind when she wrote in her acclaimed publication, *A Room of One's Own* (1929), that a woman writer needs a room of her own and enough money to support herself. Wheatley had neither, but she had a creative spirit left to her by the sainted African mothers and grandmothers. Walker uses Woolf's term "contrary instincts" to demonstrate that Wheatley, too, had contrary instincts in the form of "chains, guns, the lash, the ownership of one's body by someone else, [and] submission to an alien religion." Walker updates the Anglo foremother's stipulations for writing fiction to include African American women and women of color. Like her descendant Zora Neale Hurston, who also exhibited "contrary instincts," Wheatley had divided loyalties and a divided mind, which time and hindsight justify. Walker emphasizes that Wheatley's literary aesthetics germinated in the garden of her mind, the womb of the creative spirit. Wheatley was able to create in spite of her chattel existence. Thanks to the spirituality that stirred in her mind's garden, she created and left a legacy of creativity as a sainted foremother.

Walker shows the relationship between the mind's garden of the past and the mind's garden of the present. Contemporary women, too, create in their mind's garden. They experience more up-to-date "contrary instincts" in epithets that attack or express that which is contrary to fact, such as the stereotypes of "Matriarchs," "Sapphire's Mama," and "Mean and Evil Bitches." Walker explains that in spite of the antagonisms, contemporary African American women continue to create. They are artists and black women, an identity that lowers their status in many respects rather than raises it, yet they affirm themselves as artists. The "contrary instincts" under which the foremothers created exist for today's women as well. Neglect and exclusion represent the norm rather than the exception. However, Walker asserts that contemporary African American women and women of color artists, herself included, swim against the tide, drumming up the "living creativity" of the ancestors. This "living creativity" survives within them and grants them the stamina to continue to be unyielding African American women and women of color and artists.

Creations of the mind's garden, according to Walker, manifest literally in the mind's flowers. Walker reflects on her own living sainted mother and the creative art within her. For Walker's mother that creative spirit was the ability to grow aesthetically pleasing flowers that drew people from near and far, some of whom requested the privilege to walk among the magnificent blooms, to fuse themselves with the art and the artist. When her mother worked in her literal garden, she was the Creator who arranged her universe according to her personal concept of beauty. Like the foremothers who created against impossible odds, Walker's mother turned her experience as a poor sharecropper's wife, a wife who "labored beside—not behind—[her husband] in the fields," into a demanding garden with varied blooms of incredible beauty.

The mind's flowers not only manifested in her mother's literal garden but also in her art of storytelling. Her creative spirit increased to grow aesthetically pleasing flowers to the eye and to tell aesthetically pleasing stories to the ear. This legacy she passed on to her daughter. Walker, the inheritor of this talent, realizes that she is the recipient of the same creative spirit that Wheatley received, for Walker's mother bequeathed to her the mind's flowers, the art of storytelling in the oral tradition. Thus, the stories that Walker writes and all womanists write are the foremothers' stories. Walker realizes that the creative spirit that sparks her is very close at hand in her mother. Therefore, the impetus for searching out this creative spirit in mothers and grandmothers should be the artistic quest of all African American women and women of color. To Walker, searching through the gardens of the foremothers helps contemporary African

American women and women of color discover their own gardens. From them today's women find the creative sparks that light fires of many thousands. Many of the foremothers are unknown, leaving no signature to their art. Yet they planted seeds that sprouted so that today's women can continue to pass on the spirit.

Walker proves in this essay that African American women and women of color writers have a reserve of literary history that can be traced, a history that is not incomplete or fragmented. Just as contemporary white feminists in the literary arts sometimes trace their creative spirit to Virginia Woolf, one of their Anglo foremothers, African American women and women of color also have roots and ancestorship in their mothers and grandmothers. Walker encourages contemplation or even meditation on heritage and inheritance. Walker's essay conveys the consideration of specific inquiries, such as how African American women and women of color search for their mothers' gardens, how they redeem their mothers if they are lost in history, and how they trace a history that is not visible in American culture. When African American women and women of color search for their mothers' gardens, they find their own.

Walker ends her essay by stressing the possibility that Phillis Wheatley's mother's signature is manifest in more than her biological life. Walker wants African American women and women of color to know that there is a recognizable mother source, specific sainted foremothers, ancestral legacies of creations, histories to be inherited, and reservoirs of future creations yet unaccomplished in the gardens of the mind. African American women and women of color artists find the source of their creativity by looking back at the spirit of any African American woman or woman of color who was creative. One creative spirit births into existence another. This creative spirit must continually be passed on; the death of the body must not and cannot destroy the creative spirit.

Walker responds to the needs of those African American women and women of color who are dissatisfied with the contemporary feminist movement, who feel that it offers them no part, no purpose, no direction, and no representation. The new womanist theory embraces the consciousness of African American women who need to escape the patronizing attitude of contemporary feminists.

Walker returned to her mothers' gardens to coin this term, for it finds its roots in "You acting womanish," an old African American expression meaning "You are trying to be too much like a woman." Therefore, it has a take-charge appeal, which is the message that Walker wants to get across to contemporary African American womanists, who in being womanist seek out African American ancestors, make spiritual connections, preserve the artistic spirit, and take charge of their own existences and those in their charge. The womanist continues to pour her energies into raising women's consciousness about the decision makers' contrived inhibitors of race, class, and gender, though her approach is more toward print than platform. She champions the causes pertaining to workplace biases, including salary issues and sexual harassment. She favors Walker's definitive identity of her, which affords her more of an inclusive role in the dialogue on women-related issues; however, she is more woman-of-color-focused and friendly, more scholarly inclined rather than activist inclined, does not reject the biological maternal ancestral line, and is more male tolerant.

Continuous academic and literary contact among African American women and women of color hailed this new womanist theory. Moreover, it fed the desire for more expressions of African American feminist theory. Since the university setting increasingly became the site of protest, it was only a matter of time before a university-affiliated woman of color or writer would step forward to meet the demand. Student interest in the writings of women of color and women's studies in general also increased the necessity. This urgent need became so great because women of color were undergoing cultural change. These African American women and women of color refused to be completely absorbed into the culture of the dominant society, to have themselves dissected according to the dictates of the emerging feminist theories and existing Western philosophical theories. The whole psychology of women of color rejected such a process, creating a stirring spirit of unrest among them. The articulation of womanist theory, though, continued to manifest itself.

In essence, womanist is a theory in the creative aesthetics of African American women and women of color. Walker's preference as an artist is not to append the word *black* or *African American* to point out something. She prefers to use a word from her own culture in which all the meanings are apparent. In African American culture *womanist* implies audaciousness, but in white culture it implies weakness. A little girl who is womanist is asserting herself, acting like a woman. Walker also chose this term because it includes more of African American and women of color culture than the term *feminism* does. Unlike African American women, European white women and feminists have neither the same racial struggles nor reactions to color as African American women nor take into consideration the whole culture (*A Conversation with Alice Walker*). For these reasons, Walker feels that the womanist route is more appropriate to the needs of African Americans and women of color.

Critical and theoretical voices emerged as a result of Walker's *In Search of Our Mothers' Gardens: Womanist Prose*. Barbara Smith is the first known African American critic-theorist of record to dare to name the tradition of commentary on the works of African American women writers. Her action is bold, responsible, and serious. She officially characterizes it as black feminist criticism. She affirms this theory in the publication of her aesthetically interesting and consciousness-raising essay "Toward a Black Feminist Criticism," which appeared in Elaine Showalter's *The New Feminist Criticism: Essays on Women, Literature, and Theory* (1985). Evolving from a reactionary critical environment, Smith not only reacts to the constrictors of the critical arena in which she found herself but also establishes another way of analyzing the literary texts of African American women writers based on culture and shared black experience.

Deborah E. McDowell's essay "New Directions for Black Feminist Criticism," which also appears in Elaine Showalter's publication, is an appeal to black feminist critics to flee from analyzing literature from a perspective that generates separatism among races, classes, genders, and cultures. She proposes a move toward inculcating methodologies that unveil the use of language, literary devices, and mythic structures in the writings of African American women. Similarly, Barbara Christian's "Race for Theory," which appeared in the 1987 journal *Cultural Critique*, advances a theory that silence is not empowerment. African American women need to explore the many approaches they can take to analyze their literature. She believes that African American women need to reject the idea that Western theoretical approaches are the sum total of ways to examine literature. Christian believes that when African American women prioritize themselves, they will discover new modes of interpretation and analysis because they treat themselves as subject.

bell hooks (Gloria Jean Watkins) is a critic who examines the core issues of race, class, gender, and voice that surround sexual politics and feminism. Her groundbreaking book, *Feminist Theory from Margin to Center* (1984), a collection of theoretical essays, is an attack against traditional feminist theory, especially as it is interpreted and applied in the United States. It also sheds light on the feminist movement's weaknesses and how to move those on the fringes or margins toward the center, the place of empowerment. The late Audre Lorde's (1934–92) *Sister Outsider: Essays and Speeches* (1984) centers on African American female aestheticism, the politics of race, the difference of lesbianism, and individualism born of struggle and conflict. She challenges feminists to look the demon in the eye and acknowledge that it is she, especially if it is the feminists' actions that retard the progressiveness of feminism.

Clenora Hudson-Weems, mentioned above, contends that her model of Africana Womanism best responds to the struggles of women of African descent. She believes that the identity of women of African descent should not be based on principles of oppression and repression. She believes that identification with Euro-American feminists is problematic and polemic; therefore, separation is the answer.

Among others who accepted the challenge to illuminate African American women's literature is Houston A. Baker Jr. His "There Is No More Beautiful Way: Theory and the Poetics of Afro-American Women's Writing" appears in his *Afro-American Literary Study in the 1990s* (1990). Hazel Carby's "'On the Threshold of Woman's Era': Lynching, Empire, and Sexuality in black Feminist Theory" appeared in *Critical Inquiry* in 1985. Henry Louis Gates Jr.'s *Reading Black, Reading Feminist: A Critical Anthology* (1990) examines African American women writers and their works. Paula Giddings broke new ground with *When and Where I Enter: The Impact of Black Women on Race and Sex in America* (1984). Gloria T. Hull, along with Patricia Bell Scott and Barbara Smith, edited *All the Women Are White, All the Blacks Are Men, but Some of Us Are Brave: Black Women's Studies* (1992). Cheryl Wall edited *Changing Our Own Words: Essays on Criticism, Theory, and Writing by Black Women* (1989). Sherley Anne Williams's essay "Some Implications of Womanist Theory" appeared in Gates's publication.

African American critics who promote African American women's literature include Roseann P. Bell, Toni Cade Bambara, Melvin Dixon, Mari Evans, Frances Smith Foster, Beverly Guy-Sheftall, Trudier Harris, Patricia Liggins Hill, Joyce Ann Joyce, Nellie McKay, Gloria Naylor, Bettye J. Parker, Valerie Smith, Hortense J. Spillers, Claudia Tate, and Mary Helen Washington. This list is not exhaustive, but represents the swelling effect of Walker's womanist theory.

The Reconstruction era was preparation for the literary period that would dominate the interests of African Americans with artistic aspirations. The New Negro Movement that evolved into the Harlem Renaissance would claim the 1920s as the high point, though it began earlier, but stretched itself out until the beginning of World War II. Key players in the Harlem Renaissance were Arthur A. Schomburg (1874–1938) whose extensive collection of Africana literature would culminate into the New York Public Library's Schomburg Center, the most extensive research repository on African American life, literature, and culture in the world. Alain Locke, Langston Hughes, Marcus Garvey, and so many others contributed to the making of Harlem, New York, the mecca of African American cultural achievements. Significant publications of this period were Paul Laurence Dunbar's *The Sport of the Gods* (1902) and W.E.B. Du Bois's *The Souls of Black Folk* (1903). The National Association for the Advancement of Colored People (NAACP), founded by African Americans and whites, published the *Crisis,* which became a significant outlet for African American literary expression and criticism. Toward the end of the era Zora Neale Hurston published *Their Eyes Were Watching God* (1937); the writer and her novel would fall into obscurity before being resurrected by Alice Walker 38 years later. Of these, Zora Neale Hurston, whom Walker rescued from literary oblivion, had the greatest impact on Walker. The essay in *Ms.* magazine, "Looking for Zora," written by Walker, captured the attention of a female reading public that was hungry for literature by women writers. As a result, Hurston's groundbreaking work *Their Eyes Were Watching God* is today an important work in women's studies and in the American canon, due solely to the efforts of Walker. *I Love Myself When I Am Laughing ... and Then Again When I Am Looking Mean and Impressive,* edited by Walker, is a favorite compilation of some of Hurston's best work. This magnificent achievement occurred because Walker believed Hurston to be an inspiration to all readers.

Unlike many of her Harlem Renaissance peers who through their writings focused on an oppressive American democracy and the victimization of a segment of American society, Zora Neale Hurston established herself as a beacon to guide her people through an abyss of abasement with her writings and to shed light on their words, which had always been viewed as curious and quaint rather than artistic and creative. She determined to make her business the rescue of the black idiom from what James Weldon Johnson termed a "dwarfing, warping" reality. Hurston gave no place to race, class, and gender restrictions in her personal life; her gift to the literary public was the celebration of womanhood and woman's voice.

Hurston probably did not align herself with the woman suffrage movement or any of the popular black women's clubs of the early twentieth century. However, she is a contributor to the basic fundamentals of African American women's struggle during the founding years of African American women's activism. Hurston rejected the direct approach of racial discrimination commentary, believing that she could not do anything about the race problem. Ironically, the issues of race, class, gender, and woman's voice surface anyway in the character of Janie Crawford in Hurston's extraordinary novel *Their Eyes Were Watching God*.

Moreover, Hurston inscribed the "folk" and "folk traditions" into the national literature. She believed that pure art lies in the creations of ordinary people. Hurston also advocated the exploration of mythological archetypes that are unique to the "folk" particularly. She believed that through literature women could be social, political, and literary critics. Alice Walker shares Hurston's thematic views of African American artistic ability, female sexuality, marriage and relationships, spirituality of the "folk," creativity, and cultures that occupy society's marginal positions. Having moved Hurston from margin to center, Walker incorporates Hurston as a southern maternal ancestor into the literary tradition of the African American woman writer. Hurston's love and appreciation of the "folk" influenced Walker to value the native speech, Ebonics/Black English, of African American ancestors, challenging readers not to repudiate their ancestors' voices. Walker feels that denial of the ancestor's language is denial of the person. Using this language is also an advantage to articulating one's own reality, not having others do it. Walker uses Black English in the novel *The Color Purple*. The language articulates the reality in one's community, which is usually isolated from the larger community. This theme also upholds the significance of contemporary use of the language, a kind of switching back and forth from standard forms. The use of this language within African American culture is often misunderstood within the framework of the white value system.

The realism, naturalism, and modernism era is often referred to as the protest era. The writers of this period used their art form to protest the inequities and depravations of an insensitive American system. Two significant writers of this period are Richard Wright (1908–60) and Ralph Ellison (1914–94). Wright's *Native Son* (1940) features the character Bigger Thomas, who commits a desperate act out of fear in reaction to his racial identity. Wright used this novel to protest against racism, even though his central character was extreme. His protest equated racism with slavery. Ellison's *Invisible Man* (1952) is a contemporary slave narrative. The main character is on a personal quest for self-identity. Ellison protests the betrayals and disappointments experienced by African American males in their quest for liberation. Alice Walker adheres to similar themes in her writings. In her personal life she is an activist, and her protest activities spill over into her creative works. Her concerns are the environment, health care, women's issues, and global affairs. She manages to weave these protest issues into her creative form.

The Black Arts era began the period in which Walker was honing her craft as a writer. Those writing at this time are her contemporaries. Although the publications of men dominated the Black Arts era, the publishing arena was inclusive and appreciative of women writers. There was also more tolerance of gay and lesbian artists. Furthermore, the production of literature now had more crossover appeal, so that the writers' audiences were not necessarily exclusively African American. The women occupying the literary world were Toni Morrison, Alice Walker, Terri McMillan, and Toni Cade Bambara. Morrison, Walker, and McMillan simultaneously appeared on the *New York Times* best-seller list. Not only that, literary awards came their way. Bambara received the American Book Award for *The Salt Eaters*, Walker received the Pulitzer Prize and the American Book Award for *The Color Purple*, and Morrison received the Nobel Prize for literature. Their common themes were the woman, her romantic relationships, her friendships, her family, her past, her future, her community, and her approaches to race, class, gender, and empowerment issues.

Alice Walker's essays, poetry, short stories, and novels caused an explosion in African American women's creative fiction. The result of so many women writing and a few men writing about women writing created extra space in the canon, prompting a virtual canonical explosion. Two publications that also created controversy, written by women in the same vein as Walker and at the same time, were Ntozake Shange's choreopoem *for colored girls who have considered suicide when the rainbow is enuf* (1975) and Michele Wallace's *Black Macho and the Myth of the Superwoman* (1979). These two creative expressions produced heated debate between African American men and women, often polarizing them in the academy and public forums. The arguments centered on negative stereotyping of African American males, but women viewed the works as explicit detailing of male hegemony, calling attention to women's needs.

Other accomplishments in creative fiction followed. Toni Cade Bambara (1939–95) published *The Salt Eaters* (1980), which, like Walker's *Meridian*, is an examination of the shortfalls of the Civil Rights movement. Though Bambara published other writings, this novel is her greatest achievement. Terry McMillan is a voice that appealed to the African American populace, as well as a small crossover appeal. McMillan's *Mama* (1987), *Disappearing Acts* (1989), *Waiting to Exhale* (1992), and *How Stella Got Her Groove Back* (1996) catapulted her to national fame. Although African American scholars do not select her writings as required readings, she is one of those rare personages that has ridden the wave following the success of Alice Walker.

Toni Morrison (Chloe Anthony Wofford) emerged during this period as the literary genius that so effectively celebrates African American life and culture. Her first novel *The Bluest Eye* appeared in 1970, the same year as Walker's *The Third Life of Grange Copeland.* Morrison's winning of the 1978 National Book Critics Circle Award for *Song of Solomon,* the 1988 Pulitzer Prize for *Beloved,* and the 1993 Nobel Prize for literature places her squarely and solidly in the American literary tradition.

Alice Walker's knowledge of African American literature developed at an early age through hearing it orally in her home from storytelling parents and grandparents and later through reading the works of various writers. The African American folk tradition—that is, the oral transmission of art forms, the solid ground of her parents and grandparents—rooted Walker in the use of the proverb, that rhetorical medicine of instruction and the embodiment of wisdom. In African cultures the proverb is viewed as an effective method of instructing children, helping them to grasp fully the world around them and master their way around in it. Walker also heard the familiar call-and-response of the work songs and spirituals, what W.E.B. Du Bois called "sorrow songs," that were requisite for the accomplishment of plantation field labor and essential to religious imaging of biblical narratives. Call-and-response requires a leader who sings phrases that alternate with phrases sung by the chorus. This patterning is highly structured and rhythmic, with both the lead singer and the chorus taking some liberties, but essentially the strict form is adhered to. Secular songs, "worldly music," too, were included in Walker's upbringing, the music reserved for Saturday nights to relieve tensions and provide temporary amnesia of a laborious and oppressive life.

Similarly, folktales that Walker's family told daily served to preserve family history and to entertain, both of these phenomena she incorporates into all her writing. She explained to an interviewer that she learned African American literature by reading accessible African stories translated into English. Although both the African and American storytelling culture are oral, the influence of storytelling on Walker was not purely its oral aspect. It was a simultaneous oral, hearing, and reading of stories, not just her own but other people's stories as well. Thus, the interconnectedness of orality and written language became Walker's legacy, her artful maneuvering to create literature that would place her squarely in the literary tradition.

On the one hand, Walker's niche is within the African American novel tradition with an emphasis on literary neorealism, according to African American critic Bernard Bell in his *The Afro-American Novel and Its Tradition*

(1987). He defines neorealism as examining the human condition from both a literary method and a philosophical and political attitude. More pragmatic than idealist, Walker as a neorealist concerns herself with the effect her work has on her readers, focusing on people as social and historical beings and expressing hope for people and the world. Walker incorporates her attitude toward racism, sexism, and capitalism into her text to get the readers thinking about a new social order and, even more desirable, bringing one into existence. She takes the indirect approach, giving greater emphasis to the development of character (Bell, 245–247).

On the other hand, she is also within postmodernism, meaning that her ideas are shaped by the temper of her time. She includes herself in the fiction, taking it to new limits. Global multiculturalism is indicative of postmodernism. Though a United States location is the setting in most of her novels, the world is her home. Her participatory and observatory experiences include the Civil Rights movement, Black Arts movement, Black Power movement, Women's Liberation movement, Vietnam era, lunch counter sit-ins, building takeovers, freedom rides, and political assassinations. Her firsthand account of the injustices surrounding race, sex, and gender, and her moral responsibility to draw attention to them in an effort to correct them, become an integral, if not the central, focus of her writing.

Walker takes her place in the literary tradition as the reclaimer of southern African American women's legacies and art forms. Notwithstanding, the attention given Walker's writing by African American scholars helped to draw attention to this gifted writer, leading to her canonization in American literature, African American literature, and African American women's literature.

Although Walker's mother, a master storyteller, was the most significant influence in her life, Walker's early inspirations in her love of the creative process were novelists. She had a fondness for British novelists. The bard of Stratford-on-Avon, William Shakespeare, was an early inspiration. So was Jonathan Swift, author of *Gulliver's Travels,* a book that Walker received as a birthday gift and one that she read faithfully every year. The Brontë sisters also were favorites—Anne, Emily, and especially Charlotte, who wrote *Jane Eyre,* a favorite novel for many years. Although she loved everything he wrote, Thomas Hardy's *Tess of the D'Urbervilles* and *Jude the Obscure* were two she revered by the writer she felt expressed sensitivity to land, language, and customs. Virginia Woolf, too, was a personal influence. Russian novelists Fyodor Dostoyevsky, Nikolai Gogol, Maxim Gorky, and Leo Tolstoy were writers she read more than any others during her high school and college years. After her discovery of the Russian writers, she added American novelist Flannery O'Connor, who resided near her as a child, to her list of favorites (Bonnetti).

Gradually, various other writers became literary interests, such as Gabriel García Márquez, a Spanish-speaking novelist whom Walker feels demonstrates an awareness of and a oneness with his culture and history. The intellectual African American writer of the twentieth century, W.E.B. Du Bois, too, inspired Walker with his delight in the beauty and spirit of African American people. The African American poetic genius Langston Hughes touched her so deeply that she wrote a biography of him, *Langston Hughes, American Poet* (1974), so that generations to come would never forget him.

Alice Walker sees herself first as a writer, and then as a writer who takes several avenues of expression. She told an interviewer that her preference is to have wholeness in everything that she writes. She wants to present experiences on several levels and have the readers see the completeness of the experiences, not a sliver, comprehending even more than she is giving. She feels that her writing should first bring health and wholeness to her and then health and wholeness to her readers. Writing, in Walker's opinion, also saves lives, initially her own, which then filters down to the readers. She wants her art to help the readers grow emotionally and socially, to become better people, to become whole people. Her understanding of the people she writes about, their relationships, stems from her ability to observe human behavior. Just as she observes nature, which has many variations, she also observes people and their relationships, which vary. She uses the knowledge gleaned from these observations to construct her art in a way that benefits, as well as entertains, her readers (Bonnetti).

Walker compares her role as a writer to that of having three seeing eyes or three beating hearts—being black, a woman, and a writer. She welcomes this challenge, does not find it threatening or problematic. She considers these three places within her reservoirs from which she can draw. She remembers well the times that she despaired or became suicidal, found life bleak and difficult, but writing alleviated those slumps. Through writing she is able to keep herself in the light and away from the darkness *(A Conversation with Alice Walker)*.

Alice Walker is the consummate, authoritative short story writer, accomplished in her art form. The stories in *In Love and Trouble: Stories of Black Women* (1973) center on African American southern females and their dysfunctional relationships, the violence in their lives, and their mechanisms of redress and resistance against injustice. These stories highlight women who find themselves at the mercy of the men they love and how their passions, forces of nature, and societal expectations drive them. One story in this collection that was included in 1974's best stories is "The Revenge of Hannah Kemhuff," depicting an African American conjurer woman who seeks revenge on a white woman who denied her basic necessities during the Great Depression. The spell cast by the conjurer leads to the deaths of the white woman's children and the insanity and subsequent death of the woman. Walker decided on this approach when interest in African American folk culture piqued her interest during her research into the writings of Zora Neale Hurston. This collection won Walker the Richard and Hinda Rosenthal Award from the National Institute of Arts and Letters.

Walker's second collection of short stories, *You Can't Keep a Good Woman Down* (1981), examines closely abortion, fame, love, lust, pornography, cultural thievery, new lovers, and old friends. An interesting story in this collection is "Nineteen Fifty-five," an examination of cultural thievery. The symbolic figure is an example of white exploitation of African American music. Walker's explanation of the story is that the character is attempting to sing something that he lacks in experience and interpretation. Although faultless, he is caught up in a system of usury often found in the South, rendering him pompous with fame and finances. His character flaw is that he listens to people who fabricate the truth and care less about their prevarications. Moreover, his inability to repay what he has taken leaves him empty and unfulfilled, which causes his ultimate destruction (Bonnetti). The stories in this collection, however, differ from *In Love and Trouble* in that the characters are more optimistic, and Walker is true to her theme of surviving whole.

In addition to the short story, Walker delves into the essay literary genre. To date she has three essay collections. She edited *I Love Myself When I Am Laughing ... and Then Again When I Am Looking Mean and Impressive: A Zora Neale Hurston Reader* (1979), her attempt to restore Hurston to her rightful place as one of the literary foremothers and a major American writer. Walker almost single-handedly campaigned to preserve Hurston's dedication to the "folk," the beauty of African American expressions, and her spirit-filled audacious approach toward life, and she succeeded. Walker includes very insightful commentary about Hurston as a person and as a writer.

Her second essay collection, *In Search of Our Mothers' Gardens: Womanist Prose* is a testament to the survival of African American women. Their achievement of wholeness can be accomplished by redirecting their attention to their ancestors, where they will find a rich heritage of sister warriors to whom they must look to heal themselves. The inspiration for this collection was the reclaiming of Zora Neale Hurston and Walker's memories of her mother and her mother's art, fragrant and flowery gardens, the creative legacy of southern African American women. Walker also introduces the term *womanist* in this collection, a term that bridges the ideological differences on issues of race and gender between African American and Euro-American feminists. This collection, with its emphasis on womanist theory, is the landmark work in the development of womanist theory and criticism.

The final essay collection to date is *Living by the Word: Selected Writings, 1973–1987* (1988). She treats the environment, horses, human beings, the African American radical group MOVE, oppressed hair, the planet, tobacco, and the Uncle Remus stories, to name a few subjects, and she includes writings from her personal journals. Walker compares the relationships between social violations of sexism and racism and violations against nature. She also delves into the relationship between human beings and nature. Walker's selection of the book's title was revealed to her in a dream, a spiritual connection that relates her work to prayer.

In addition to short stories and essays, Walker also writes poetry, which to her is communicating with herself at the most vulnerable and deepest levels. When she takes an excursion into this place, she sees vividly and takes control of whatever force has control of her. Earlier in her life, whenever she composed poetry, it was always in a state of sadness and depression; however, she has more control over her emotions now because of the healing effects of her writing, allowing her to construct poems when she is bubbly and elated *(A Conversation with Alice Walker)*. Her poetry, though not overly anthologized, is a welcome exploration into the recesses of her soul. Her way of expressing human emotion, her use of language, description, and tone give her poetry a dramatic quality, as well as a resemblance to song.

Walker's first book of poetry *Once: Poems* (1968), most of which were written in less than a week and slid under the office door of poetry professor Muriel Rukeyser at Sarah Lawrence College, was Walker's introduction to the world of professional writing. The poems are about her life in the South and her travels to Entebbe, Uganda, and Kenya, where she lived with the Bugandans and the Kikuyus. Some of the poems center on African images and civil rights in the South. A series of poems focuses on Walker's abortion ordeal, as well as love.

The Southern Regional Council's Lillian Smith Award for poetry and the nomination for the National Book Award were given to Walker for her second mainstream poetry publication, *Revolutionary Petunias and Other Poems* (1973). These poems focus on resistance against injustice and the decline of the southern revolution. Walker also praises the role of African American women such as Sammy Lou and Mrs. Johnson in the Civil Rights movement, establishing them as the s/heroes of the resistance.

Walker's third collection of poetry, *Good Night Willie Lee, I'll See You in the Morning* (1979) is a tribute to women's healthy love of themselves. The fourth collection, *Horses Make the Landscape Look More Beautiful* (1984), centers on relationships, the connection between nature and human beings, and violations against nature. Walker also considers connections between racism and sexism. Walker collected all of her poems in her fifth collection, *Her Blue Body Everything We Know: Earthling Poems, 1965–1990* (1991). Such a compilation is rare for an African American woman, especially one who, most likely, will write more poems. Another volume, *Absolute Trust in the Goodness of the Earth: New Poems* (2003), focuses on grief, life, and spirituality. Walker's latest volume of poetry is *A Poem Traveled Down My Arm: Poems and Drawings* (2003), a development centering on her signature. To avoid the monotony of signature repetitiveness at book signings, Walker included drawings along with her signature, giving readers something unique within the book.

Walker's fame comes primarily from her novels, and Walker views the genre of novel as the medium that permits her the greatest amount of freedom in her creation of a literary work that is uniquely hers in her own words. This construct is ideal for her, allowing her to create a form that interests and entertains her, becoming an entity that she has not seen before, for she does something different each time she writes a novel (Bonnetti). Walker is a skillful novelist, successfully weaving story lines into dialogue and introducing readers to the most intimate thoughts of characters.

During the course of her literary career, Alice Walker has invigorated the study of literature. She brings to the field remarkable energy and expertise in the telling of women's stories. Her special appeal stems from her ability to develop the stories of African American women who are noticeably absent from American literature, being very careful to balance women who find themselves weakened by their position with women who are strong and rise above their unfortunate circumstances.

3

The Third Life of Grange Copeland (1970)

Alice Walker's first novel introduces thematic factors that will prove essential in all her subsequent works. Treatments of familial cruelty precipitated by racism, sexism, and economic deprivation are the crux of *The Third Life of Grange Copeland* but will recur consistently wherever Walker applies her creative hand. The patriarch in this novel, Grange Copeland, travels three roads that represent three lives or three lifetimes: the road of economic suffering as a sharecropper in the South, the road of urban degradation in the North, and the road of self-respect and improved personal development in his return to the South. The novel also explores a 60-year period of trigenerational male cyclical violence that establishes a pattern of trauma and terror in family members. It provides an in-depth exploration of the destructive nature and compulsive abusive behavior of Grange and his son Brownfield in their determination to wreak havoc on their respective wives Margaret and Mem. Even though Grange Copeland acquires redemptive qualities and strives to change the course of destructive familial patterns and right some of the wrongs evident in his family members' chaotic lives, he proceeds toward greater disorder. However, Grange's final act, though violent, opens the door of change for the future of the Copeland biological line. Alice Walker's family's sharecropping existence in Eatonton, Georgia, provided the stimulus for this novel.

STRUCTURE AND PLOT

The novel's structure is like that of an old tattered and torn family quilt held together by snippets of fabric that once were whole pieces of family members' garments. The arrangement of the quilt's pieces is random; they are not laid out according to any apparent carefully constructed plan, just held together with hope and prayer. The novel is divided into 11 parts of unequal length, with 48 smaller chapters that chronicle the saga of degeneration and regeneration of the Copeland clan. The first half of the novel probes the degenerative process of family destruction under the Argus-eyed observation and far-reaching hold of southern racism. The novel's second half plots a chart of regeneration brought about by knowledge of human fallibility and social pathology that had been passed on from father to son. Realization of wasted youth and adulthood causes within Grange the desire to amend the negative trends chosen as life's options. Part 1 details the daily, weekly, monthly, and yearly cycles of first-light-to-last-light labor in the sharecropping existence; fear and hatred of southern white men and their control over the division of labor; rituals of merriment found in song, dance, drink, and fight every Saturday night, and the periods of wife abuse in between; and the desperate grasping for spiritual solace at Sunday church services. The novel focuses on the monotony of Grange's sharecropping life, broken only by weekend social life when he loses himself in the sinner's indulgences of alcohol and brutality. Grange's violent behavior toward his wife Margaret, her child, and their son Brownfield is a norm that becomes the pattern of Copeland life. This section culminates in Grange's desertion of the family to the North and Margaret's infanticide of her son and her suicide.

The second and third parts show Brownfield's inheritance of Grange's methods and madness, as he becomes both sharecropper and wife abuser. It also marks the reappearance of Grange to exchange marriage vows with Josie the prostitute, who is also his son's lover. Ruth's birth takes place in part 4. She is the youngest of Brownfield's daughters and the precious granddaughter who will become the hope of the Copeland line and the reason for Grange to turn his life around. Brownfield's intensified violent nature and his spiteful treatment of his wife Mem and their daughters are the central points of parts 5, 6, and 7. Briefly, Mem becomes assertive, threatening Brownfield with a shotgun, but her newly found empowerment diminishes. The plot climaxes in this section with Mem's murder and Grange gaining custody of Ruth. In part 8 Brownfield and Josie, a prostitute and Grange's abandoned second wife, become conspirators to petition a white judge to void Grange's custodial rights and return Ruth to her father following Brownfield's release from prison. Parts 9 and 10 depict the tender bond that develops between Ruth and Grange. He provides wise responses to her interrogations and recounts his life in the North. In part 11 Grange murders Brownfield after he successfully gains custody of Ruth, and the police, in turn, kill Grange at Ruth's cabin in the woods, which he had vowed to secure against white men's assault.

Walker develops the themes of the novel through the eyes of an omniscient author-narrator who is privy to every tightly held secret of Copeland family life. The narrative voice is all-knowing, unrestricted, and free to comment at will but also the creator of a tale that stems from personal instruction of and participation in sharecropping life. Moreover, Walker bases the story line of this novel loosely on the murder of a Mrs. Walker (no relation), killed by her husband, of Eatonton, Georgia, whose 13-year-old daughter Kate was Walker's friend and classmate. Walker similarly witnessed violence among her relatives, although not as extreme as death, when the males in their need to dominate females resorted to violence. The narration proceeds not in chronological order but in patchwork, rearranged quilt style. The reader receives pieces of information about each character as events unfold. The theme of death marks this novel: Margaret's suicide; the murders of Mem, Brownfield, and Uncle Silas in the North; the justified killing of Grange; infanticide, the killing of the human spirit; and the killing of free-spirited womanhood through wife beatings. These events take place against a background of institutionalized racism in the South. Thus, Walker weaves a story of the futility of violence and the advantage of personal responsibility.

SOCIOHISTORICAL CONTEXT

Following the end of the Civil War, Congress established the Bureau of Refugees, Freedmen, and Abandoned Lands, shortened to Freedmen's Bureau. The agency provided assistance to recently freed men of the postwar period in their transition from slavery to freedom. Former slaves, who were destitute as a result of the war, petitioned the agency for assistance in the acquisition of education and land, negotiation of labor contracts with white farmers, resolution of legal matters involving African Americans and whites, and provisions of food, medicine, shelter, and transportation. The bureau was underfunded and inadequately staffed; the demand for assistance was too great for the agency to honor the deluge of requests.

One significant blunder of the agency was its mishandling of land distribution. Government "set-asides" included 40-acre plots seized from Confederates that were to be distributed to freedmen, but President Andrew Johnson, who ascended to the presidency after the assassination of Abraham Lincoln in 1865, revoked the arrangement almost before distribution could take place and ordered any distributed land returned to its former owners. Therefore, former slaves who believed that they had become landowners had to reconcile themselves to the fact that they were landless, literally and figuratively, and the country's one-time Confederate enemies became the recipients of the spoils of the North's victory. Agency officials advised freedmen to dismiss their bitter feelings and reconcile with their old masters, to once again work the land that they had previously worked without compensation.

Another blunder was the formation of the sharecropping system, which exploited the labor of unskilled field workers. Agency officials pressured freedmen to agree to contracts with former landowners, arresting those who rejected the agreements. Seldom did the landowners offer wages; instead they agreed to forfeit a one-third portion of the harvested crop to the freedmen, which benefited them little since the best of everything went to the landowners. Furthermore, landowners demanded that workers remain on the land for a full year without striking or quitting. The late historian Benjamin Quarles (1904–96) wrote in *The Negro in the Making of America* (1964) that the sharecropping system rarely operated in honesty, for the system was evil within. The landowners charged exorbitant prices for commodities sold to the sharecroppers and attached excessive interest charges. Sharecroppers were required to purchase the farm tools, seeds, and provisions needed to work the land owned by others. In addition, the landowners kept the accounting records, and the illiterate sharecroppers had no way of verifying inaccuracies in price fixing. On "settling-day" sharecroppers often found themselves in debt to the landowners with no money owed to them from the sale of their one-third portion. Consequently, they had to surrender their services to the unscrupulous landowners for another year. The shackles and chains of the freedmen ended with the surrender of the South at Appomattox, but they were just as bound to a system of perpetual exploitation as they had been before the war. The system offered no incentives to improve their lot in life; the harder and longer they worked and the greater their output, the less their reward (Quarles, 246–247).

The Freedmen's Bureau, in its desire to appease the southern land-owners, became partner to a system that co-opted whole families. The landowners refused to relinquish their grip on their former slaves. Deeply entrenched in the regional culture of white superiority and the inferiority of all others, the landowners demanded that the freedmen work the land as families—without wages. Thus, the system put into play generations of laborers who were always destitute, fearful, and illiterate, especially those who lacked the fortitude to seek out an alternative. Therefore, most sharecroppers realized that their effort resulted in "a lazy descent to hell." The uncompromising system robbed many of their good-natured postures and positive outlooks, causing many of them to become angry, frustrated, and violent.

The Third Life of Grange Copeland emphasizes the Copeland family's endurance under slavery's replica, the sharecropping system. The men in the family are so oppressed and unable to escape their frustration and rage that they turn on family members, whom they love and oppress or even kill, especially their wives. Because white men dominate them, offering no release of pent up emotions, the Copeland men insist on the complete subservience of their wives. If the wives dare to resist the men's domination, they become the victims of verbal, physical, mental, and emotional abuse. The Copeland men believe that their identity as men stems from how much they threaten and intimidate their wives, demanding that they be silent when men talk and that they are obedient when men make demands. Because the white men under whose bondage they labor treat them as if they are children, the Copeland men feel that they can dominate only in the white men's squalor shacks that house their families. In the white men's presence they respond to his queries with "yassur," prohibited from making direct eye contact and denied the privilege of demonstrating any intelligence on a level equal to them. They feel helpless and entrapped. They are in search of any semblance of their manhood. Unfortunately, the only part of it that they retrieve is the physical, abusive, territorial part, the part that is more animal-like than human. They are pawns in the curse of violence that permeates and swallows up the South.

Walker's novel is a passionate work, a multilevel commentary on life, a realistic depiction of lives lived. One level sheds light on a farming system designed to keep in place an antebellum system. Another level examines the violence that such an inhumane system causes. A third level looks at relationships between husbands and wives, fathers and children, mothers and children, and women and women. Walker's interest lies in the message. She wants her concerns to be readers' concerns. This novel exposes an oppressive sharecropping system that has its origin in seventeenth-century colonial beginnings. Walker shows how this system dehumanizes the labor force on which it depends for its existence and continuance in its perpetrators' quests for profits. Walker feels that she is the artist whose duty is to illuminate the system's menacing effects on an entire group of people. Her message is that people need to be saved, need the strength to evolve from the drudgery of forced enslavement, and need to discover their own redeeming qualities and self-worth. Only then can they manifest love and emerge as whole human beings.

GENRE AND NARRATIVE TECHNIQUE

The Third Life of Grange Copeland has qualities of the *bildungsroman*, that is, the novel deals with the development of a key character from youth to experience. Grange, the Copeland patriarch gradually intellectualizes the lessons of life as he progresses from a young man to an adult to a wise geriatric character. The novel also functions in the genre of the *Erziehungsroman*, the novel of education. The ultimate lessons Grange learns are self-love and then familial love. His progression to this level of inner examination leads to the remarkable transformation that he makes toward the end of his life.

The autobiographical genre is closely akin to Walker's works because she bases her works on the truth as she experiences it. Slave narratives or emancipatory narratives (see Literary Contexts/Chapter 2) began the tradition of African Americans articulating their innermost feelings. Walker continues the tradition in this novel with her perceptive insights and observations and detailed accounts of the inner workings of the human spirit. She writes as if she gives a firsthand account of personal experiences that rocked her to the core. Walker explains in the "Afterword" to *The Third Life of Grange Copeland* the true events that are the foundation of this narrative. Seeing the lifeless human form of her classmate's mother, dead from spousal physical abuse, spread out on the enameled table in the morgue created in Walker's mind an image that found a resting place. Only after she created her manuscript could Walker shake the image that had pressed her for years. Walker's autobiographical contribution in this novel thus helps to keep autobiography a constant in the African American novel tradition.

Walker's literary accomplishments can be categorized as part of the neorealism movement within African American literature. This movement references the European realism movement of the nineteenth century in which writers reacted against the idyllic presentations of the romantic era. Similarly, African American neorealists react against the stylistic devices employed by writers of the protest movement, particularly in their effort to understate so as not to offend readers. Protest writers seemed overt at the time; however, in hindsight scholars observe that the messages produced in their writings were under the radar range. Conversely, Walker's approach is overt, explicit; she conceals nothing and makes no attempt to evoke empathy. Nor does she write for shock value. Her purpose is to privilege the message. African American neorealists create in a somewhat improved racial climate, and readers are more receptive to topics of controversy taken on by writers. Moreover, writers create for themselves rather than target specific audiences. Toni Morrison once remarked that she writes the books that she likes to read. Alice Walker, too, takes the stance that she writes what is important to her. Time has not swept away the problems of racism, and as a writer of the neorealism movement Alice Walker uses her art form to inform readers of the many masks it assumes and to dissuade them from embracing its negativity.

Walker's narrative style does not lean toward the complex. Her use of language is amazingly clear and plain, not intimidating to readers. Her syntax is a masterful aggregate of detail and effect that produces density and depth. Readers proceed quickly through the novel, not slowed down for want of clarity, but they may pause at the section that chronicles the life of Brownfield and Mem, not because it confuses but because it mesmerizes. Not pure chronology, the novel's numerous twists and turns and positional shifts contribute to its wide scope. It is epiclike without being pure epic, as a series of adventures centered on characters who form an organic whole in their connection to the patriarch. For example, its characters come from the dregs of society rather than high positions; even the landowners are not representative of the genteel aristocracy the South has to offer. In addition, Walker builds on a historical record that is significant to a race of people and the nation as a whole. The novel's patriarch is not of legendary significance but is crucial to the life-changing events of his family. The setting covers both the South and the North, and while the characters' deeds are not valiant in the pure sense, a certain kind of determination is needed to commit even the most heinous antisocial acts. Walker, as the Greek Homer would have done, recounts the deeds of the protagonists with objectivity and acuity.

THEMES

Themes are controlling ideas or central insights of imaginary works. They reveal aspects of life or support perspectives about life. *The Third Life of*

Grange Copeland incorporates themes of abuse, blame, death, economic enslavement, entrapment, marriage, neglect, relationships, and racism. Walker's writings are often social commentaries; therefore, many of the themes in this novel center on social issues. Knowledge about abuse is key to understanding the characters of Grange and Brownfield. Both their wives are victims of physical, psychological, mental, and emotional abuse. Blame is another idea that permeates the novel. Grange and Brownfield blame whites for the wrongs in their lives, refusing to be responsible for their actions. Another central focus of the novel is the economic enslavement enforced by the landowners who control the sharecroppers and, therefore, any material wealth that they might accumulate. Landowners insist on whole families working, forcing Brownfield to be overseer over his own children and exercising control of generations of the family line. The Copelands are perpetually indebted to their white employer, the debt endless and greater with the increase in family members working.

Grange, associating Brownfield with family ties and responsibilities, feels trapped. Thus, Grange experiences guilt for his inability to improve his son's life and his powerlessness to protect Margaret from her white lover Shipley. The house is also significant because it is Mem's gift to herself, a material possession that Brownfield is unable to give, a status symbol and a symbol of accomplishment. Marriage as a theme in this novel begins as something hopeful, passionate, and idyllic but soon becomes painful, given over to suffering and Saturday night beatings.

The theme of death abounds in this novel, especially family killing. It takes several forms. For example, spiritual, emotional, relationship, and inner-self death occur with all the characters. Then there is the death of loved ones. Margaret commits suicide, putting into place the demise of the Copeland wives. Finally, the physical death of Mem and the infanticide of the newborn son result in the end of the Copeland biological line and the clean sweep of Mem's memory from future generations. Neglect is a subtheme that focuses on Grange's treatment of Brownfield. Relationships between parents and their children, husbands and wives, and women with each other figure prominently as a theme in the novel. All of the relationships are dysfunctional until Grange has a spiritual wakening.

Like the slave narratives that precede it, this novel uses the image of the North as a salient element. It represents an escape route for slaves, in this instance escape from sharecropping and white control. For Brownfield, the North initially is a sanctuary where family members appear to be free. It is analogous to Frederick Douglass's North Star, a guiding point in reaching freedom. Moreover, the North is the Promised Land, a place of hope and liberty.

Central to this novel is the theme of racism, the terror of the South where the wheels of change never turn in a positive direction. Racism is cyclical and repetitive, an institution that is woven into the fabric of the South. The system of racism reverses familial roles, making the male the dominant provider but unable to provide sufficiently. The system holds African American men in a childlike position, requiring that they seek permission for all requests. Women, too, are the victims of role reversal. Southern ladies subscribe to a system in which as agents of purity and beauty they are the recipients of male affection, but the reverse is true for Margaret and Mem. The attention they receive is cruel and brutal. Racism in the South fosters mental genocide and permanent hopelessness, where the days center on agriculture and debt, laborers and debt, work and debt, and the hot sun.

CHARACTER ANALYSES

The Third Life of Grange Copeland contains two fully developed male characters, Grange and Brownfield Copeland, and two developed female characters, Margaret and Mem Copeland. Walker's wordplay on the name *Grange* has reference to farmer or farm, which relates to the character that she develops. His life centers on farming, although for others and not for himself. When readers meet Grange, he is already a married man who is abusive to his wife Margaret. Readers are not privy to his developmental changes as he transitions from childhood to adulthood or the patterns that contribute to his flawed reasoning and moral attitudes, but as a young adult husband and father he is ineffective. His neglect of his son Brownfield begins the child's cycle of descent into a place from which he cannot successfully emerge. Grange is uncomfortable with his masculinity, feeling that he is less than a man. This sense of unmanliness results from his inability to free himself from the surmounting debt that he owes his white boss. Unable to deal maturely with the situation in which he finds himself, he seeks solace in alcohol and in the arms of the local prostitute Josie as an adulterer, creating greater complications in his marriage. Drinking and wife beating become ritualistic events in his life.

Grange manages to muster up enough gumption to travel to the North, where he believes he can improve his life, leaving behind Margaret, who commits suicide as a result of his abandonment. New York holds even greater degradation for Grange. Hunger and helplessness drive him to criminal behavior for survival of self. In a haze of despondency he indirectly causes the death of a pregnant white woman as he attempts to convince her that he should keep more than half of the $700 that she discards following a quarrel with her married lover. Encumbered by racism and fear of an African American male she jumps to her death into an icy pond to escape his approach, refusing to accept his helping hand of rescue. Her death leads to the resurrection of his suppressed manhood in a hostile earthly existence. To Grange, her death represents the death of white oppressors and oppression, restoring in him a passion and zest for life. Therefore, he returns to Georgia with his sanity intact, a changed man, a complete person. His respect for African American women is at a height surpassing any experienced in his previous life. Upon his return to the South he marries Josie, but the bliss he seeks in this relationship is fleeting. Grange eventually neglects Josie just as he abandoned his first wife.

By now Grange understands and achieves socially responsible behavior and assumes the responsibility of rearing Ruth, his youngest granddaughter, following her mother's vicious murder by his son. He prepares to make a sound home environment for Ruth, but this attempt at harmonious family life is marred by Brownfield's success in regaining custody of the daughter whose mother he has murdered. To correct the inadequacies of the white justice system that determines that he cannot rear Ruth, Grange reverts to past behavior and murders his son so that Ruth can have a good life. As a sacrificial lamb for the sake of the family that he wants to preserve and protect, Grange has the most redeeming qualities of the men in the novel. Although the police end his life, he ends Brownfield's life, which to him is the performance of a last good deed before he closes his eyes forever.

Walker's wordplay on the name Brownfield symbolizes decaying farmland vegetation. Fields of green represent bountiful harvest, but fields of brown are rejected plants suitable only to be mowed over and turned over into the soil year after year. Thus, Brownfield is a permanent fixture of the enslaved sharecropping system. Men like Brownfield are essential to the success of the system, making any escape improbable. Though Brownfield struggles to comprehend his lack of advancement in material accumulation, he resigns himself to his life of slavery and drudgery and copes with the land (Copeland) in the way the system designed—perpetual servitude as the chattel of the southern landowners.

Brownfield has no redeeming qualities; he is dysfunctional to the core of his composition. At the age of 16 he already exhibits signs of an antisocial personality. His behavior stems from being deserted by his parents, who show him no outward signs of love or affection. What dreams he has as a youth of going to the North soon dissipate under the calamity of obstacles that he confronts. He has a clear understanding of his gender role as a man, for when he is told to watch over his mother's illegitimate infant son, he resents the responsibility, mumbling to himself that he feels like a "sissy." Unable and unwilling to attach himself and bond to his younger half brother in a meaningful way, Brownfield sees child care as strictly women's work. Alone most times and painfully shy, he moves away from direct lines of communication, preferring instead to ask and answer questions from an indirect path—back turned, eyes askance, or from another location. He lurks in the shadows, avoiding direct contact with those he fears, including his mother and father.

In an effort to fit into a social environment, Brownfield finds himself on the path established by his father. As an employee at the Dew Drop Inn working for Josie, he releases sexual tensions by sleeping with her. Not completely incapable of emotional attachment, he meets and falls in love with Mem, Josie's schoolteacher niece, whom he subsequently marries. He wins her affection and confidence, only to take advantage of her. Whether masking his true personality or speaking honestly about his intentions, Brownfield offers Mem hope and escape from the South—both unfulfilled. Instead, he duplicates the abusive patterns of his father but to a greater degree. Intolerant of everyday frustrations, he sinks deeply into an abyss of depression, searching for the meaning of manhood and for his own manhood. His feelings are identical to those of his father; he believes that he is less than a man. Like his father, he turns to the person closest to him to express in physical, mental, and emotional abusive ways his dissatisfaction with the hand life has dealt him. Beating his wife becomes as ritualistic as working daily on the plantation.

When Mem demonstrates her womanly strength by threatening Brownfield with a shotgun, her audaciousness temporarily unnerves him. Her retaliation is unexpected and unbelievable. Like a boxer who suddenly is hit with a surprising uppercut, he retreats into a safe zone, waiting for an opportune moment to strike back. During the time he waits to reclaim the authority Mem has seized, he mimics compliance. His inner self plots, plans, and schemes for the perfect moment of intervention to remove Mem from her high place. He exists for the exact moment to bring her down. His need to dominate Mem and their daughters far exceeds any desire to have a peaceful home or a content wife. Brownfield's destructive behavioral patterns allow him to function deceptively and feign emotions that he no longer feels.

Brownfield needs to justify his impoverished life. To do so, he fulfills his desire to deprive Mem of her schoolteacher education, middle-class ambitions, and her articulate speech, all reminders of his own less-than-adequate education; this duty he accomplishes through a series of abusive techniques. He forces Mem and their children to return to the hard labor of sharecropping after she successfully finds them a home that is not a shack, something that he was incapable of doing. His selfish nature causes him to treat Mem and their children as objects, his wife to be used when he wants sexual gratification and discarded when he does not. His calculating, devious mind conjures up ways to break her down step by step, resenting the fact that her womanly mental strength exceeds the mental strength he has as a man. He accuses her of being the paramour of white men, which she vehemently denies. To scar her even more emotionally he places their three-month-old newborn albino son in the winter cold so that he will freeze to death. Without any guilt, he sleeps comfortably beside his wife, having committed the ungodly act because his only son showed a resemblance to Grange. Turning Mem into a toothless hag and a constant nag fails to satisfy his insatiable appetite for wife abuse. His murder of Mem in a drunken stupor and deranged mind-set is Brownfield's final destructive act, and it sends him to prison for nine years. However, prison does not put a limit to his vile scheming because he conspires with Josie, the prostitute he shared with his father and who is now married to his father, to get custody of Ruth. Upon the expiration of his prison sentence he convinces the judge to return custody of Ruth to him, a decision that leads to his death at the hands of Grange.

Mem is a composite character. Alice Walker writes in the "Afterword" to *The Third Life of Grange Copeland* that she derived this character's name from the French *la même,* meaning "the same." Mem is the same as all women, symbolic of all women who suffer physical, mental, psychological, and emotional abuse from their spouses. Mem's descent into abject poverty begins when she marries Brownfield. Although she desires to advance socially and strategizes a more humane existence for herself and her daughters, Brownfield circumvents any steps toward progress. Because the sharecropping system emasculates Brownfield to the point that he is intellectually and professionally nonproductive, Mem apologizes to him for her accomplishment. For the assurance of her husband's love she relinquishes her reproductive power, remaining with Brownfield for nine years even after he destroys the fruit of her womb. His charges that she is ineffective in the bedroom—not as good as Josie—and ignorant about birth control are not enough for her to leave him. Surmounting physical abuse drives her to reinvent herself as a woman, choosing to become a witch rather than remain a demure southern lady with intellectual abilities. Her physical appearance suffers, her speech imitates informal and unschooled "folk" language, and her constant nagging falls on deaf ears. In her metamorphosed personality she threatens her husband with a shotgun and destroys his defense mechanism, but even this dastardly act fails to check his deviant behavior.

Mem remains with Brownfield for the preservation of the family unit. She is a victim of gender-role socialization. Her acceptance of Brownfield as dominant partner, family defender, and economic provider contributes to dissolution of the family she so craves. Her willingness to endure his abusive behavior renders her incapable of weighing her options. Mem's educational advantage qualifies her to shift to survival mode and provide a new beginning for her and her daughters. However, she opts to keep the children with their abusive father, further jeopardizing her own safety. She brainwashes herself into believing that a positive family relationship results from the husband remaining in the instrumental role as the head. Therefore, Mem follows Brownfield obediently back into the slavery of the sharecropping system, defeated by his adversarial comments, continual sarcasms, and dominant posturing. For her reluctance to leave an extremely abusive environment she pays the ultimate sacrifice meted out to women who endure abuse—death.

Margaret is also a defeated woman. Although betrothed to Grange she finds herself in a joyless marriage. The two of them share a plantation squalor shack but develop separate lives. Margaret, too, reinvents herself as a woman. Emotionally scarred from the physical abuse she has suffered at Grange's hands, Margaret exploits her own sexuality in retaliation for the treatment she receives from her husband. Discarding her marriage vows she transforms herself into a slut and takes many lovers, including the white men responsible for the sharecropping system. She bears an illegitimate son as a result of her promiscuous behavior. Despite the unhappiness she feels in her marriage, she is content to remain with Grange in an oppositional relationship. Margaret becomes dependent on the prevailing anger, frustration, poverty, and abuse, preferring the daily sounds of discontent to the silence of nothing. Therefore, when Grange abandons her and makes his way to the North, his absence from the household is more than she can bear.

Rather than live without him she commits suicide by poisoning herself and her illegitimate child.

Josie, a minor character, is an example of how a father's rejection alters the future and expectations of a young girl. Full of promise and possibility, she becomes pregnant at the age of 16 and incurs the wrath of a disappointed father. To win back his love she uses her body to earn money to purchase gifts for him, but her well-intentioned gestures are unappreciated. Nevertheless, her introduction into the world of prostitution leads to quick and easy money. Josie finds herself in an adult world where she is expected to fend independently. The lessons of her youth teach her to feed on male despair, becoming the happy medium between their downtrodden livelihoods and broken marriages.

Daphne, Ornette, and Ruth are the living children of Brownfield and Mem. Daphne is the precious darling in the eyes of her father until she is about five years old. Around this age Brownfield realizes that he has nothing to offer his daughter, materially or otherwise and, thus, ceases to treat her as a little darling. Daphne assumes the role of griot, repository of family secrets, granting her younger sisters revelations of their father's good period before he becomes a viper. Brownfield's aberrant behavior affects Daphne negatively though, even his nicknaming her "Daffy," for she develops into a nervous child and as an adult will become a mental patient. By the age of eight, the middle daughter, Ornette, has a tough exterior and an exuberant interior. Ruth by age four shows promise that she will determine her own way independent of family turmoil; even at this tender age she has the temerity to call her father a "sonnabit."

Shipley, Captain Davis, Mr. J. L., and the judge are white men who represent the solidarity of the power of the South. They hold intact the southern tradition of lifetime servitude of African Americans. Although the Copeland family men are freeborn citizens and have the right of mobility, these inherent rights do not alter their status as land laborers. Southern authority figures are not to be undermined by literacy or Christianity. These systems are outlets that essentially reinforce the cultural and physical repression of the workers. The judge's decision to return Ruth to a violent father demonstrates a lack of compassion concerning the legal affairs of African Americans. Returning Ruth to her father guarantees that the sharecropping system will inherit another laborer. Grange thwarts the plan through gun violence. In turn, the power structure ends Grange's life because he represents resistance to their system, and resistance is the enemy of the sharecropping system and the South. Men in authority who reinforce hypocrisy and violence uphold the system. Nothing and no one usurp power from those who control the forces of government and the systems of economics.

A SOCIOLOGICAL READING

Several schools of thought make up sociological theory and criticism. Scholars take many avenues in analyzing, interpreting, perceiving, and understanding social constructs. The consensus among critics who apply sociological theory to literature is that the perspectives can be categorized into two primary schools of thought: Marxism and feminism. Marxist critics explore literature for images of how dominant value systems lead to the suppression of the laboring class. Feminist critics evaluate patriarchal culture, examine the place of women as authors in the canon, and recover neglected women writers of the past.

German philosopher and theorist Karl Marx (1818–83) authored *The Communist Manifesto* (1848) along with fellow thinker Friedrich Engels (1820–95). The ideology expressed in this publication focuses on socialism, which Marx calls "scientific socialism." Fundamental Marxist theories include five major points: economic determinism, dialectical materialism, class struggle, theory of surplus value, and theory of the inevitability of communism.

According to Marx economic determinism is at the foundation of all human institutions. Changes in economic conditions affect the production and exchange of goods, that is, economics determines the exchange of goods. Dialectical materialism involves a historical timeline of evolutionary change and development created by material conditions. One economic system becomes a contradiction of itself and gives rise to another economic system, in an unending process of class struggle. Those in charge of production (thesis) struggle with those who produce the goods (antithesis). In the final analysis there is the emergence of an economic system based on a classless society (synthesis). Marx's theory of class struggle stipulates that the historical chronology of the world outlines an indefinite struggle between free men and slaves, later bourgeoisie and proletariat. The struggle between the two groups will manifest a utopian society, one that is classless.

The theory of surplus value emphasizes the connection between wealth and the value of goods. Marx theorizes that the value of goods, the selling price, is a result of the effort of workers, but workers are recipients of subsistence wages earned from the goods they produce. The capitalists or bourgeoisie reap the profits or surplus value of goods; they are the recipients of the creations of workers. Thus, the theory of the inevitability of communism points out that destruction of the middle class is the effect of the conflict between the bourgeoisie and the proletariat. With wealth and ownership of production concentrated in the hands of the capitalist few, the middle class will be eradicated from the equation and swallowed up by the proletariat. In the end a technological society brought about by the capitalist few through the introduction of machines will replace the laboring class. Capitalists, then, will have no market for the goods produced because the consumer class, the proletariat replaced by machines, will face mass unemployment. Because job displacement and financial failure do not allow them to purchase goods, the laboring class will start a revolution, assume control of production of goods, abolish the bourgeoisie, and create a classless society void of economic divisions.

Literary scholars who apply sociological Marxist theory to imaginary works focus on the relationships among the classes and on the roles money, politics, and power play and how best to redefine and reform society's distribution of wealth among the classes. Critics view literary works as products of the particular economic and political climate at the time the works are composed or the time described in the action of the literature.

Feminism as a literary theory has four basic principles. First, found throughout Western civilization is a system of patriarchy that is male-centered and male-controlled and that subordinates women to men. It manifests its power in all arenas, including art, culture, economics, family, politics, religion, and society. Next, men through their patriarchal biases formulate cultural constructs of gender, defining masculine and feminine traits. Further, patriarchal ideology defines among imaginative narratives the canonical great books, the majority of which are written by men for men. Finally, the pervasiveness of patriarchal ideology is responsible for the aesthetic criteria for analyzing, interpreting, perceiving, and under-standing literary works, making the critical assumptions overwhelmingly gender-biased.

Feminist literary critics include Sandra Gilbert, Susan Gubar, Adrienne Rich, and Jane Tompkins, as well as Barbara Christian, Barbara Smith, Claudia Tate, and Mary Helen Washington. Elaine Showalter has been particularly influential in the feminist literary movement. In *A Literature of Their Own* Showalter argues that literature by and about women sheds light on literary subcultures that undergo three significant developmental phases: feminine, feminist, and female. The feminine phase centers on imitating the dominant tradition and internalizing the standards pertaining to it. The feminist phase expresses opposition to the dominant tradition and aids the cause of minority rights. The female phase ceases to be opposition dependent, reversing the course and turning inward; it is the place of self-discovery and self-identity.

Feminist literary scholars value the political and theoretical discernment of women's personal experience, that "the personal is political." They highlight "gynocentrism," examining works of literature for a woman-centered frame of mind. They are interested in what assumptions about women exist and how to communicate those assumptions. These scholars bring together communities of women to inform female culture and consciousness.

Both Marxist and feminist critics examine literature for issues of oppression, especially as pertaining to those underserved and underrepresented in society. In the "Afterword" to *The Third Life of Grange Copeland,* Alice Walker ponders the question of whether she could influence her readers to see connections between the oppression of a woman and the oppression of an entire people. Even more, she wonders whether she can get her readers to care. Many scholars see no value in sociological and political approaches to literature. However, to read Walker's writings is to confront the interconnections between literature and lives lived. Walker's literature and societal events are intertwined with economic and political connections. The literary critic Priscilla B. Clark in "Literature and Sociology" asserts that sociological perspectives are advantageous in showing the connections between individuals and collective phenomena, groups, institutions, and forces. Taking a sociological approach helps readers to glean a greater understanding of the phenomena and the work of literature.

The Copeland family men have a culture of their own. They struggle to establish their identities and sustain their traditions while simultaneously making adjustments to meet the demands of the dominant society. Moreover, they are at society's margin, and their behavior clashes with the expectations of the wider society. For example, the Copeland men's definition of manhood is distorted; they have a false representation of masculine gender. Their need to define themselves as men is inextricably tied to their need for control. Because they cannot exert authority over the wider community, women or wives become the targets of their frustration. The distortions that emanate from their confused minds are directly related to the racism that is inherent in their society.

Racism in the community where the Copeland men reside functions because those in power agree to sustain certain group boundaries and foster identities of superiority for the empowered. Those on the fringes are then left in inferior positions and have no power. Moreover, the elite's access to higher paying jobs introduces a competitive edge to the equation. Those with the power dismiss those on the fringes as inhuman or unworthy in order to restrict access. The Copeland men, then, are victims of the racism of the dominant society. They function under restricted freedom and exercise limited control, their families becoming the outlet for them to express their resentment of the restriction.

Walker's novel points out the preponderance of violence in poor African American households. She elucidates the occurrence of violent acts in an isolated rural poor community where the family's housing is substandard. The Copeland men use their families as sacrifices for their inability to exercise control as men. Violent behavior is also an inherited phenomenon, passed down from father to son. Grange's family undergoes weekly abuse, and he ultimately neglects and then abandons them. Brownfield emulates the behavior of his father, making his own family a scapegoat for his inability to attain power in a white man's world. His wife and children are the recipients of his regular beatings. Brownfield justifies his behavior by placing the full blame on white men.

While patterns of racism are systemic in the South and in sharecropping, to blame negative behavior on the whole lot is unjustifiable. Brownfield denies that he has options in determining his behavioral patterns. Although he finds himself looking down on those higher up, white men are not totally responsible for his choosing to become a brute. His decision to remain in slavery by becoming an overseer on Shipley's plantation stems more from his fear of white men than from their domination. While white men do play a power game and keep him in a stranglehold, they do not advocate that he brutalize his wife. Mem becomes the brunt of all of Brownfield's inadequacies. Stripping her of her womanliness, knowledge, diction, and power is a conscious decision on his part without any intervention from white men. His behavior is more a result of his jealousy of his wife—of her intelligence—than of any injustices inflicted upon him by white men. Brownfield takes the necessary precautions to maintain Mem's unattractiveness, making certain that she has sufficient blows to the face and kicks in the side. Not only is he successful in maiming her constantly, he also succeeds in killing her character and her body. Brownfield makes these decisions outside the parameters of racism, which is not to blame for his determination to respond to frustrating situations with anger and violence.

A significant aspect of sociological examination is problem solving. Coming to terms with the reasons for the existence of negative entities is a major breakthrough. Walker's novel helps to shed light on sharecropping and the futile existence that it offered African American families of the 1920s. This system provided no outlet for economic advancement and contributed to feelings of powerlessness in the people who provided their labor. The landowners reaped all the benefits and the profits, leaving the laborers without hope. Walker's novel also presents Grange's character as an instrument of redemption and love. His trip to the North contributes to his spiritual rebirth and revelations about the meaning of a man's existence, namely, that manhood and family destruction are not synonymous. Similarly, the injustice of white men does not justify violence toward family. He puts spiritual rebirth into action when he assumes parental responsibility for Ruth and extends to her his undying love. His individual transformation is the inheritance that Ruth receives so that her family will be one of compassion, honesty, and love.

4

Meridian
(1976)

Meridian is the follow-up to *The Third Life of Grange Copeland*. Alice Walker examines the role of women in the Civil Rights movement in her second novel and explores similar thematic issues. She explores the sexism within the movement, an often-neglected aspect. She also shows how African American women made sacrifices in their lives to join the campaign to free their people. Meridian, the main character, begins her life in the traditional way offered to women—marriage and motherhood—but finds herself pursuing higher education. Becoming politically awakened her involvement in the movement leads her to a higher calling, resulting in a decision to devote her life to freedom causes.

Meridian is the antithesis of the stereotypical African American mother figure. Believing that she is the epitome of failure at motherhood, she relinquishes her son, has her tubes tied to prevent future pregnancies, and devotes her life to activism in order to be an agent of change. Walker advances Meridian to the position of symbolic mother of the African American race. Thus, *Meridian* is a novel about the interconnectedness of personal change and movements for social change.

The novel *Meridian* challenges the African American male stance on the nationalist position, which idealized African American manhood. The contribution and oppression of women went unacknowledged. Student

Nonviolent Coordinating Committee (SNCC) leader Stokely Carmichael (Kwame Ture) once remarked that the only position women would hold in the organization was the prone position. Walker's novel opens the way to a consideration of a different aspect of the nationalist position, angering many, especially African American males. Despite the controversies, Walker's volume of publications is evidence of readers' demand for her work, for she treats subjects that are engaging to readers.

STRUCTURE

Walker begins the novel with a quote from Black Elk in John G. Neihardt's *Black Elk Speaks*. She returns to the repository of Native American myths, stories, and histories. As a holy man Black Elk inherited the name of his father, grandfather, and great-grandfather; Walker similarly uses three generations of matrilineal heritage for Meridian. Having the ability to transform his human spirit and travel back in time, Black Elk often explained the meaning of Native American symbolism and history. He acknowledged the omnipotence and omniscience of the Great Spirit even as he reported historical travesty in his lament for the Oglala Sioux tribe that returned to the earth spirit during the Indian Wars of 1860–90. In like manner, Walker's epigraph from Black Elk refers to the death of a people's dream of a nonviolent approach to demonstrating and the death of the hope for equality and freedom. Thus, she references the death of the Civil Rights movement, for passive resistance gave way to overt violent action.

Walker's next page begins with two lists of definitions of the word *meridian,* one list defining the word as a noun, the longer of the two, and the other defining it as an adjective. Both lists share the common symbol of circles spiraling, intersecting, and ascending toward an apex.

Walker divides the novel into three sections: the first is Meridian, the second is Truman Held, and the third is Ending. The first part allows the reader to experience time travel as Walker explores Meridian's matrilineal roots, descending to the time of her mother, grandmother, and great-grandmother and then suddenly being propelled forward to the 1970s again. The descent of the second part entails a journey to a brief time prior to the 1960s and then a return to the 1970s. The last section travels forward to a time out of the sphere of Chicokema (the only Native American identity preserved in the town) where Meridian receives resolution and Truman's quest begins, which is actually the start of the novel. Walker takes readers on a circular journey and evolves full circle.

The journey is also embryonic, a return to a time before conception when decisions regarding life's paths are made. The spirit that is to become agrees to follow certain paths before entry into a specific realm is allowed. This journey is personal. Then the spirit that is to become agrees to interact with other spirits and share discoveries and experiences. The spirits are in a constant state of travel, spiraling, intersecting, and interacting toward a higher understanding. This journey is social. Both journeys are explorations into history, and at a given point personal history and public history intersect to bring revelation and resolution.

The novel has 34 chapters, but the initial chapter is an outline of what is to come. The first chapter in the first section relates the sequential events in the novel in the order of their presentation. Walker titles the first chapter "The Last Return," suggesting a type of finality at the beginning. Most of the novel focuses on the 1960s; however, it begins in the 1970s. Therefore, the reader looks back to the 1960s from a historical perspective, for example, observation in a present time to a past time or looking back as in hindsight. Each subsequent chapter develops a specific motif relating to spiritual beings, the coexistence of spirit and body, nature, or music. Walker's introduction of animism (the belief that everything is immaterial spirit) as a spiritual construct is central to the development of the novel. Walker's approach is that spirit consciousness is the highest form of understanding, and it is the vitality of the universe. *Meridian* is Walker's first experimentation with time travel in novel form. With this novel she looks ahead to time travel in *The Temple of My Familiar*.

SOCIOHISTORICAL CONTEXT

The Civil Rights movement in the United States has its origins in the Reconstruction era following the Civil War, from 1865 to the 1890s. The 13th Amendment to the Constitution, passed January 31, 1865, prohibited slavery in the United States. The 14th Amendment guaranteeing citizenship and the 15th Amendment giving suffrage soon passed. Unfortunately, the Supreme Court in 1883 nullified many of the federal initiatives passed on behalf of African Americans during Reconstruction. Secret societies formed in the South intent on intimidation, lynching, and violence against African Americans, which led to successful efforts to oust reconstructionists, putting former Confederates back in power. In 1896 the Supreme Court dealt another blow to African Americans in its rendering of the *Plessy v. Ferguson* decision that established the doctrine of "separate but equal," also called the Jim Crow Car Law. Homer Plessy, more white than African American, rode a section of a Louisiana train reserved for "whites only" and was arrested. Plessy sued for protection of equal citizenship under the 14th Amendment, but the Court upheld the practice, introducing segregation, or "Jim Crow," as a standard in American life. Similarly, the Atlanta Compromise stirred up controversy when Booker T. Washington's (1856–1915) speech at the Cotton States and International Exposition in Atlanta, Georgia, on September 18, 1895, encouraged African Americans to content themselves with inferior roles, dismiss desires for social equality, and focus on economic prosperity. The establishment praised Washington's delivery, but African American spokesmen refuted the speech at every opportunity.

From 1900 to the 1930s African Americans protested against the practices of Jim Crow. W.E.B. Du Bois was an instrumental force in the formation of the Niagara Movement in 1905 to reaffirm the struggle for African American equality; born from this organization in 1909 was the multiracial National Association for the Advancement of Colored People (NAACP), with its mandate to achieve equal citizenship for all Americans. The organization's publication the *Crisis* was a vital print medium to supplement the deeds of the NAACP. The case that shocked the nation involved nine young African American boys in Scottsboro, Alabama who were arrested and charged with raping a white woman. The guilty verdicts of three trials resulted in the Supreme Court overturning their conviction on April 1, 1935. Their ordeal became a cause célèbre for supporters of African American justice. School segregation and Jim Crow were the focus of the NAACP beginning in the 1930s.

The civil rights struggle of the 1950s focused on legal strategies and courtroom tactics. With Thurgood Marshall, successor to Howard University's law school faculty member Charles Hamilton Houston (1895–1950), at the helm members of the NAACP developed a plan to overturn *Plessy v. Ferguson*. Under Marshall's tenure the NAACP Legal Defense Fund financed the association's legal campaigns. After a South Carolina test case showing the repercussions of segregation, the Marshall team decided to sue Topeka, Kansas on behalf of Oliver Brown, whose daughter Linda crossed railroad tracks and took a bus to a segregated school everyday, passing a school for white students near her home. Several segregation cases were consolidated under *Brown v. Board of Education of Topeka, Kansas*, going all the way to the Supreme Court, which issued a unanimous decision on May 17, 1954, that separate but equal educational facilities were unequal and segregation unconstitutional. white supremacists in the South called the decision "Black Monday," but it was the most significant civil rights case of the twentieth century. Nevertheless, implementation of the decision required a more public participatory approach. Following the Supreme Court decision an event occurred that prompted widespread public action in the fight for civil rights. A 14-year-old African American boy from Chicago's South Side visited relatives in Leflore County, Mississippi. Emmett "Bo" Till and his cousin Curtis Jones rode the train to visit their sharecropper uncle, but the August 1955 trip was Bo's last. Responding to a dare from several local African American boys, Bo entered Bryant's Grocery and Meat Market country store in Money, Mississippi, purchased bubble gum, and reportedly said to two-time beauty contestant winner Mrs. Carolyn Bryant, "Bye, baby," which he followed up with a wolf whistle. Mrs. Bryant informed her husband of the incident, and Roy Bryant and his brother-in-law J.W. Milam went to Bo's uncle Mose Wright's cabin and dragged the youngster into their car and drove away. A young white boy fishing in the Tallahatchie River discovered Bo's decomposing body nearly three days later. He was the only child of 33-year-old Mamie Bradley Till, who had her son's corpse returned to her in the condition in which it had been found. Thousands lined the streets of the Roberts Temple Church of God on State Street in Chicago to view Bo's remains. Outrage engulfed the nation.

The two men charged with the murder embraced their wives following the jury foreman J.W. Shaw's reading of the "not guilty" verdict after deliberation of little more than one hour. The *Pittsburgh Courier,* a leading African American newspaper, headlined the September 23, 1955, decision "BLACK FRIDAY!" Other newspapers from various communities editorialized about the injustice of the verdict. Contributions to the NAACP Defense Fund reached record levels, and African Americans prepared themselves to become activists.

The December 1, 1955 action of Rosa Parks, who disobeyed Jim Crow law by refusing to give up her bus seat to a white male passenger, sparked the Montgomery bus boycott, a form of protest involving nonviolent mass action. African American leaders in Montgomery, Alabama decided in a meeting to call a boycott of the Montgomery City Bus Lines, electing 26-year-old Reverend Martin Luther King Jr. (1929–68) president of the boycott committee of the Montgomery Improvement Association (MIA). Leaders assigned Reverend Ralph Abernathy to negotiate with city officials, who refused to concede to African American demands of desegregated seating on the buses, hiring of African American drivers for their communities, and courtesy toward African American passengers. The Supreme Court in November 1956 invalidated the Montgomery,

Alabama law of intrastate segregation, and the boycott ended after 381 days. However, disgruntled southerners bombed the homes of Reverend Abernathy and other church leaders, resulting in the formation of the Southern Christian Leadership Conference (SCLC), with Reverend Martin Luther King Jr. as president. The teachings of Mohandas Karamchand Gandhi (1869–1948) inspired Dr. King to adopt the protocols of passive resistance. Political and social revolutionary tactics of nonviolence became the protest method of choice in the next decade.

Direct-action protests began in the 1960s. The Congress of Racial Equality (CORE) sponsored workshops in Miami, Florida, from April to September 1959 on sit-ins and interracial nonviolence, giving birth to the movement. Sit-ins and freedom rides began February 1, 1960 when four freshmen from North Carolina Agricultural and Technical College entered Woolworth's, purchased toothpaste and school supplies, and requested service at the lunch counter, which they were denied. Each day the college students returned to protest segregated public facilities and "whites only" serving policies, until the sit-in movement spread to 54 cities in nine states and included white students from prestigious schools. Organizers called for a nationwide boycott of Woolworth's, a call heeded by thousands. In May 1961 workshops began in Washington DC, on freedom rides that became another tool in the arsenal of nonviolence. The movement sparked nonviolent protests against segregated public accommodations in all forms and supported the admittance of James Meredith into the University of Mississippi. A conference held at Shaw University in Raleigh, North Carolina, spawned the Student Nonviolent Coordinating Committee (SNCC); its first president was Marion Barry, future mayor of Washington, DC. The organization coordinated sit-in campaigns and media coverage. An effective tactic of the demonstrators was their choice of jail over bail, literally filling jails over capacity to draw attention to the cause.

Martin Luther King Jr. went to jail in Birmingham, Alabama, where he composed "Letter from a Birmingham Jail," and local firemen used high-pressure hoses to disperse demonstrators while the police used dogs and tear gas. Demonstrations took place all over the South and the North, growing to include high school students to replace adults who were fearful of job loss. President John F. Kennedy (1917–63) and Attorney General Robert Kennedy sought a resolution to the behavior of Alabama police authorities against African Americans and whites. The behavior of these authority figures embarrassed the United States in the eyes of the world. The president agreed to the peaceful assembly of demonstrators at the August 1963 March on Washington for the redress of grievance; here King delivered his renowned "I Have a Dream" speech. Governor George Wallace prohibited desegregation of schools in Alabama, and President Kennedy federalized the Alabama National Guard to enable African American students to enter the school system. In September segregationists bombed the Sixteenth Street Baptist Church in Birmingham and murdered four African American girls. President Kennedy, assassinated in Dallas, Texas November 22, 1963, had agreed to the Civil Rights Act, later signed by President Lyndon B. Johnson in 1964, outlawing discrimination in voting and public accommodations and requiring fair employment practices. By June 1964 segregationists had abducted and murdered three young civil rights workers, Michael Schwerner, Andrew Goodman, and James Chaney, in Neshoba County, Mississippi. The summer of 1964 brought hundreds of volunteers to Mississippi to register voters, culminating in Freedom Summer; the summer was highlighted with violence, but people continued to register to vote. Selma, Alabama became a violent scene when police attacked marchers, driving them back across the bridge they were crossing. Nightly news programs flashed the images across television screens and named it "Bloody Sunday." The public mobilized in support of federal legislation, and President Johnson responded with the Voting Rights Act of 1965.

Reverend Martin Luther King Jr. was the victim of an assassin's bullet on April 4, 1968 in Memphis, Tennessee. Outward images of Jim Crow disappeared from public places only to reveal ingrained racist patterns woven into the fabric of the South. De facto segregation in the North continued with the isolation of African Americans in poverty stricken areas of decaying urban cities. Urban rebellion exploded in cities across the United States for another three years. A new African American militancy surfaced in the Black Panther Party for Self-Defense, created by Huey P. Newton and Bobby Seale in Oakland, California, in 1966. Eldridge Cleaver helped formulate the party's ideology, a rebellion against the politics of integration and passive resistance. Thus, a new era of civil rights began (Wexler).

Alice Walker was knowledgeable of the history of protest in the South and was an eyewitness to the 1960s Civil Rights movement's tradition of resistance. Oppression is her history and her heritage. Stokely Carmichael's plea for "Black Power" was the next evolution following the integration focus of the 1960s, but the issues of economic and political empowerment and race pride were rallying cries in the late 1960s and early 1970s, the period that ushered in the Black Arts movement. *Meridian* is a behind-the-scenes examination of the inner workings of the Civil Rights movement through one woman's story. The protagonist Meridian becomes an activist to help change an American society that oppresses women and African Americans by placing restrictions on them.

GENRE AND NARRATIVE TECHNIQUE

Meridian is a novel, an extended prose narrative presented in episodic format dealing with characters in both human and symbolic form. The stringing together of loosely connected episodes one after another to complete the interconnected cycles of the narrative is the strength of *Meridian*. It is panoramic in its coverage of characters and events. It is a fictional account of characters, events, and situations that parallel real lives and events surrounding the Civil Rights movement. Wide in scope, it also has depth because of its multifocused character development. Walker combines the collective history of a people with the personal history of the main character.

The novel is also one of sensibility. The characters have heightened emotional responses to the circumstances surrounding the movement. Moreover, Walker is conscious of readers and wants her readers to experience similar emotional intensity. Because the Civil Rights movement was a life-changing entity in Walker's life, she involves readers in this experience and takes readers on the journey to relive events that were supposed to have international ramifications.

In addition, *Meridian* is a historical novel in the sense that Walker pays homage to the movement. Her concern here is historical, not autobiographical. She weighs the conflict between institutional southern ideals and African American hopes for a brighter future, the death of racist politics and the birth of democratic goals. Walker's fictional characters are participants in the historic Civil Rights movement and knowledgeable of Walker's roll call of fallen heroes. She comments on a past era and the impact that real events had on the people of the movement. Walker gives her personal testament about a historical time that she frames in a social context.

Finally, *Meridian* is an exploration of ideas. Walker searches for the meaning of the Civil Rights movement and for its significance beyond its existence as a movement. She works out philosophically the movement's connectedness with other movements in whatever time or place or space. Walker seems clear about the internal significance of the movement; however, its external significance is unclear. To understand the true significance of the movement, looking back in time helps to illuminate the meaning, to expose the truth. Walker's search for meaning requires an analysis of the history of the South and of the African Americans who were integral to it, for no separation exists between the two. Walker strives to understand the universal circle of destiny that intersected with the South, placing African Americans in that moment of experience. Walker rationalizes the uniqueness of southern African Americans and the energy that enabled them to endure extreme struggle, for they were the backbone of the movement. She wrestles with her material to make sense of the philosophical, political, and social issues of the movement.

Walker's narrative style is anecdotal, humorous, lyrical, and gossipy. Walker writes interesting narrative lines detailing personages and events from the Civil Rights movement. She also writes witty expressions about personages and events that are effectively comical. Music frames this novel, the kind of music that represents the culture of a people. The music is everywhere—protest songs, church songs, work songs, love songs, and party songs. The music is there because it was part of the survival of the South. Like Toni Morrison's *Jazz*, where the words and the chapters cooperate in syncopated expression, so too does this novel evoke music in its word and chapter associations engulfed in improvisation, chapter lengths representing long, short, high, and low notes. The reader feels privy to secret information, as if Walker were sharing information that only an insider would know. She keeps alive the African American oral tradition of storytelling, bringing to remembrance centuries-old voices of protest.

PLOT

The protagonist, Meridian Hill, is guilt-ridden for her inability to play the traditional roles of daughter, wife, and mother. Deserted by her young husband, she chooses college over motherhood and gives away their child. She becomes romantically involved with Truman, the movement's organizer, an artist who speaks French fluently. However, she aborts the child she conceives with him over his unfaithfulness when he leaves her to marry Lynne, a white exchange student. He subsequently deserts Lynne and the child they have together. Meridian decides to have her tubes tied, a procedure suggested by an unethical physician, to avoid the entrapment of sex and motherhood. She is then free to pursue her goals of movement participation, organizing the community, teaching, and writing poetry in the rural South. Meridian's enlightening moment comes at a 1968 memorial service for a civil rights martyr; the epiphany releases her from her many guilt-ridden burdens. She finally commits to killing in the name of the revolution if necessary, a loyalty she previously rejected. In the end Meridian extends to Truman her forgiveness, at last accepting the Civil Rights movement's failure to change the social order completely and leaving him to work through the same insecurities that once plagued her.

THEMES

Themes function as universal ideas explored in literary works. Walker's novel *Meridian* embodies the fundamental ideas of the Civil Rights movement, socialism, women's struggle, children, history, social change, violence, relationships, change, and wholeness. The pervasive theme of *Meridian* is the Civil Rights movement. Walker uses the movement to illuminate continuities, describing how love of the ideology of a cause challenged the prevailing beliefs of the American system. She also develops a theme around the shakiness of revolutionaries, exposing vulnerabilities and less-than-perfect behavior. Socialism is also a theme, in that Walker focuses on group living and group responsibility in the distribution of goods and services.

Meridian is a womanist novel. It points out the audaciousness and courage of African American women in the movement and their willingness to sacrifice and struggle on its behalf, as well as their ability to take charge and become agents of social change for the liberation and wholeness of people. Walker centers on race and class issues, as well as incorporating feminist issues of gender. African American women's struggle to cope in life is a central theme in the novel. Walker concerns herself with the maternal ancestor and the wisdom of the ages. As Walker explains in the essay "In Search of Our Mothers' Gardens," reconnection with the mother is essential to women's survival. She develops the connections between generations of women in the novel. Walker elevates women to sainthood and builds a theme around the radicalization of saints.

The figure of the child represents continuance and possibility. Children are the future, but they are also the past. Meridian has aborted children, and Lynne has a deceased child. Walker uses the child thematically to show that life and death are a cycle of regeneration, that where children are there is new beginning.

The history of the generations of southern African Americans from their beginnings to the 1960s is an important component. Their past is crowded with agony, pain, powerlessness, suffering, and violence. With conglomerate negative energies shadowing their past, they must reform and reshape those energies into something positive for the future. In other words, they take the best from the worst and forge ahead. Similarly, Walker explores the history of oppression—if the world has ever been without it, and whether the world can move on without it. She looks at groups oppressing groups, men oppressing men, men oppressing women, and women oppressing women.

Social change and its twin connections to the past and the future are significant. Walker explores the relevance of past events and their influence on future possibilities, that the events of the past are not just baggage but important to future decisions. Walker delves into the impact the movement has on its participants' personal development. Likewise, societal change is a major theme, whether society's behavior promotes immediate change, relevant change, global change, or no change. Walker probes whether diversity in the world, a part of the natural process, is also responsible for so much discord.

Violence as a main theme emerges in the exploration into whether it is a necessary evil to effect change. Walker explores the relationship between revolutionary sacrifice, or killing, and change, whether it is necessary to destroy life in order to preserve it, whether good naturally proceeds from bad, whether peace, justice, and nonviolence emanate from disturbance, injustice, and violence.

Walker also explores relationships in this novel. The relationship between Meridian and Truman is contentious. While he professes to want to be with her, he chooses not to. She also explores the relationship between Truman and Lynne, an interracial relationship that is complex on many levels. Truman allows the color of Lynne's skin to determine his decision making, and Lynne sacrifices everything to have Truman in her life. The relationship between Meridian and Lynne is a love and hate one. They both involve themselves with the same love interest, and one of them must accept rejection. Walker delves into whether the two of them can maintain a friendship, knowing the history that impacts both of them.

Personal change, self-discovery, and transformation are important themes in the novel. Meridian is on a journey to discover who she is and why there is a need to make personal changes. She also transforms herself once she comes into full realization. Other characters, such as Truman and Lynne, also engage in a cycle of change, discovery, and transformation.

Wholeness or surviving whole is another important theme. Walker's interests lie in emerging from conflict a complete restored human being. Walker believes that change comes about only when people learn first to love themselves and then to love others. She suggests that this revelation is followed by forgiveness of self and then forgiveness of others. These two steps are the essential requirements in surviving whole.

CHARACTER ANALYSES

Meridian Hill, an African American woman, analyzes herself and, therefore, is receptive to all ideas. She is a rural Georgia resident, a Saxon student, and a rebel without a cause, for the Civil Rights movement is dead. She sees herself as a traitor to the ideal of African American womanhood and to her mother for placing her child up for adoption, thus rejecting motherhood and all of its symbolic images. Meridian works through personal conflicts of the nonviolent ideal. She needs a place to proceed philosophically with the nonviolent ideal now that the movement is over, leaving her alone to struggle. A killer she is not; she is unwilling to kill for the "revolution," but she has a willingness to die for the cause of freedom for her people. By the novel's end she vows to kill if required. At the conclusion of each march Meridian loses consciousness and becomes paralyzed; she enters a death zone, as close to literal death as she is willing to go. She prefers life to remain connected to her people. Feelings of unworthiness overshadow her because she prioritizes art over revolution; she is, therefore, a revolutionary artist. Her responsibility is to preserve the cultural history of the people and be one with the people. Meridian also struggles with spiritual conflicts. She is stuck in a time zone, wearing Afrocentric attire when everyone else dons the dress of militancy. Nonviolence to Meridian is more than an act or a reaction; it is a spiritual journey. She can no more abandon nonviolence than she can abandon her own skin. Her commitment to the people is strong, and she holds herself personally responsible for their future success. The African American church, or a new form of it, returns to her the understanding of herself, that she has a place in the world and that she has a place for her ideology of nonviolence. Meridian irons out life's importance, which is living for the cause and not for romantic gratification. The cause is all.

Truman Held encapsulates the ideal of blackness except in his marriage choices. While he professes his love for Meridian and her beauty and suggests that they make black babies together, Truman dates white exchange students because of their interesting skin color. He has temporary amnesia that Meridian aborted his child and decided to sterilize herself. His preference for white women stems from the fact that they were historically off limits. Therefore, marrying a white woman is a defiant act against the power of white men. Wearing African robes and reading

W.E.B. Du Bois have no bearing on his romantic interests, for he chooses to marry Lynne, whom he intimidates. He surrounds himself with African American paintings and sculptures of African American women while married to her, and Truman with all his black imagery chooses another white woman after he and Lynne part ways. Truman's conflict is with the movement participants whose ideology excludes whites. Therefore, Truman suppresses his love for and attraction to Lynne in order to gain acceptance from movement participants. In the end he wrestles with the identical issues of the meaning of nonviolence, freedom, and revolution that plagued Meridian at the novel's beginning.

Lynne, the Jewish woman married to Truman, loves the South and southern African Americans, their itinerant communal culture and mores representing the pinnacle of art to her. Lynne's insistence that she and Truman move permanently to Mississippi results from the desire to escape the sterility and monotony of life in the suburbs. Lynne views the South and southern African Americans in the same way that an explorer views undiscovered terrain, a personal romanticized venture. She fails to see their humanity; rather, she sees their community strength, agrarian existence, and interdependence as the ideal. Tragically, Lynne becomes a rape victim, the attack coming from African American civil rights worker Tommy Odds. Lynne subsequently offers no resistance, rationalizing that Tommy, too, is a victim of the racist whites who shot off his arm, of the color of his skin, of a hopeless existence. Therefore, she succumbs to guilt, the guilt of her white privilege and the knowledge that reporting the crime would bring about his certain death. Her liberated thinking opens the door of alienation, for she has no white friends to call, no family to come rescue her, since they have forgotten her name because of her involvement in the movement, and no white authority figures to report to because they consider her an outside agitator. Ultimately, Lynne becomes every African American man's sexual desire, passing her body around freely as if it were an offering plate, convincing herself that the men love her and prefer her to African American women because of her whiteness. As an abandoned wife and the mother of a deceased biracial child, Lynne has deep psychological issues that she suppresses and avoids.

A NEW HISTORICIST READING

New Historicist critics examine literary works as reflections of authors' lives and times and their economic, social, and political contexts. They apply the same principles to the characters that the literary works include.

A historical approach is also beneficial in placing implied and indirect references in the literature in their proper background. *Meridian* takes place in 1960s America, a violent and gruesome time. It was the era of black protest, sit-ins, freedom rides, marches, federalized National Guard units, assassinations, attack dogs as weapons, fire hoses as tools to wash away people as if they were street debris, and tear gas as a means of crowd control. America's people put their hope in a young charismatic president, John F. Kennedy, and his brother Attorney General Robert Kennedy, only to watch them fall to assassins' bullets on nationwide television, the recorder of America's history. Other victims of violence fell with them: Medgar Evers, Che Guevara, Dr. Martin Luther King Jr., Malcolm X, and so many others. Alice Walker returns to this direct-action protest time, the excitement of it and the unity of blacks and whites acting together, as historical contexts in *Meridian*.

Meridian reflects the issue of activism, its significance and value. The Civil Rights movement awakened Walker to indignities endured by some at the hands of others and connected her to the humanity of African American people and the history of their struggle. She wrote in "The Civil Rights Movement: What Good Was It?" that "if it gave us nothing else, it gave us each other forever." Walker's character Meridian attaches herself permanently to the South and southern African Americans because of the affinity she develops for its people. Walker's novel also works through anxieties about "the dream." The iconic martyr Dr. Martin Luther King Jr. in his March on Washington speech inspired the northern exodus to the South to help bring "the dream" to fruition (although he knew that the problem was nationwide). Walker, perched in a tree in Washington DC, heard Dr. King's speech and responded to the challenge, returning to the South for two summers to do significant work and living in Mississippi later to continue work of relevance. Dr. King's death reinvigorated "the dream," just as Meridian discovers that she is a worthy contributor to the cause in whatever capacity she serves, that relevant work is needed in the background as well as on the front line.

Above all, the novel works through the construct of struggle. Walker noted that African American women who struggled alongside the men received little recognition for their contributions, for nationalist men desired to subjugate women in traditional roles of wives and mothers. Walker writes in "Choosing to Stay at Home: Ten Years after the March on Washington" that "this is heartbreaking. Not just for black women who have struggled so *equally* against the forces of oppression, but for all those who believe subservience of any kind is death to the spirit."

While working in the South she listened to the stories of these women's lives and determined to resurrect their histories as women of struggle. Meridian exercises her option of choice. Guilt over the inability to nurture or be a model daughter, wife, and mother no longer torments Meridian. The character Meridian actually chooses the struggle of the rural South (organizing, teaching, and poeticizing) over motherhood and liberates herself from any limitations and restrictions that patriarchy—whether in African American or white form—would impose on her.

Meridian is an important cultural novel. It sheds light on the African American male leadership in the movement and the ideology of Black Nationalism. Because the leadership manifested a masculine agenda, little knowledge of the women's work surfaced. The assumptions and beliefs of that period relegated women to second class and second place. Many African Americans outside the inner circles of the movement did not know that Coretta Scott King was so intelligent and articulate until after her husband's death when they heard her speak for the first time on television. They did not know that she was musically gifted, with a voice that she could lift high in song. Mahalia Jackson was the soloist often heard at churches where organizational strategies materialized—at least this is what was televised. Walker frames the behind-the-scenes strife among men, their bad behavioral choices and abuse of women, both black and white. Theirs was a culture of power that in some ways mimicked the white male power structure. Stokely Carmichael (Kwame Ture) dismissed all the white volunteers when he took over SNCC. Walker works through such annoyances in the novel but does not detract from the overwhelmingly positive commitment and loyal dedication of the volunteers of the movement, both male and female. She gives glimpses into the cultural force of sharecroppers and working-class people who were the faithful, the redeemed who heeded the call to democratic justice.

Relationships of power are a concern of this novel. First, at the background are the white power structure and its Machiavellian principle of "power in force and fraud." The Civil Rights movement existed because those with the power chose not to share or give it up without violent confrontation. They chose a doctrine of superiority and inferiority over equality; therefore, the countervoices of the few, intolerant of past injustices, demanded the rights that had been denied them by the dominant many. Second, the novel explores the relationship of African American men and white women. These men empowered by the movement exercised power over white women because this antagonized white men, especially the southerners. The women volunteers, liberated in their thinking and committed to their calling, accepted African American male dominance. In some cases African American males exploited the "black and white together" theme, taking on white wives and girlfriends while at the same time confessing to be "solidly black." white women volunteers endured endless abuse because white southerners perceived them as traitors to their Anglo-Saxon heritage; many of these women had white color but no Anglo-Saxon heritage. Their presence in the protest marches stirred up the kind of hostility among whites, southerners and northerners alike, that exposed the most depraved of human emotions. Truman Held wrestles with his feelings for Lynne, once loving her and later denying that love. He allows the Black Power militant fringe of the movement to define his blackness and similarly whom he loves. Truman holds in his hands the power to keep Lynne or to let her go.

The novel *Meridian* acts as a vehicle for analyzing the successes and the failures of the Civil Rights movement and as a mechanism for dealing with issues of guilt. It also is a historical public document that gets passed on to future generations.

5

The Color Purple (1982)

Alice Walker described to African American critic Mary Helen Washington in 1973 three types of African American characters excluded from the literature of the United States: physically and emotionally exploited women who lead narrow and confining lives and are often driven to insanity, psychologically exploited women who endure cultural alienation, and surviving women who achieve wholeness out of oppression and prepare spaces for other oppressed communities. Alice Walker gives the reader some of the first two and all of the third in *The Color Purple*, a novel about womanhood and the awakening of consciousness and spirit (Washington, "An Essay on Alice Walker").

Walker's explosive epistolary novel, her third, won her the 1983 Pulitzer Prize and the 1983 American Book Award, as well as a nomination for a 1982 National Book Critics Circle Award. She is the first African American woman writer to win the Pulitzer for a novel. *The Color Purple* explores the issues of spousal abuse, incest, lesbianism, subjugation, and dehumanization. Walker's protagonist Celie writes to God, Nettie to her sister Celie, and Celie to Nettie. The letters reveal the injustices women incur from men in the United States and in Africa. This novel chronicles Celie's growth from a dependent, defeated personality to an independent, liberated woman with purpose and drive.

The novel is not without its controversial aspects, and the film adaptation directed by Steven Spielberg in 1985 intensified the controversy. The novel's detractors complained of its depiction of African American family structure, suspicious historical inaccuracies with regard to Africa, and references to lesbianism. Moreover, Spielberg's supposedly overly negative portrayal of African American men and the Hollywood flair of the film caused dismay among many critics and admirers of the novel, including some African American women. Walker refused to comment publicly about her novel's reception among African American literary critics, specifically males. By remaining mute on the subject, Walker escaped the entrapment of personal controversy, retained her reputation as a writer, and assured the success of the novel. She permitted the critics to fight things out among themselves until the issue diminished. She later commented that Spielberg's film brought Celie's story to women who do not necessarily read books. Walker examines the controversy in hindsight in the 1996 autobiographical writing *The Same River Twice: Honoring the Difficult: A Meditation on Life, Spirit, Art, and the Making of the Film The Color Purple, Ten Years Later.*

STRUCTURE

The Color Purple's epistles are correspondences between two sisters over a period of approximately forty years. Walker assigns no dates or numbers to the letters; therefore, the reader's task is to number each letter meticulously if the goal is reader-response criticism. Otherwise, the novel is a great read without numbering. Letters 1 to 51 are Celie's correspondence, and letters 52 to 90 belong to Nettie.

Unusually for Walker, an omniscient narrator is absent from this novel, meaning that there is no explanatory feedback or intervening commentary. In the omniscient perspective authors are the storytellers, having total knowledge of the characters' lives, actions, and thoughts. Here, one singular voice controls the narration, that of the undereducated protagonist Celie. Walker heavily engages readers in the novel because a close reading is required to become aware of the specific details that inform the lives of Celie and Nettie. The correspondence sometimes has long breaks, as much as five years between letters.

SOCIOHISTORICAL CONTEXT

African Americans faced numerous challenges in their efforts to gain economic stability after Reconstruction. Transitioning from slavery to freedom required the determination to proceed full speed ahead and not falter. Second-class citizenship handicapped them in their efforts to meet the demands of competitive society, although they were bent on an unwavering course of action. Most African Americans continued to live in the South during the last part of the nineteenth century and the beginning of the twentieth century, until the Great Migration changed this pattern. Some were fortunate enough to operate small businesses such as confectionaries or dry goods stores. Others had no choice but to farm. Some type of farming—as sharecroppers, tenant farmers, farm laborers, and casuals (work for food)—provided the means for them to eke out a mere subsistence.

However, in the late 1800s and early 1900s some African Americans purchased their own land and had enough capital to purchase farm tools. Others inherited small farms or ample acreage from the previous owners as settlement after the war. Although they suffered from poor harvests and declining prices and meager profits yielded over to losses, they owned their farms. There was much agricultural discontent among white farmers after the war, and they organized and formed the Southern Farmers' Alliance, from which they excluded African Americans, to function on a cooperative basis. They encouraged African Americans to form their own self-help group, which was the Colored Farmers' Alliance and Co-operative Union, which enrolled approximately one million members.

Acquiring land in the post–Civil War period was a gateway to freedom through land ownership. Becoming independent farmers was a way to seek wealth and economic security. At the turn of the century African Americans were less than 10 percent of the United States population but owned no fewer than two hundred thousand farms. Family and community revolved around farm life and helped to develop the vital link of interdependence of relationship and consciousness. Women also were mandatory contributors to the family farms, indicating that their physical stamina mirrored their mental stamina for survival (Logan and Cohen, 126–152).

Alice Walker's *The Color Purple* uses the poor independent farmer and his community to frame her narrative. Albert, whom Celie refers to as Mr. _____, inherited the farm that was passed down from the white slave owner to Old Mister to Albert, who hopes to pass it on to his oldest son Harpo. The stepfather, Alphonso, by entitlement through marriage takes over the dry goods store owned by Celie's biological father. Walker, a child of the South, is knowledgeable about agricultural hierarchal systems. She builds on *The Third Life of Grange Copeland*, this time having the characters as poor landowners rather than sharecroppers. The two novels, though, share similar themes of gender bias and sexual abuse.

In a June 1982 *Newsweek* interview Walker acknowledges that the model for Celie's character is her own grandmother, a 12-year-old rape victim of a slave owner. Walker links the despicable behavior of Alphonso and Albert to their white ancestry. Just as the enslavers sexually abused slave women, these two sexually abuse Celie. The stepfather impregnates her twice without remorse and then secretly arranges to have the children removed. This behavior recalls the conduct of pre–Civil War slave owners. Albert twice examines Celie with his eyes, as if she were a product for the auction block, before taking her to his farm to be homemaker, farmhand, and sex partner. Walker links slave history to the behavior of the two African American men but not without the possibility of transformation. Albert in the end undergoes a renewal and asks Celie to marry him again.

GENRE AND NARRATIVE TECHNIQUE

The Color Purple is an epistolary novel, a narrative presented in the form of written correspondence (epistles, or letters) between the characters. Alice Walker as writer reveals the characters' emotions without personal intrusion into the novel. This genre allows the writer some flexibility because the same occurrences are presented through multiple points of view via the correspondents' epistolary records. In like manner, Walker as the writer retains verisimilitude (the appearance of truth and actuality) as she edits the correspondences of fictitious persons. However, Walker exceeds the parameters of editor to become medium or clairvoyant. The first epigraph to the novel addresses spirit: "*To the Spirit*: Without whose assistance/Neither this book/Nor I/Would have been/Written." She concludes the novel courteously on the final page: "I thank everybody in this book for coming. A.W., author and medium." Sandwiched between this opening and this closing are the epistles. Walker takes the reader on a visitation, opening the door to another dimension and closing it at visit's end.

The earliest epistolary novels, a form invented by men to shape the literary images of women, trace back to England and France. Seventeenth-century varieties include *Poste with a Packet of Mad Letters* (1602) by Nicholas Breton, *Five Love-Letters from a Nun to a Cavalier* (1678) by Roger L'Estrange, and *Love Letters Between a Nobleman and His Sister* (1682) by Aphra Behn. Eighteenth-century productions were a popular format for the sentimental novel (indulgence in pity and tears). *Pamela* (1740), which is officially recognized as the first epistolary novel in the English tradition; *Clarissa Harlowe* (1748), the longest epistolary novel; *Sir Charles Grandison*

(1754) by Samuel Richardson; *Humphry Clinker* (1771) by Tobias Smollett; and *Evelina* (1778) by Fanny Burney expanded the form. Nineteenth-century use was largely unsuccessful, but a twentieth-century revival of the form materialized. *The Late George Apley* (1937) by J. P. Marquand, *Pal Joey* (1940) by John O'Hara, *A Woman of Independent Means* (1978) by Elizabeth Hailey, and *Letters* (1979) by John Barth were favorites. A genre primarily formed by men, the epistolary novel received new treatment in *The Color Purple*. Like her foremothers Harriet Jacobs, Harriet E. Wilson, and Hannah Crafts, Alice Walker usurps the authority of the traditional Eurocentric literary standard and asserts her control over the form. She articulates the literary image, representation, and female narrative voice of previously silenced poor African American women. She allows them to be confidants engaged in intimate communication.

The narrative technique Walker employs is language appropriate, given her subject of choice. Walker reclaims the diary, letter, and journal tradition associated with the culture of women. With her poor African American characters Walker uses "folk" language as female narrative voice, embracing and reclaiming not only poor African American women but also their language. Walker in *The Color Purple*, like Zora Neale Hurston in *Mules and Men*, prioritizes African American culture, folklore, and folk expression, treating the language of the "folk" as praxis, an art form or a skill. Zora Neale Hurston wrote in *Mules and Men* that "[w]hen I pitched headforemost into the world I landed in the crib of negroism." Part of that culture is formulating words and meanings through black vernacular English or Ebonics, which reflects the experiences of African Americans and the preservations of certain Africanisms. Therefore, Walker takes the language of a primarily oral culture and applies words to paper, essentially liberating "folk" language from the strictures of Western standard forms. This language, too, is written; it is legitimate, for Western scholars do not give credence to anything that is not written. Walker deconstructs the Western standard and reconstructs the oral standard. Her reconstruction of the foremothers' language promotes acceptance of them, their histories, their speech, music, religion, and community.

PLOT

The protagonist Celie writes letters to God after her stepfather Alphonso rapes and beats her. She conceives two children, a girl and a boy, Olivia and Adam, both presumed to be stolen and killed by her stepfather. Alphonso takes advantage of her because her mother is ill, physically and mentally, her illness a result of the lynching of her first husband, an ambitious country small business owner. The white southerners envied his success. Celie's mother dies and her stepfather marries again, but his remarriage does not end the sexual abuse.

A widower farmer in the community, Albert, shows interest in marrying the unattractive Celie, although he really wants the pretty Nettie, who is too young and also a virgin, rendering her valuable. Celie, no longer a virgin, is considered "spoiled" goods. Albert reluctantly accepts Celie as his wife and takes her to his house to be his cook, field hand, and lover. Moreover, she is to be stepmother to his four uncontrollable offspring. Not long after Celie enters a loveless marriage, her sister Nettie escapes the amorous desires of her stepfather and seeks refuge with Celie and Albert. When Albert makes a play for Nettie, she rejects his affections and leaves his house. Celie believes Nettie is dead.

Albert has a part-time love interest named Shug Avery, a sultry, Bessie Smith–type blues diva, who comes to town to make an appearance at the local jook joint, but Celie is not permitted to go. In spite of Albert's desires for Shug, she comes at whim and leaves the same way. When Shug contracts an illness and Albert brings her to his house to recuperate, Celie nurses her back to health. This decision spins into motion Celie's eventual transformation. Shug stays longer than required when she learns that Albert physically abuses Celie in her absence. Shug and Celie foster a close bond that escalates sexually.

Albert's son Harpo falls in love with the full-figured, independent and assertive Sofia. Albert opposes the relationship, but Harpo marries her anyway after she becomes pregnant. Neither Harpo nor Albert can intimidate the strong-willed young woman. Sofia's resistant disposition surprises Celie, who encourages Harpo to beat Sofia in order to bring her under submission. But Sofia proves too much of a challenge for Harpo, for he has as many bruises on him as Sofia has on her. These two contending forces cannot hold a marriage together.

When Sofia comes to visit, she unleashes her anger on Harpo's new girlfriend Squeak. While in town the white mayor's wife admires Sofia and asks her to come to work as her maid. Sofia's response to Miss Millie is "Hell no!" The mayor then physically abuses Sofia for her disrespect toward his wife, and Sofia returns the blow. After being sent to jail, Sofia is sentenced to 12 years' labor as Miss Millie's maid.

A new husband, Grady, accompanies Shug on her next visit to Albert's. The friendship between Celie and Shug is impenetrable. Celie shares information that she believes her sister to be dead, but Shug tells Celie that she has seen Albert hiding letters. Searching through Albert's trunk Celie and Shug find the letters Albert has been hiding for years. Celie reads the letters one at a time, containing but not forgetting the anger toward Albert that she is yet to release.

Celie learns of Nettie's missionary life in Africa and her disillusionment over the Africans' arrogance. Nettie discovers that she is with the biological children of Celie, who were not dead but had been adopted by Samuel and Corrine, a childless missionary couple. Corrine's death paves the way for Celie to reconcile with her children. After confirmation from Alphonso, who tells Celie that he is her stepfather, not her biological father, Celie begins to lose the faith in God that has sustained her for so many years. Shug convinces Celie to imagine the God she needs, not the traditional image of a white God.

Released from servitude six months early, Sofia dines at Albert's home with the extended family, their Fourth of July dinner. Celie comes full circle, releasing the emotions that years of physical and sexual abuse prohibited her from articulating. Shug informs everyone that she and Celie are moving to Tennessee, and Squeak decides to join them. Celie's livelihood is sewing tailored pants, which she turns into a successful business. She returns to Georgia for a visit and learns that Alphonso is dead, and her inheritance is the house and the land.

Nettie marries Samuel, and Celie's son Adam marries an African girl named Tashi, who undergoes the traditional African ritual of facial scarring and female circumcision. Adam, too, performs the ritual of facial scarring to show his solidarity. Tashi and Adam will appear again in *Possessing the Secret of Joy*. Nettie and Samuel return to the United States with Adam and Olivia, and Celie gets to meet her children. Sofia remarries Harpo, and Celie and Albert are platonically involved. Celie emerges from years of oppression a whole human being.

THEMES

Themes are implicit concepts around which imaginary works of literature revolve. The dominant themes of *The Color Purple* are female assertiveness, female narrative voice, female relationships, and violence. Female assertiveness is Walker's way of delimiting women's space. She liberates Sofia from submissiveness, making her a mouthy free spirit, a challenge to a powerful system. Shug is an adventuresome blues singer with fine tastes and without limits on her sexual preferences. Nettie, too, asserts herself by escaping her stepfather's house rather than succumbing to his unwanted advances. Her escape takes her all the way to Africa.

Female narrative voice is a significant theme in the novel because Celie finds hers. Alphonso, Celie's stepfather, rapes and threatens her, telling her that knowledge of the act is information only for God. This threat silences Celie. Maya Angelou's *I Know Why the Caged Bird Sings* tells the story of her muteness after a rape, causing her to put her energy in writing. Walker's protagonist, too, uses letters as a confessional tool and an emotional escape. Her silence is representative of her invisibility, and she entombs herself in years of silence. Initially, Celie is submissive to Albert's dominance, internalizing the values imposed on her. She becomes a defeated soul, a victim of abusive patriarchal power, believing that beatings are the norm, the power men exercise over women. When Nettie comes to live with Celie, she cannot successfully be her protector or her advocate in Albert's house. However, away from the house she helps Celie to discover her voice through letters. When Sofia confronts Celie about her recommendation to Harpo to beat Sofia, Celie takes the first step of being literally stunned out of silence. To her amazement she stands face to face with a woman empowered to challenge a man physically. Sofia even challenges Celie verbally. Having been abused at such a tender age, Celie lacks the experience or the knowledge of retaliation. If Sofia causes Celie to ponder Albert's authority over her, Shug Avery provides her with all the answers. With Shug's assistance Celie recoups Nettie's letters, which provide her with internal strength and enable her to discover her voice. Most importantly, she overcomes her passivity and uses her voice to transform herself.

Female relationships or connections are another theme. In this case a strong bond exists between Celie and her mother, who is unseen and helpless, but an unspoken maternal bond is there. A tender sisterly relationship establishes a secure bond that holds even through years of separation. Nettie and Celie are sisters but also friends, and Nettie's letters are the same as her presence. When Celie reads Nettie's letters, she is able to summon the courage to endure Albert's brutality. Sofia and Celie share a familial connection; however, Sofia is instrumental in arousing Celie's curiosity about being assertive. Sofia explains that her strong bond with her sisters is the source of her feistiness. Shug and Celie share a relationship that crosses over into many levels—sisterlike, girlfriends, host and guest, teacher and student, caretaker and patient, and lovers. Celie's circle of friends is a safe haven for her, a place where she can be reclusive and an escape from a man's world.

Violence among the men plays a major role in the novel, the act of gender violence almost handed down from father to son. Walker shows the generational implications of violence. Albert is much like his father, who controlled his household through abusive behavior. Harpo finds it difficult to carry on the cycle only because Sofia is resistant to masculine dominance; she refuses to be beaten. Celie takes on an attitude of violence, telling Harpo to beat Sofia because she cannot assume Sofia's independence. Race and class violence are a result of societal influence, the result of one group subverting the assumed power of another. Walker demonstrates the South's reluctance to release the stronghold it once held over humans who were considered property. Similarly, the men in the novel represent the attitude of the Old South, sanctioning the use of violence to bring about enforced submission.

CHARACTER ANALYSES

Albert is the character whom Alphonso chooses to become Celie's husband. He is a wife beater and an adulterer, but his character is ambiguous: he shows Celie great cruelty and Shug great love. Albert's insensitivity is a result of improper parenting by his father, a mean and abusive man; he is a product of his instruction. His first wife commits adultery because his hard outer shell never softened, and emotional detachment was the norm for him. However, he has a soft side. His attraction to Shug stems from her beauty; she awes him so much that he places her on a pedestal in the tradition of the southern belle, someone to be admired and cherished. However, Walker deconstructs Western paradigms. Shug is a transformed southern belle, an independent thinker and doer. Albert allows Shug to determine the course of the relationship, when she comes and when she goes. Her company gives him pleasure; therefore, he waits patiently for her to return. Although he hides Nettie's letters from Celie, he does not destroy them. In the end he regrets his behavior. Walker reforms Albert from a despicable, brutal character for whom readers cannot develop empathy into a kind, understanding figure; this new side of his personality supersedes the sinister character at the novel's beginning.

Readers are introduced to Celie as a teenager who has been raped by her stepfather and then used as a bargaining chip in marriage to Albert. She is nearly uneducated and her first letter is to God, written in southern "folk" language. Her letters reveal that she searches for the person within; she has been ostracized by her stepfather and Albert, who compound matters by calling her ugly. Knowing that her stepfather sent away the babies that she conceived as a result of his sexual intrusion, she needs to find love, self-esteem, and empowerment. Celie's letters to God are honest expressions of her internal feelings. She is an inherently good person but the victim of many bad things. She devalues her own worth and comes to accept all the negative treatment that comes her way. At 14 she assumes the role of Albert's wife, the mother figure to his children and the keeper of his home. She endures a slavelike existence. Almost like a Job character, in all this misery she does not curse God. Her transformation comes through the assistance of Shug, who gets Celie to see her inner beauty as well as her external beauty, to discover her strength and self-worth, but most importantly her voice and her independence. She emerges womanist, reclaiming the matrilineal creative art of sewing.

Shug's boldness is her asset. She has an independent sexy style, a dragon tongue, a quick wit, and a claim on Albert. Shug's behavior—that is, her free will—is that traditionally ascribed to men, but Walker wraps her in class and sass. Shug appears to be loved by all, but when she becomes ill friends vanish, and Albert brings her to his house to recuperate. However, Celie is the life preserver. Both experience rejection—Shug from her family for her lifestyle and Celie from Albert—that helps them to forge a bond. Also, Celie has flashbacks of her mother when she looks at Shug, which may be an underlying factor in Celie's need to be around her, making Shug the constant in her life. Moreover, Shug brings comic relief where too much sadness abounds. Her ability to bring out the best in Celie reinforces the many roles that she plays in Celie's life.

Sofia is uncompromising almost to a fault. She fails to realize when her strength might turn destructive. Refusing to adhere to the dictates of her day, Sofia rejects oppression from Harpo and the dominant society. She represents the new thinking developing among women who ride the trains to New York. Her value system is troublesome in the South, where African American women are expected to be maids in the homes of white women. A positive representation of sisterhood, she does not blame Squeak for being Harpo's mistress but instead offers to rear Squeak's child until she can establish herself. Sofia pays a heavy price at the hands of the power structure that imprisons her and beats her, emerging from bondage nearly a broken spirit. She is a warrior woman though, taking up the cause against systemic power and having the courage to fight.

Nettie knows that education is the great equalizer. She goes after intellectual pursuits successfully, but knowledge does not replace family. Her separation from her older sister Celie makes Nettie lonely and distraught. Just as Albert silences Celie into a state of denial of her personhood, he overpowers Nettie and silences her by hiding her letters to Celie. Nettie's experiences in Africa reveal to readers that oppression of women is common practice in many cultures.

A WOMANIST READING

A womanist approach embraces practice and theory and criticism all at once. Womanist criticism subverts classical Eurocentric feminist criticism. *Womanist* refers to women of color who embrace universality rather than separatism. According to the articulator of womanist theory Alice Walker, *womanist* is the most appropriate term for defining black feminists because the term is inclusive of the culture without color delineation. The term *womanist* does not reference race, ethnicity, or skin color or trace its literary foremothers to the European tradition. Womanist critics are contributors to an interpretative community that traces its United States ancestral matrix to Lucy Terry, Phillis Wheatley, Anna Julia Cooper, and Zora Neale Hurston. Literary ancestral mothers vary for women of color, but womanist scholars develop ways to reclaim their forebears' art and acknowledge their contributions. Fully aware that a Western patriarchal ideology charts the course of literary history and catalogues official literary works, womanist critics do not privilege the patriarchal system but map their own compass direction to celebrate and critique imaginative writings by women of color.

Defined in Walker's *In Search of Our Mothers' Gardens*, womanist is "outrageous, audacious, courageous or *willful* behavior." The term has its genesis in "black folk expression of mothers to female children, 'You acting womanish,' i.e., like a woman." Womanist scholars explore female literary characters who are unrestrained in their attitudes toward society's dictates. They often surpass the limits of the usual restrictions demanded of females, refusing to be confined or compartmentalized by rules of propriety. In many instances womanist characters exemplify adventurous and daring qualities; they are willing to take risks in order to accomplish desires and goals. They have the mental capacity and moral fiber to face difficulties, endure hardships, and resist fears. Their determined minds and intentional purpose in pursuit of the self demonstrate their bravery and tenacity of spirit. Practitioners of womanist theory claim qualities identical to those they analyze in female characters.

Scholars who are womanist explore a liberated, free spirit. They identify women writers and women within literature who free themselves from debilitating historical patterns of patriarchal dominance, racism, and discrimination. They are not racially or culturally oppressed beyond restoration but are freethinkers who assert their rights and are instrumental in changing the institutionalized inequality of the sectors of life in which they exist. Womanists are authoritative and defiant. Women writers and female characters that exemplify these qualities value themselves and recognize their importance in society. They connect spiritually and emotionally to a sisterhood that abounds with deserving women, offering assistance and challenging trends that might undermine the community of women.

Further, women who are womanist are survivors, and they love and appreciate other women and women's culture. They form bonds by empowering themselves and other women. Through exploration and education they instruct members of the sisterhood about the twin evils of racism and sexism and the necessary paths to take to triumph in light of the presence of these destructive forces. They research the literary accomplishments of women, form circles of exchange, and share the literary productions of women long forgotten, their diaries, histories, journals, letters, and stories. They have a sense of who their sisters are and demonstrate a deep sensitivity to the needs of their sisters. The ideal womanist always emerges as a whole human being.

Walker's *The Color Purple* exhibits all the characteristics of a womanist novel. The protagonist Celie fits the criteria of womanist, for she is a survivor, develops a liberated spirit, acquires inner strength, bonds with other women, and fights the evil of sexism. She triumphs over incest, wife beating, and abject poverty. Her quest for freedom and wholeness begins at the age of 14, when she lacks the stamina required to resist the sexual advances of her stepfather, who impregnates her. The attack continues when she enters a loveless marriage with Albert. Even her relationship with a white patriarchal God suppresses her development. Her journey to wholeness is a psychological one in which she must free her mind of male dominance. Discovering that Alphonso is her stepfather and not her biological father helps her to release some of the agony. Knowing that her children are not the result of incest helps her to remove a layer of pain. Walker affirms that the key to wholeness is forgiveness; thus, when Celie manages to pick up the pieces and move on with her existence, accepting herself and forgiving herself, not seeing Albert as an enemy or holding a grudge against him, the two of them begin a friendly relationship. Albert loses out because had he been more emotionally attached to Celie rather than treating her as an object, he could have had years of positive relationship development.

Equally important is Celie's indomitable spirit, her desire to overcome her struggles. In spite of all she endures, such as losing her children, rearing Albert's children, surviving Albert's physical abuse, and being denied love and attention, she has the courage to rise above the monstrous forces of negativity that engulf her. Grounded in the strength of southern African American culture, Celie refuses to relinquish control of her mind. Although she retreats inward, she protects herself from insanity until the time of her flowering.

Even more, Celie is an example of strength against all oppression. Women have historically been divided by oppression, with men oppressing women and in some cases women oppressing women. Before Celie comes into her own, she attempts to oppress Sofia indirectly by suggesting to Harpo that he beat her. Celie's envy of Sofia's spunk blinds her to the fact that Sofia is her sister self. Her sojourn in the valley of the shadow of death begins at adolescence, a time when girls her age enter a zone of discovery and come into their own. However, male dominance swallows Celie, crushing her pride and her sense of self. Even Albert's children disrespect her, refusing to extend simple courtesies to her. From this abyss she rebounds, thanks to her circle of female friends who enliven in her what seems to be the last flicker of hope. The dominance of patriarchy and hypocrisy hold her temporarily, for righteous indignation rises up in her at the Fourth of July family dinner, her liberation day.

Another reason *The Color Purple* is a womanist novel is its focus on the bonding of women. The female relationships develop around a community of women. Sofia extends a helping hand to Squeak, her husband's mistress. Nettie becomes the stepmother to Celie's children, ensuring that they will reunite with their mother. Liberated Shug, with her un-Christian-like behavior is the moral compass that carefully guides Celie into a brave new world. Shug and Celie take Squeak with them to Tennessee to begin life anew. They form a sisterhood whereby they tend to each other's needs. Their survival does not depend on being the pampered servants of men or performing domestic chores. They are the masters of their own liberty, not the recipients of perceived liberties granted to them by men. Their dedication to each other supports and sustains them.

The Color Purple also warns against sexism. Old Mister, Albert, and Harpo are ineffective in their efforts to subdue the women. Harpo's brutality brings him more resistance than submission, and Albert's abusiveness detracts from a happy home. Some critics find Walker controversial, indicating that the men in the novel are dehumanized when they make certain demands of the women. However, when Walker exercises the right of sexual egalitarianism, the men appear redeemed. For example, gender role transference has Harpo developing a love for housekeeping and cooking and becoming a stay-at-home dad while Sofia works in a store. Albert acknowledges Celie's independence and makes quilts with her, a womanist artistic creativity. Walker's statement, essentially, is that sexism has no place in a civil society. Sexism is a universal evil, and the concerns of women in general and African American women in particular are universal. Celie's victimization is the result of sexism on a small scale, but Nettie witnesses sexism en masse in Africa. The novel conveys the message that women everywhere need to unite and resist the patriarchal influence of sexism.

cosmologies, accounts of the creation of mankind, and causes of death. Unlike the anthropomorphic Greek and Roman gods and goddesses, African supreme deities refrain from interference in human lives. Lesser gods, or orisha, approach the supreme deity, not the people themselves. In addition to polytheistic practices, animism (the belief that everything in nature has a spirit) is a unifying concept.

Ancestor worship is another branch of African indigenous beliefs and practices, a key entity in the well-being of earth dwellers. Tribal and familial ancestors are the recipients of tribal members' honor and worship. The hierarchal order of the deities is comparable to a triangular shape: supreme deities at the top; lesser gods and ancestor worship at the sides; and forces of animism, magic, and medicine at the base. Worshippers are in the middle because they live in harmony with the forces. Another description of the hierarchal order is a pyramidal shape: Supreme Being at the top, orisha or lesser deities beneath the Supreme Being, ancestral deities beneath the orisha, and high-ranking humans, such as kings and queens, and regular believers at the base level.

In African cultures myths differ from tales, which are of two types. Entertaining stories about animals and people are *tatsuniyoyi*, tales that teach lessons in social, moral, and personal behavior. Stories geared toward male members of the tribes are *labarai*, tales of cultural, family, or tribal history. Exportations of some African tales resurface in other cultures, for example, in Hindu and Buddhist tales.

The African Aesop (c. 620–560 B.C.), reportedly at one time a slave and who continued the tradition of animal tales, gains the favor of the goddess Isis, who rewards him for his devotion with the gift of speech, which he uses to outwit his masters, gain freedom, and advise kings in one account of his life. Another account has him falsely accused, convicted, and thrown from a cliff. A third account has him as Croesus's ambassador in Delphi whose job was to distribute gold among the people; however, they so irritated him by their covetousness that he returned the gold to Croesus; this angered the people, who labeled him a criminal and executed him, an act for which they incurred various natural calamities, spawning the adage "the blood of Aesop," indicating evil is punishable. Credited with writing beast fables, though not the inventor of the genre, Aesop wrote timely primers on how to live life, narratives featuring animals with human virtues and vices as characters whose exploits teach moral lessons and highlight human foibles, mostly through oral tradition. Interestingly, Aesop's animals talk, have voice, and experience an oral culture while voicing human ideas and concerns.

During Aesop's time these fables were sophisticated political and social satires (Saunders, 71).

Alice Walker is now a practitioner of ancient spirituality. Her characters Shug Avery and Miss Celie from *The Color Purple* discuss the meaning of God, who to them is everything that is, was, and will be. Celie alters her opinion from her original belief in the traditional white Eurocentric God in the sky. Walker gave those words to her characters years before she came to believe them herself. She discovered that Isis, ancient goddess of Africa, spoke similar words, and she now views Isis as the spiritual mother of all people. Religion, Walker believes, imprisons people by teaching hatred of women, love of violence, and greed, the ultimate destroyer.

Walker identifies herself as a pagan, which means "of the land, country dweller, peasant." In fact, this is what she always was, having grown up in rural Georgia on a farm. She sees her parents, who were farmers, as lovers of the land with the utmost respect for it; they were one with nature, and their primary spiritual relationship was with nature and the earth. Walker's rationale is that African Americans are held captive by a religion that sanctions their destruction, whose ties to their indigenous practices and connections to All Creation are severed. *Heathen* is another word that contemporary religious leaders apply to pagan practices, but Walker indicates that African Americans are empty without their pagan-heathen ancestors and need to instill them within themselves.

Walker concludes that people need to decolonize their spirits, and if they are reluctant to exchange the Jesus that they have come to know, then an option is to expand him to include the "wizard," the "dancer," and the female-reverencing deities. Releasing of the pagan earth spirit allows people to become one with the earth and flow into the universe. Evolving from this unification with nature is the natural activism process, which Walker defines as the need to eradicate whatever oppresses and join collectively against all injustice. People then discover that Creation loves them, chooses to place them in loving earth, and wants them to find their place in the makeup of the cosmos. Walker lives by these principles.

Walker uses her knowledge of ancient spiritual practices to frame her narrative *The Temple of My Familiar*. In it she takes the reader on a cosmic journey of man, myth, magic, and memory; the origins of knowledge production and discourse and the significance of language; the interconnectedness of precolonial, colonial, and postcolonial constructs of race, class, and gender oppression; and numerous realities, to name a few of the excursions. Walker weaves a multidimensional, multifaceted tale where humans and animals communicate with each other, incorporating the storytelling tradition, myths, and archetypes to demystify time immemorial and multiple incarnations.

GENRE AND NARRATIVE TECHNIQUE

Alice Walker's term for her novel is a *romance*. At its base level a romance emphasizes the occurrences of the plot rather than reflecting ordinary life experiences. Close relations of romance are myths and adventure and/ or detective stories. Walker combines these components of romance to invent a setting wide in scope and a history of immeasurable dimensions, including human primary characters that bond with familiars (the near equivalent of pets).

Countermyth operates on one level of the novel. Walker rewrites the Genesis creation story and its Edenic ramifications, as well as the Beatitudes. In Walker's version humans and animals share lives as equals, in contrast to the way humans and animals coexist today. In one of Lissie's incarnations she is a white boy in search of a mate who couples with a girl who has a familiar, a serpent. After intimacy he sees his reflection in a pool and realizes that his skin color (which his mother hid with pigmented oil) differs from the girl's. He is so traumatized by the difference that he rejects the girl and kills the familiar that tries to defend her. The story of Genesis portrays Eve as the temptress of Adam following her beguilement by the evil serpent. The two then become knowledgeable of their nakedness, that is, their sexual differences, and cover their exposed genitalia. Walker kills the serpent, thereby eradicating the source of patriarchal institutional separation, racism, and sexism through the construct of difference—color or sexual difference. In addition, Walker wishes to rewrite the history of witches, most of whom were Moors during the Middle Ages and whose stories do not appear in Western records. She writes that the Spanish Inquisitors made bonding with animals illegal, a habit of witches. Their goal was to separate humans and animals, to establish that the two are different, and to silence the Moorish witches' correspondences with animals. Therefore, they burned witches who disobeyed the law, forming "witch-hunts." Walker reclaims their untold stories.

Autobiography is another narrative technique exercised in the novel. The major character Lissie describes her lives through detailed oral history, indicating that her story is meant to be heard rather than read. Walker's narrative voice distrusts the recorded histories of Western paradigms (the embodiments of literary philosophical and theoretical frameworks) that repress oral history or the cultural memory of people of color. Walker gives legitimacy to Lissie's memories of past lives and the accuracy of her memories.

Walker uses the fable to give legendary accounts of the lives of animals, that is, to recover their origins and to illustrate a moral lesson. The novel explains that animals' inability to use language is the single difference and method of separation between animals and humans. Mythic fantasy also seems to operate here; however, the narrative lines blur between fantasy and reality.

This novel is also a narrative of ideas and social commentary. Walker includes in the novel commentary regarding society's responsibility to animals, consciousness raising, the environment, government, and Middle East issues. To move the narrative along Walker uses lengthy narration, conversation, dialogues, and monologues that are whole chapters, occurring mostly between and among women of African heritage.

PLOT

This is a tale of three pairs of lovers, including two couples who need to reconcile their relationships. African American professor of American history Suwelo takes the train from California to Baltimore to honor his uncle with a funeral and to place his inherited house on the real estate market. His wife Fanny (granddaughter of Miss Celie of *The Color Purple* and daughter of Olivia) discovers womanist views and wants a divorce—not because she has fallen out of love with Suwelo, but because she no longer wants to be married. Freedom from the limitations of marriage is much more enticing to her. In Baltimore Suwelo meets his uncle's friends Miss Lissie and Mr. Hal, who visit regularly to converse and share ideas. Miss Lissie's memory is remarkable, revealing that she has lived in different incarnations since the beginning of time; she is even able to relate the origin of women's loss of dignity and integrity. This story sets into motion the myriad voices that explain the interconnectedness between the ancient order and contemporary times. The third couple, rock musician Arveyda and his Latin American refugee wife Carlotta, has marital woes over "the other woman." The intervening tales span three continents and thousands of years of evolution. The tales explore the depths of human character, history, myths, and legends to uncover truth and beauty. The couples discuss themselves and reconnect the missing pieces of the past. Truth is revealed in their oral accounts and collective oral memories, prioritizing orality over written records. They unfold truths about gender, race, and other species that reside on planet Earth.

THEMES

Themes are commentaries on human conditions in literary works, essential components that give works meaning and relevance. Major themes in *The Temple of My Familiar* are racism, sexism, and oppression; violence; nature; time; and saga of the self. Racism, sexism, and oppression as central themes relate the oppression inflicted upon the inhabitants of Africa and the American South, the subjugation of women by all men, and the patriarchal powers that suppress ancient African deities. Violence is also a theme. Fanny is both participant in it and victim of it, a method of escape extremely difficult for her to manage. Whether white or black, violence is a consistent strain throughout the novel. In an effort to understand the reason for so much violence Fanny's father explains to her that the deaths of whites do not lead to psychological liberation or additional oppression, just freedom from the imprisonment of those things and a place in the world for his children. Another theme is nature, which represents an orderly world. However, Walker's novel shows the disorder that results when transgressions plague the cosmos. Time, covering five hundred millennia, is a theme that reveals the intricacies of the interconnecting lives. Walker also explores the saga of the self, indicating constant exchange between the universe and the self. The legendary and historic experiences of the three couples in their efforts to comprehend the self reveal to them some surprising truths.

CHARACTER ANALYSES

Arveyda is a musician who adorns himself in headbands, capes, and peacock feathers. Gifted with the flute and guitar, he mesmerizes women into cosmic unconsciousness. Unlike the piercing sounds of the average rock musician, Arveyda's music is low toned and soft. Secure within himself and an admirer of womanhood, his mind is open to receive new knowledge. Because he is so receptive to consciousness raising, Arveyda and Fanny share an intimate moment, merging in such a way that they are one and one with the universe. Arveyda's lust leads him to intimate involvement with his mother-in-law.

Carlotta is born in prison. Her mother Zedé one day during the final sessions of college finds the doors to the university locked without explanation.

She takes a job in the hills as a teacher in a school without walls but is arrested on suspicion of being a communist. She is sent to prison, where her daughter is born, but manages to escape to San Francisco where Carlotta grows up and attends the university. Working in an import store Carlotta learns to pilfer peacock feathers for her mother to make capes for rock stars. One day she delivers a cape to the musician who becomes her husband, Arveyda.

Fanny (Celie's granddaughter and Olivia's daughter from *The Color Purple*) is Suwelo's ex-wife and finds her true self through dreams that house her archetypal memories and through journeys back to Africa to meet relatives. She learns meditation and masturbation and dissociates herself from organized religion. She achieves an elevated consciousness and becomes one with the cosmos.

Hal, a gentle man, frequent visitor to Suwelo, and friend of Suwelo's deceased uncle, is the character who provides background information on Lissie in the present time. He and Lissie are inseparable, for they have been companions for many years. Hal gradually loses his eyesight but receives a miracle at novel's end. After Lissie's death Hal marries Miss Rose so that they can be companions for the time that they have left and live together in the geriatric home.

Miss Lissie is an ancient goddess incarnated multiple times as a woman, man, lion, and white male. One incarnation is a white-skinned man with insufficient melanin to produce color in his complexion. He leaves the heat of Africa and animal familiars for Europe, where he creates an angry god in his image. Another is a pygmy at a time when visits occur between sexually segregated male and female tribes, who fraternize with apes. Men invent war that extinguishes the peace, and they endanger the apes and impose themselves on the women who become their familiars (companion animals). In another incarnation Lissie is a slave during a time when Europe and monotheistic Islam war against the Great Goddess of Africa, sever her head, and use it as a Gorgon emblem.

Suwelo (Fanny's ex-husband), an African American history professor, finds his true self through absorption of Lissie's messages. He learns to prioritize, that is, television watching and philandering are unimportant. He ultimately reconciles with Fanny, and the two move into a bird-shaped house with separate wings. They find a way to be married and free. Suwelo's challenge in the novel is to become informed about histories other than American history and to reach a higher understanding of the needs of his wife and, therefore, all women.

A MYTHIC OR ARCHETYPAL READING

Mythic/archetypal criticism as a literary approach discerns recurrent mythological and ritual patterns in cultures and religions worldwide. Philosopher and theorist Carl Gustav Jung believed these repetitive models to be psychic dust traceable back to mankind's ancient ancestry which survive in humanity's "collective unconscious." The images surface in a wide scope of literary expressions of writers, as well as varied psychological experiences, myths, and religions.

All critics do not embrace Jung's theory. For example, Canadian literary critic Northrop Frye (1912–91) accepts the fact that the archetypal duplications exist but argues that Jung's theory is an unnecessary explanation of their existence. In his publication *Anatomy of Criticism* (1957), Frye redefines Jung's approach to myth and archetype. Frye examines literature from four perspectives: theory of modes, theory of symbols, theory of myths, and theory of genres. The theory of modes describes an assortment of levels of realism in literature. The theory of symbols describes five levels ranging from the mundane to the spiritual. The theory of myths associates four seasons (spring, summer, fall, and winter) with four principles ("mythoi") of comedy, irony/satire, romance, and tragedy. Frye then subcategorizes these into phases. The theory of genres explains the dissimilarities among drama, epic, lyric, and others. Frye's theories have their central focus in Western literature.

Mythological/archetypal approaches to literature presume that readers everywhere are affected similarly and experience the same responses in relation to universal characters, images, motifs, and symbols. Myth critics contend that this universal composite of archetypes is the stuff that gives good literature its punch. Specifically, certain images have the same referents everywhere. Universally, desert denotes spiritual emptiness, water means purification, serpent translates to wisdom or evil, green indicates fertility, and seven stands for perfection, among other interpretations similarly shared. Moreover, myths are communal and contribute to the wholeness of society reflected in the literature of various cultural groups. For example, underground journeys and heavenly ascents are archetypes in the Italian epic poem *The Divine Comedy* by Dante Alighieri (1265–1321), death and rebirth are archetypes of the New Testament found in the Bible, the scapegoat or sacrificial lamb is an archetype in *The Strong Breed* by Nigerian dramatist and poet Wole Soyinka, the hero is an archetype in the *Iliad* by Greek poet Homer (8th c. B.C.), and the goddess mother is an archetype in Alice Walker's *The Temple of My Familiar*.

Some of the most interesting African myths are about primeval times and primordial energy. Following the lead of her literary foremother Zora Neale Hurston, who developed an interest in the paranormal through the study of anthropology, Alice Walker seeks the metaphysical basis of reality through the study of ancient beliefs and practices. Hurston and Walker both probe the relationship between memory and identity. Like Hurston, Walker discovered that many of the beliefs and practices have their genesis in feminine energy that unveils the truth of universal energy. Walker incorporates some of these discoveries in the novel *The Temple of My Familiar.*

Walker builds her story around Carlotta, Zedé, whose birthplace is Mesoamerica, and Lissie, whose recollection of the beginning times reveals African matriarchal origins. Close parallels exist between the indigenous spiritual practices of Mesoamericans and the Yoruba people of Africa. Walker's narrative line links the physicality of Zedé, Carlotta, and Arveyda to African origins, an assimilation of the two cultures. For example, Zedé finds Arveyda's hair "Kinky, firm, softly rough. Exactly the feel of raw silk. The only hair like this—*pelo negro*—in the world." Moreover, the three of them share pigmentation, although Zedé has the lightest complexion of the three. Thus, Walker discloses African physical traits in Mesoamericans and later ties in their spiritual practices and the revelations of Miss Lissie.

Bird and serpent imagery are some of the symbols that Walker uses in the novel. Grandmother Zedé, mother of Zedé, showcases her talents in the peacock-feathered costumes and headdresses she crafts for the dancers, musicians, and priests at village festival time, eventually handing down this art form to her namesake, Carlotta's mother Zedé. Peacock feathers are the adornment of the capes in which Arveyda wraps himself in his performances as onstage musical prodigy. Walker develops the connection between knowledge and symbols. Indigenous cultures use symbols as encryptions of their language and knowledge. Birds and serpents are mysterious symbols of immense power, and when combined they represent awesome power. The deities of indigenous people take the forms of birds or serpents alone or combinations of bird and serpent, feathered serpent, or serpent woman, all representations of positive rather than negative principles. Among the Yoruba people is the very old festival "Gelede," a celebration of the ancestral mothers and the life-giving powers of women, similar to the celebration that young Zedé witnesses.

Orality as energy is another focus of the novel. One major complaint of Walker's critics is that the novel is too talky. However, indigenous cultures preserve their knowledge over many millennia not in written form but through oral transmission. The imparter of knowledge is the ancestor, as represented by Lissie in the novel orally passing down knowledge to Suwelo and Hal. This ancient method of transmission demystifies history, since words passed down are never inaccurate or deceptive. The power of oral forms is that there is no place for untruth, for the words are always pure—unlike written history, which is often corrupted. The practice is personal and responsible, the passing down of information to the sons and daughters who will inherit the same personal and responsible roles, recognizing the assurance of cultural preservation. Words are also energy, always fluid and embodying the energy of the universe. Written forms are stagnant, without motion, and therefore do not interact with the energy of the universe. Above all, in indigenous cultures the ability to transmit orally is an art form, a creative internal force that makes the transmitter a constant connector to the universe.

Walker also references ancient African female deities, specifically the beheading of the African goddess figure by the Inquisitors, information revealed by Lissie. Ancients believed in the existence of one primordial mother from whom other mothers emerge, for example, as qualities of her personality. One female deity that Walker considers a spiritual mother is Isis, ancient goddess of Africa, called Aset in ancient Kemet. Often portrayed with the infant Horus in her arms, Isis was a dark-skinned deity considered a spiritual mother among indigenous people. High in the universal order as well is Ma'at, a teenage goddess often portrayed as a twin pair. She represents truth and order, constant strains and essential principles of the universe.

Another spiritual mother is the Yoruba goddess Obudua, copartner and wife to Obatala or Orishala, as well as cocreator. Also Yoruban is Oshun, whose symbol is the vulture, regarded as the opening to the powerful forces of the primordial mother and who promises rebirth following the process of death and decay. Other qualities of the primordial mother include Iyanla, who is the great wise mother, the water deities Yemoja and Osun, and Oya, strong deity of the forest and the hunt. Incorporating all of these qualities of the feminine, Walker crafts a novel centered on women's spiritual practices, emotions, and culture.

Lissie relates a story about being burned at the stake under suspicion of being a witch. Indigenous people worshipped witch goddesses who became so, in some cases, through violence and ultimate death. Some of them have the ability to replace their lower extremities with bird legs and talons. The power of sorcery is often their trademark, but they are not evil or the equivalent of the Western perception of devil. Instead, they operate on behalf of the petitioner but can also work against those who are disruptive to universal order.

Walker's *The Temple of My Familiar* is a metatext. Just as Frederick Douglass's *Narrative of the Life of Frederick Douglass, An American Slave, Written by Himself* can be read and interpreted on more than just its base level, Walker's narrative can as well. Gloria Steinem once said of Walker that she "comes at universality through the path of an American [B]lack woman's experience.... She speaks the female experience more powerfully for being able to pursue it across boundaries of race and class." Alice Walker is not the image of the "girl-next-door" writer, with all the prerequisites of the novel tucked into a neat little package of plot, theme, and character, as some critics apparently desired. In her effort to reclaim womanhood, especially that of women of African heritage, she returns to the dawn of time to give them a place, not only in the world but also in the universe. This novel answers the lines of Sonia Sanchez's poem, "there is no place/for a soft/black/woman." Walker provides such a place by exploring the universal on her terms, and exploring it provocatively.

7

Possessing the Secret of Joy **(1992)**

Three characters who make brief appearances in *The Color Purple* (Olivia, Adam, and Tashi) and in *The Temple of My Familiar* (Olivia and Tashi) resurface in this controversial protest novel. Clitoridectomy (female circumcision or female genital mutilation) is the focus of *Possessing the Secret of Joy,* which chronicles the life of one African woman traumatically scarred by this millennia-old practice and her struggle to comprehend its impact physically, mentally, and emotionally and survive its consequences. The novel explores phallic control of women's lives and the indoctrination of women to make the procedure a tradition, offering no options to unsuspecting young women. Written from a womanist perspective, it shows how one woman musters the strength to stand up and react to a situation, even if after the fact. The protagonist Tashi retaliates against the woman who carries out the surgical procedure on her. Walker in this novel verbally goes to war against this pervasive African and Middle-Eastern misogynistic practice, which continues where immigrant groups develop their own communities in foreign nations.

The sequels to the novel are the nonfiction companion book *Warrior Marks: Female Genital Mutilation and the Sexual Blinding of Women* (1993) and the film documentary *Warrior Marks* (1993) both with Pratiba Parmar, creating a trilogy. Walker successfully centralized this topic in the United

States, and indeed the world, creating national debate over the issue. In Walker's fictionalized version, the protagonist undergoes infibulation circumcision, the complete removal of the female genitalia.

Several media critics expressed shock and dismay that such "primitive" practices still occurred in underdeveloped nations. Other critics suggested that Walker discontinue her Western signifying and leave African women to their customs and traditions. They argued that clitoridectomy is deeply entrenched in African women's rites of passage to wifehood and motherhood, and felt that Walker, as a Western African American woman, failed to understand how her meddlesome ways could have a negative impact on African women's positions in their own society. Walker brings to this novel her characteristic political ethos of protest, resistance, and liberation, offering a sympathetic perspective while championing, in her view, a worthy cause to bring about change.

STRUCTURE

Walker begins the novel with a dedication: "This Book is Dedicated/With Tenderness and Respect/To the Blameless/Vulva." She follows the dedication with something of a repudiation of the racist thinking exhibited by some experts or scholars: "There are those who believe black people possess the secret of joy and that it is this that will sustain them through any spiritual or moral or physical devastation." The idea is that some people believe that people of African heritage have a capacity to survive the many tragedies heaped upon them. However, by the novel's end Walker reveals what she considers to be the true secret of joy. She follows this with an excerpt from *The Color Purple* about the failure of the missionaries to prevent the Olinka's practice of scarification and female genital circumcision. Preceding the first part of the novel is a quote from African folk culture: "When the axe came into the forest, the trees said the handle is one of us," apropos for the narrative that follows.

Multivoice narration dominates this 21-part novel. There are 72 narratives of a horrific nature, 42 articulated by the multiple Tashi personas; 30 in-tandem discourses featuring Adam, Benny, and Olivia; Lisette and Pierre; M'Lissa; and Mzee. The afterword cites statistics of the millions of women in Africa, the Far East, and the Middle East who have undergone female genital circumcision as a rite of passage.

SOCIOHISTORICAL CONTEXT

African societies are not monolithic in their beliefs, customs, and traditions. Although within the African continent there are amazing similarities in cultural practices, there are also wide differences both in the agrarian communities and the thriving urban areas. Advantaged Africans who gain access to Western education and knowledge adhere less strictly to time-honored practices than the minimally educated Africans who cling to traditional customs and resist any changes in tradition. Many Africans begin their lives in the bush or farming communities that have tribal connections and, therefore, are immersed in the practices that give them their identity and acceptance within the society.

African societies are both monogamous and polygamous, depending on the economic stability of the men, for the more affluent the men, the more wives they can afford. Men are the overall providers and take additional wives only if they are in superior economic situations. Multiple marriages assure men many children, who add to the prestigious advantages of their families. Initially, children receive instruction from the mothers, but as the children mature other teachers who are members of the tribe replace the mother's tutelage (although she remains a vital connection throughout the child's life), which leads to the ultimate ceremonial initiation into manhood or womanhood.

One step taken toward becoming an adult is scarification, a process of lasting injury undergone by both male and female children, as well as adults who are initiated into specific tribal societies. Usually cut on the cheeks, these marks are tribal identifications and are distinguishable from marks made by other tribes.

Both young men and women are participants in coming of age ceremonies; some initiations take place with and some without simultaneous male and female participation and contact. Young men's initiation ceremonies include circumcision. The door to manhood requires responsible actions, the first of which is marriage. Certain dictates and processes to be followed are prescribed for marriage, such as exogamy, a requirement that the bride must come from outside the tribal or village unit. The union of the two young people is not so much theirs alone as it is a benefit to and an involvement of whole clans, villages, or lineages. The ceremony involves elders, families, men, and women. Chinua Achebe's novel *Things Fall Apart* has an excellent marriage section that helps to explain the bargaining and ceremony pertaining to marriage in the Igbo culture. Following marriage young males take on other responsibilities that assure their continued elevated status in African society—perhaps more wives, titles, and/or memberships in secret societies (Shelton, 4–7).

Young women's initiation ceremonies include circumcision as well. Female children receive all of their instruction from their mothers and their mothers' cowives and some from other influential women of the tribe or clan. Almost from birth their mothers prepare them for the day when they will become wives and mothers. Except for the knowledge that it exists, female children receive little preparation for the act of circumcision, which is a life-changing event governed by secrecy. After initiation the senior women admonish the young women not to discuss the occurrences and swear them to silence. Moreover, according to tribal policy self-respecting African men refrain from entering into marriage with uncircumcised women because they have not gone through the processes of womanhood, but remain children. The act itself prevents women from exploring their sexuality, ostensibly renders them more suitable for marriage, less likely to seek divorces, and keeps their minds on the preservation of the family. Walker sees female circumcision as taking sexual gratification out of women's control, making pleasure a practice enjoyed only by men, and relegating women servants rather than participants in the act.

Clitoridectomy is of four types. Mild sunna circumcision is nicking, slitting, or removing of the prepuce of the clitoris, leaving the gland and body of the clitoris intact. Modified sunna or Muslim circumcision is partially or totally removing the body of the clitoris. Clitoridectomy is detaching the clitoris totally, including sometimes the labia minora, resulting in extensive scar tissue leading to obstruction of the vaginal opening. Infibulation or pharonic circumcision is the cutting away of both sides of the vulva followed by scraping the area raw and sewing together the raw edges, leaving a small opening for the vagina. This procedure provides sexual gratification for men but creates life-threatening situations for women, making urination, menstruation, intercourse, and childbirth extremely painful and difficult (Lightfoot-Klein).

Prior to Walker's novel becoming such a controversial rallying cry for abolishment of the circumcision practices, others, such as informed Western feminists and missionaries, expressed outrage over the practice of female circumcision, and members of the United Nations included it in its human rights initiative. However, some native Africans are not impressed by Westerners' intrusion into their cultural practices. For example, Jomo Kenyatta, Kenya's first leader after the cessation of colonial rule, rebutted Western views in his study *Facing Mount Kenya* (1965), asserting that the practices of circumcision for males and females are significant components of the sacred rituals for birthing young people into adult membership in the tribal family. Kenyatta's stance was that he stemmed from a culture as elevated and complex, although different from, as European culture. He encouraged his countrymen to return to the ways of the ancestors and cease to allow European agitators to detribalize them.

Clitoridectomy remains a heated issue in the national debate; women who underwent the procedure speak publicly, giving voice to this contentious issue. Some see the practice as essential to their national heritage and continued group identification. Others see no place for it in the twenty-first century and recommend its phasing out. Women who are personally and culturally attached to the rituals continue to debate the issue, and they will determine its modifications or abolishment.

GENRE AND NARRATIVE TECHNIQUE

A political novel centers on politics or political issues. Walker's novel focuses on one aspect of political life, female genital circumcision, which is a primary component of the novel, not just background fodder. This novel is extended political discourse on African customs of tribalism and sexism and the complicity of African leaders, male and female, in upholding the rituals of female mutilation as passage into adult life. It has a political mission to draw attention to an issue of which the world had little knowledge.

The story line progresses through the narrative accounts of important events in the characters' lives. The narratives are not chronological but arranged as flashbacks so that readers are involved in the memories of the characters and at the same time receive instruction and information, which is sometimes shocking but also readable. It connects rather than polarizes human emotions of anger and joy, love and hate, and courage and weakness. At the end of the novel the readers come away with not only understanding but also empathy.

PLOT

An English rubber manufacturer is the catalyst that begins the slow degeneration of Olinka society, reducing them to beggars. Outsiders whose guiding principle is the profit motive derived from the natural resources available in the village threaten traditional Olinka society because of their insensitive nature and determined motives. Realizing the threat imposed on her village, Tashi, an indigenous Olinka woman, rationalizes that preservation of Olinka culture requires its people to remain receptive to traditional tribal rituals, the practice of which is their only identity as Olinka. Resistance to the colonizers' influence is resistance to eradication; therefore, Tashi makes the decision to embrace the tribal practice of scarification, the marks on her face uniquely specifying her Olinka, differentiating her tribal identity from all others. As an older woman, she later consents, indifferent to Olivia's vehement pleas not to have the procedure, to the initiation ceremony of female genital circumcision as an additional external identification of tribal unity.

"Our Leader," the seat of power among the Olinka, sanctions continuance of tribal mores as a method of resistance against colonial law. The colonizers in power instituted a law that prohibited the leader's name from being spoken; thus, the Olinka referred to him as "Our Leader." His intent is political, for he is the Olinka revolutionary figure in opposition to foreign colonizers. In his view the Olinka maintain control of their culture by using their bodies as visible signs of physical protest, which include scarification and circumcision.

Following female genital circumcision, Tashi's body changes, developing a pervasive odor from the procedure and lengthy menstrual cycles; she is also unable to resume a normal way of walking, shuffling instead. Moreover, as a result of the procedure the sexual act with her husband is not pleasurable for her, and Adam, an African American, derives no satisfaction from the presence of blood or his wife's pain. Devastated over what has happened to her, Tashi retreats inward, assuming multiple personas as coping mechanisms to compensate for her tragic error: not realizing that she is innately Olinka, whether or not she acquiesces to participation in the life-altering initiation.

Years later Tashi undergoes psychoanalysis under the care of Mzee because she represses the memories that are the sources of her sadness and mental anxiety. As a child the sight of blood frightens her, a fear that continues into adulthood. With the doctor's prodding, using talk and dream therapy Tashi begins to unravel slowly the reason for her pain. As a child Tashi loses her favorite sister Dura to female genital circumcision, although at the time she is told that her sister bled to death. Dura's death causes Tashi to develop a blood fixation, panicking at the sight of it. Dura's death is the genesis of Tashi's trauma and her own victimization.

Tashi and Adam have a son together, Benny, but his painful delivery and the crushing of his brain during labor discourages Tashi from subsequent pregnancies, leading her to abort the child of her next conception. Adam is a loyal supporter of his wife, in spite of her physical and psychological imbalance, but he turns to another woman, the French born Lisette, the niece of Mzee, for a more stable man-woman friendship and then a romantic relationship. They have a son, Pierre, whom Tashi at first despises but later learns to appreciate. Pierre helps Tashi to comprehend the archetypal symbols of her dreams. As Tashi goes through the healing process via psychoanalysis, she concludes that she must avenge what happened to her and to countless young women who have endured similar mutilations. Her decision is to return to Africa to end the life of M'Lissa, the *tsunga* or circumciser, just as M'Lissa murdered her sister Dura.

Before Tashi ends M'Lissa's life, she listens to M'Lissa's story of how she became the *tsunga*, a national monument, as well as midwife and healer. Learning that M'Lissa, too, is a victim of the same procedure by the tribe's witch doctor, and that Catherine, Tashi's mother, assisted M'Lissa in holding Dura in a secure grip so that the procedure could be done to her fails to create a dilemma for Tashi or to convince her to spare M'Lissa's life. M'Lissa is an expendable commodity in a society that devalues the contribution of women except as vehicles of progeny; the tribe can always produce another national monument, another *tsunga*. The death of M'Lissa is the final step that leads to the restoration of Tashi as a healed whole human being, although she pays the price of death for the life she took; her victory is thus also a defeat.

THEMES

Themes are the primary topics of artistic representations in literary productions. Themes dominating *Possessing the Secret of Joy* are Africa and America, dreams and memory, and female genital circumcision. Africa is a central theme in this novel, as well as America. Walker engages in a unification process, linking them as continents through the characters. During the Harlem Renaissance of the 1920s and the Civil Rights movement of the 1960s African Americans idealized Africa. Proponents of black pride focused on the beauty and majesty of Africa, its history, art, music, dance, literature, religion, and people, reconnecting severed ties centuries old. However, Walker deconstructs the perception of idyllic Africa held by pro-Africa converts, pointing out the tribalism inherent in African male leaders that maintains intact a patriarchal institution responsible for the circumcision of millions of African women. Africa is also not a panacea, as Walker points out in the novel, when male leaders deny women's autonomy by enforcing female cultural rites and denying sexual pleasure and gratification to women, making the joy of sex a "men only" club. At the same time Walker depicts the African continent and the African body as domains colonized by exploitative European imperialists.

Dreams and memory are dominant themes in that Walker incorporates the theories of Carl Gustav Jung in the psychoanalysis and dream therapy of Tashi. To recapture memories through dreams is essential to psychological well-being. Tashi's conscious, personal unconscious, and collective unconscious memories are prerequisite avenues required to make progress toward completeness and wholeness. The characters also reveal their emotions through providing accounts of their memories.

Female genital circumcision, viewed as genital mutilation, is the dominant theme of the novel. Through the novel readers learn about the whole of the issue through the experience of one young woman who submits to the ritual. The *tsunga* performs the most extreme form of the procedure on the protagonist, disrupting her order and creating chaos that requires years of psychoanalysis to unravel. The procedure is a cultural rite of passage overseen by society's matriarchs, whose complicity with the patriarchy avoids change and keeps the practice firmly entrenched. Walker, a supporter of Jungian theory, attacks the rigid adherence to sexual roles assigned in African society. Jung's theory of the personal unconscious points out the importance of forgotten experiences, for example, the female elements of men and the male elements of women. However, African culture prohibits such an experience because all individuals are the totality of the sex they represent and are socialized into that particular sex role, incapable of supporting both sexes.

CHARACTER ANALYSES

Adam (Miss Celie's son in *The Color Purple*) vacillates between duty to uphold Christian dogma and disobedience of the commandment against adultery. He is missionary minister to the Olinka African tribe, marries Tashi, and eventually takes her home with him to America. He and Tashi have one son. A progressive minister, he has an opportunity to address the congregation about the horrors of circumcision but refuses to do so, fearing the subject would be too divisive. Following Tashi's trauma and eventual mental incapacity, he first befriends and then commits adultery with Lisette, fathering a son Pierre.

Benny (Bentu Moraga) represents the challenges of the mentally underdeveloped. He is the only son of Tashi and Adam and is mildly mentally challenged as a result of his trip through the birth canal. Tashi's infibulation creates a small vaginal opening that impedes his birth process, causing Benny's brain to be crushed during labor. His memory is also poor as a result of his traumatic birth. A constant note taker, he writes down all communications to safeguard his recall. His mother is emotionally detached from him, unable to bond with her son, often boxing his ears; this limitation is an effect of the mental distress from her infibulation.

Dura represents the thousands of defenseless young women who lose their lives to ancient practices of sexual binding. She is Tashi's older sister, a victim of the female circumcision process who bleeds to death from a botched procedure. Walker uses the euphemism "bath" to refer to female genital circumcision.

Hartford, an AIDS victim, represents the devastation of the AIDS epidemic on the African continent. Working for a medical laboratory in Africa as a hunter and decapitator of green monkeys, Hartford articulates the troubling genesis of the epidemic in Africa, tracing it back to the conspiratorial Americans, Australians, Dutch, Germans, and New Zealanders who, in their zeal to use the green monkeys to discover a cure for polio, disseminated contaminated vaccines to the African population, which was used as disposable test subjects. Walker bases Hartford's narrative lines partly on the research of journalist Tom Curtis, an investigative reporter who documented his findings in equatorial Africa.

Lisette is the "other woman" character who provides an escape from the stresses of a marriage that has too many challenges. She is the French mistress to Adam, and the niece of Mzee the psychoanalyst. She gives birth to Adam's son Pierre. Before her execution Tashi composes a letter of reconciliation to the deceased Lisette and informs her of Pierre's importance in her life.

M'Lissa represents the female conspirator with the patriarchy to maintain a tradition of sexual oppression against women. Inheriting the position of *tsunga* from her mother, it is she who performs the procedure on Tashi. A victim of genital circumcision herself, she is left with a malfunctioning left leg that she drags behind her as she walks. Her mother's plan was to perform the mildest circumcision on her, but the suspicious male witch doctor sensed a violation and performed the infibulation himself, cutting even the tendons of her leg. M'Lissa is emotionally detached from the young girls whom she mutilates, concentrating more on her economic stability and her autonomy as a *tsunga*. She believes that the young women themselves are the mistresses of their fates, whether through foolish naiveté or patriarchal domination. She has no pity on the young women.

Mzee or "Uncle Carl," the Jungian analyst, portrays the value of psychology. He helps Tashi to progress through the three phases of Jungian analysis of the psyche. Olivia and Adam take Tashi to his tower in Switzerland for analysis; there he treats her through Jungian dream symbology.

Olivia (Miss Celie's daughter in *The Color Purple*), voice of reason and best friend of Tashi, pleads with her not to undergo female genital circumcision. She and Tashi are lifelong friends and sisters of the heart who met when her missionary parents first arrived in the Olinka village. She is sympathetic toward Tashi and the aftermath of the procedure, helping her to discover a way to maintain feminine cleanliness. Olivia is also by Tashi's side when she is imprisoned.

Pierre is the personification of the coming together of disenfranchised groups—black-white biracial and gay intellectual. He is the son of Adam and his French lover Lisette. He is rejected by Tashi, who throws stones, a Jungian symbol of wholeness, at him when he comes to visit Adam. He is a student of anthropology at the University of California, Berkeley. Interpreting Tashi's termite dream, he links it to African symbology, helping her eventually to begin recovery from her disorders.

Raye, an African American female analyst, symbolizes women helping women. She encourages Tashi to recall her female genital circumcision experience. She also helps Tashi to peel away the masked layers that prevent her from seeing herself completely. She, too, is at Tashi's side when she is imprisoned.

Tashi, protagonist of *Possessing the Secret of Joy,* is the representative trope of all women who undergo female genital circumcision. As Adam's wife she gives birth to the mentally challenged Benny and aborts their second child because she could not bear a caesarean delivery. She demonstrates ethnocentric pride and arrogance in her decision to undergo female genital circumcision, which ultimately causes lifelong pain and suffering and mental anguish and strips her of her sexuality. She devotes the rest of her life to attempting to understand the meaning of the ritual. Mzee stirs her repressed memories by showing her a film of an African initiation ceremony and using clay as a reference to fertility dolls as symbols of matriarchal empowerment. Tashi begins her journey to mental wholeness through art and psychology.

A JUNGIAN READING

The Austrian neurologist Sigmund Freud and his followers investigated psychic experience in part through one of its unconscious aspects, dreams. They discovered a split consciousness where there were traces of memory of the dreams. The split consciousness revealed a symbolic language. When left alone to "free associate" from their dreams' symbolic elements, Freud's patients released psychological determinants that were at the root of their illnesses. He believed, then, that symbolic language shed light on evidence of the repression of infantile sexuality.

Freud's contemporary Carl Gustav Jung expanded Freud's theories of dream symbolism to include not so much repressed unconsciousness but collective unconsciousness. Freud called his process psychoanalysis and Jung called his analytical psychology. Jung's focus shifted from Freud's personal symbols to the concept of universal symbols of the psyche, noting that all individuals held certain archetypes in common to all experience and recorded them in all forms of cultural expressions. Jung called the process from which individuals shift their center of gravity from the ego to an integrated human being "individuation." Alice Walker credits the writings of Jung with influencing her individual "self-therapy," but she also evinces reliance on Jung theories in the development of her novel's protagonist Tashi in *Possessing the Secret of Joy.*

The first level of Jungian psyche is consciousness, the "persona" or mask. Tashi begins masking after her first traumatic experience. Tashi's sister Dura undergoes the procedure of female circumcision, suffering in agony and screaming in pain; the outcome is bloody and fatal. Tashi is fully conscious of this unfortunate occurrence and develops a phobia from the sight of blood, but repressing the memory of this traumatic event, she agrees to take the first step of cultural identification with her vanishing tribe—scarification. Although while undergoing the process she is fully aware of the impoverished conditions and the disintegration of her fellow tribal members, she consents and follows through, masking the reality of her world. Later, over the objecting cries of Olivia (Miss Celie's daughter from *The Color Purple*), missionary in Africa and Adam's sister, Tashi consents to the infibulation procedure as an additional cultural identity and accepts the code of silence imposed on her fully conscious, that is, with awareness of her actions. When she removes the veil or mask of cultural arrogance that blinds her reality, Tashi renounces the two powerful elements of African tribalism and sexism that are the source of her grief and haughtiness, sending her on a descent into insanity.

The personal unconscious, a mirror image of the persona containing unrealized possibilities and forgotten experiences, is the second level of Jungian psyche. Tashi slips into a recessed inner self, the shadows of her mind, telling stories and creating from her imagination multiple personalities. At this level she exhibits her most aberrant behavior. Her multiple personas include Tashi, the little girl of the Olinka tribe who undergoes scarification and circumcision as an act of tribal identity. The next is Evelyn, the Tashi who accepts American citizenship. The third is Tashi-Evelyn, who remembers her African past through nightmarish dreams. Another is Evelyn-Tashi, who is a fusion of her African and American cultures. The fifth is Tashi-Evelyn-Mrs. Johnson, the aged murderer of the circumciser M'Lissa. She commits this crime to avenge the deaths and sufferings of the female victims of genital mutilation and to affirm female sexuality. Tashi's behavior is indicative of the Jungian anima/animus archetypes of right and wrong qualities. Murdering M'Lissa is wrong, but Tashi murders her for the right reasons. The last is Tashi Evelyn Johnson Soul, who reconciles her various internal oppositions and makes the steps toward wholeness. Her sister Dura's death and the blood phobia she develops as a result of Dura's death contribute to her mental decline.

Benny and Pierre are the specific victims of Tashi's shadowy self; she often boxes the ears of the first, and she hurls rocks at the second. She requires extensive analysis to reach self-knowledge of her shadowy side. While existing in the shadows, Tashi and her multiple personalities return to Africa intent on murdering M'Lissa, considered an African national monument. One personality purchases razors as murder weapons; another personality is audience to storyteller M'Lissa's horrific accounts of her life as a *tsunga;* another personality denies involvement in the murder; and yet another affirms her involvement. Tashi's behavior evinces again the rightness or wrongness of the anima/animus archetype, how each is unshakable in its convictions. Walker makes M'Lissa's murder premeditated, but all of Tashi's personalities commit the murder because M'Lissa's crimes were against all Olinka women. However, the capital punishment imposed on Tashi is not for M'Lissa's murder, national monument or not. It is for breaking the code of silence the patriarchy demands around the female circumcision issue. Coming out of the shadows, moving toward wholeness, and using the colors of the American flag (representing freedom of speech) Tashi creates protest signs, becoming herself a national monument to the scores of women who stand with her in solidarity and appeal to the president to commute her sentence. In this way Walker unites the best of America with the possibility of a better world for Africa. This is then a real cause that enjoins both sides of the ocean. On the day of her execution the protest sign most obvious to Tashi reads "RESISTANCE IS THE SECRET OF JOY!"

The third level of Jungian psyche, the collective unconscious, which contains the whole psychological heritage of the human race, uncovers specific African archetypes relevant to Tashi's cure from mental aberration. The termite hill dream is symbolic of the reserved places men hold in African society, and of African men's tendency to use African women as breeders. Tashi's artistic drawing of a foot, fighting cocks, and a large strutting cock waiting to receive the unclean vulva tossed to it by the foot reveals the role of women in upholding the tradition. The foot is M'Lissa, and the large cock is really a hen, all the women who play a participatory role as oppressors in holding down the young women so that the procedure can be finalized. The boulder in Tashi's throat is the repression of her memory, but when she has total recall the boulder explodes.

Wholeness, or the individuation process, occurs when Tashi accepts the truth of her experiences, recovers her memories, and faces her accusers. Just as Dura's death causes Tashi's repressed memories, Dura's death also triggers her cure from insanity by once again remembering it. She then chooses to be a change agent for the countless women wronged by the defeatist actions of a patriarchal society and other women who succumb to its pressure by supporting the tradition. Resisting the prevarications of the establishment and facing the truth of female suffering, Tashi goes to her execution a whole woman and amidst the fertility symbols of corn, flowers, seeds, beads, and herbs brought by the women supporters.

8

By the Light of My Father's Smile (1998)

Alice Walker's *By the Light of My Father's Smile*, her sixth novel, is an erotic fantasy filled with serious commentary about female sexuality. She continues in this novel the subject she began in *Possessing the Secret of Joy*. She does not, however, write about female sexuality that deprives women of self-esteem and self-worth but treats the subject as a celebration of pleasure and expectation. The novel is also about hypocrisy, masquerade, and deception, the qualities needed by the lead characters to accomplish their anthropological goals. An African American married couple, the Robinsons, relocates to the remote Sierras of Mexico in the 1940s to study a cultural group near extinction. They live among the Mundo, an ancestrally mixed-race tribe of escaped African slaves and Native Americans. With them are their two daughters, whose lives will change dramatically as a result of the Mexican experience. Spirituality and afterlife are at the center of the novel, including the idea that men of African American heritage can acquire an angelic state of grace.

STRUCTURE

Alice Walker begins her novel by informing readers that it is "A Story of Requited Love, Crossing Over, and the Sexual Healing of the Soul."

Indeed, the narrative unfolds an exciting story line of love avenged, disembodied humans, and sexual intimacy. She follows this page with a poetic tribute to instructors, awareness, and kinship. Much of the novel centers on the acquisition of knowledge and the development of a circle of friends who become extended family. A third page includes a quote on friendship, love, lovers, and angelic envy from author Father Matthew Fox, as well as one of Walker's insightful maxims in the same vein. This reference foreshadows her fictional version of the intersecting line between life and death and the connection between the living and the departed. She ends this section with a brief Mundo prayer to Mama. The allusion is to literal mothers who continue the earthly lifeline and to the figurative universal source of planetary life.

The narrative is a division of three sections. The long first section, "Angels," begins with a chapter of the same title and introduces readers to the characters, alive and deceased, and to the issues they face through life's journey. "A Kiss between the Dead Is a Breeze" is the title of the second division, a segment of poetry and conversations among the characters on the other side of life. The final and shortest section is "Fathers," a focus on eternity and guardianship of the living through the divine state of grace. Walker ends her novel with acknowledgements of assistance from the spirit of Eros and spiritual helpers who encourage her in consciousness raising and new understandings of the universal cycle.

SOCIOHISTORICAL CONTEXT

In this novel Alice Walker introduces readers to the presence of Africans in Mesoamerica. She creates a group of people called the Mundo, a cultural group that is a fusion of African and Amerindian bloodlines in Mexico. Within the mainstream scholarly community, African presence in the Americas is a subject that is either rejected outright or treated as controversial. However, African American scholar Ivan van Sertima asserts in his publication *They Came Before Columbus: The African Presence in Ancient America* (1976) that historical evidence documents the participation of Africans in Mexico in the pre-Columbian period. More widely accepted is that Africans accompanied Spanish conquistadors to Mexico in the sixteenth century.

Juan Garrído, a man of African heritage, was with Hernán Cortés when he arrived in Veracruz in 1519. He was active in the conquest of Tenochtitlán, the Aztec capital, and in expeditions to explore the country. Cortés and Spanish settlers depended on Hispanicized enslaved Africans and enslaved people from the African continent, mostly men, to provide the labor for the mines and plantations. This introduction of Africans into Mexico began the process of miscegenation (mixing of African and Amerindian bloodlines) that would fuel an Afro-Mexican population. By the seventeenth century enslaved and free Afro-Mexicans outnumbered the whites who had settled in the region. Importation of enslaved Africans continued, for European diseases decimated the Amerindian population. Limitations on the importation of slaves brought about a decline in the Afro-Mexican population in the eighteenth century. In addition, they fell victim to disease such as tuberculosis and were often worked to death. Another contributor to the declining numbers of Afro-Mexicans was the Spanish distaste for dark skin. Afro-Mexicans were encouraged to mate with lighter-skinned partners to improve their positions in the Mexican caste system. Individuals with dark skin endured harsh treatment and marginalization from officials of the Spanish government and from the clergy of the Catholic Church.

By the nineteenth century Mexican countrymen demanded their independence from Spain, and slave revolts led to the abolition of the system of slavery under the leadership of the part Afro-Mexican Miguel Hidalgo. Before emancipation in the United States, some escaped North American slaves found their way to Mexico, settled in the region, married Seminole Indians, and assimilated into the community. Miscegenation continued into the twentieth century, and the reduction in the numbers of Afro-Mexicans was precipitated by marriage for the purpose of skin lightening, making Afro-Mexican heritage undetectable. The Mexican leadership used the phrase *mejorar la raza* (improve the race) to sanction marriages between lighter-skinned Amerindians and darker-skinned Afro-Mexicans to create lighter skin in their offspring. Today, at the beginning of the twenty-first century, dominant Afro-Mexican settlements are in Costa Chica, Veracruz, Coahuila, Zacatecas, Sinaola, Yucatán, and Quintana Roo, among others.

Government leaders of Mexico take pride in the nation's mixture of diverse peoples, identifying it as a nation of *mestizos* (indigenous and European ancestry). However, the 1990s brought about a change in governmental policy. Mexican officials now recognize its third ancestral root, the Afro-Mexicans. The government will further the study of this cultural group through the project Nuestra Tercera Raíz (Our Third Root). Interest in Afro-Mexicans by anthropologists inside and outside the country has prompted officials in the government to amend their attitudes and acknowledge the population that they ignored and marginalized (Appiah and Gates). Also during this decade Afro-Mexicans from 30 Afro-Mexican settlements convened the Encuentro de Pueblos Negros (Gathering of Black Towns) to discuss their history, improve their communities, and organize against marginalization.

Walker's novel also highlights the African American middle class. Access to quality education is one criterion for admittance into the professionally and financially successful world of the African American cultural elite. Its members are associated with artistic, business, educational, legal, medical, and political endeavors. The urban lifestyle is another criterion, that is, African American city dwellers (in large and small cities) demonstrate an appreciation for social festivities that revolve around theatres, museums, restaurants, colleges and universities, fraternities and sororities, and charitable organizations. These criteria form the distinctions among African Americans; however, more than education and lifestyle determine inclusion in the middle class.

Members of the African American middle class affirm each other. Employment status and the inheritance of wealth and property are less significant than decorum, refinement, reputation, respectability, and morals. Even within class structure there are gradations of identification. Langston Hughes, expressing his views in his essay "The Negro Artist and the Racial Mountain," illustrates African American class distinctions, calling the middle class not wealthy but not uncomfortable, and the high class white imitators. As with most groups there are gender issues and some biases centered on skin hue, a carryover from antebellum society, but these do not detract from their middle-class ideals. While they are not monolithic, they are connected by a common thread and a common call.

They have a commitment to the African American church, the hub of religious life, organizing, and politicizing. Moreover, they address the needs of African Americans and citizens of the African diaspora as a whole. They retain the spirit of resistance to oppression and injustice that was embedded in their ancestors, and they work hard to advance the cause of marginalized and disenfranchised people (Harley, 786–789). Vigilant in their duty to those whose lives are weighed down by societal pressures, they are instrumental in bringing about change where it is needed. The Robinsons in Alice Walker's novel are members of the African American middle class. Their contribution is an anthropological study of the people that the world does not see. Their primary research and documentation of the existence of the Mundo is lasting evidence of their dedication to African causes.

Finally, Walker's main characters the Robinsons are practitioners of agnosticism, a doctrine that holds that the existence of God and other spiritual beings is unknown and probably unknowable. Agnosticism takes center place between theism, which affirms the existence of God and spiritual beings, and atheism, which denies the existence of such beings. Individuals who embrace agnosticism do not deny all belief systems; they deny the reliability of metaphysical and theological beliefs. Scottish philosopher David Hume (1711–76) and German philosopher Immanuel Kant (1724–1804) are responsible for modern agnosticism. Both concluded that the argument for the existence of God and the soul lacked validity, pointing out the logical fallacies in the arguments. Walker's characters find themselves in an afterlife existence, but not the heaven or hell of Christian doctrine and not the nothingness and termination of consciousness of atheism.

GENRE AND NARRATIVE TECHNIQUE

Genre refers to the grouping of literary works into categories according to their formal or technical characteristics. The literary compositions of Alice Walker, however, never fit easily into ideal traditional classifications. Walker likes to experiment with forms, giving herself leverage to combine some forms and disregard others. The publication *By the Light of My Father's Smile* is an extended work of fiction about life and experience, and thus a novel, but Walker extends its magnitude to incorporate a variety of prose forms. This creative work has elements of the romance (love story) along with some aspects from the chivalric tradition of the knight and his deeds (gallant in battle and courteous to women, some of Manuelito's character traits). The father, Señor Robinson, interrupts the romantic bliss of the happy young couple (Magdalena and Manuelito), severs their romantic ties, and separates them for an indefinite period of time. Magdalena pines over her lost love, replacing passion with food and becoming morbidly obese. Her lover, Manuelito, massages his crushed heart through Vietnam War quests that result in injuries, causing his broken body to be held together with metal. They reunite by chance when both are booked on the same airline flight, only to have him lose his life in a freak automobile accident following a romantic dinner together at a New York restaurant.

Incorporated in this creative work is also a novel of manners (customs and habits of a social class at a specific time and place). Walker is detail specific in her descriptions of the social behavior of the African American middle class post–Harlem Renaissance (artistic creative period of African Americans from the end of World War I to the beginning of World War II). With accuracy she narrates the Robinsons' social mores—education, court-ship, marriage, home life, and family building. She chronicles their par-ticular lifestyle, built around love of art, literature, and music, as well as their appreciation of anthropology. They are well educated and instill their values of accomplishment and success in their daughters. Because they have anthropological interests that they wish to pursue, they devise a plan to relocate their family to the heart of the Mundo cultural laboratory, afford-ing their children a unique opportunity to learn and to travel. Walker's rep-resentation of the Robinsons as members of the African American middle class is realistic, for their middle-class values are powerful controls over the way Walker develops them as characters in the novel.

The genre of myth is a central point of development in the novel. Myths have their genesis in the storytelling traditions of primitive people. The stories have no traceable author but are reflections of primitive cosmology used for the purpose of comprehension of the natural world and natural events. The core belief systems of primitive cultural groups are mostly centered on myths pertaining to the supernatural. They provide explana-tions of life and death, natural phenomena, creation of the world, divine nature, and existence outside of flesh. Walker's Mundo people provide the mythological embodiments of truth and teach their ways to the Robinson family. The perceptions of the Mundo inspire revelation into the purpose of love and healing, lessons for the Robinsons to learn in life or in death.

Walker uses the genre of narrative poetry (nondramatic poems that tell stories) to embellish her novel. She has exceptional power with words and rare sensitivity to human emotions. Though the poems are succinct, they express intense feelings of love and otherworldliness. Just as the dominant romantic poets (Byron, Keats, Shelley, Wordsworth) infused their poetry with images of nature as a means to express their subjective reflections of its struggle to thrive, Walker uses poetry in her novel to justify the existence of nature beyond the physical and into the metaphysical. Walker not only explores varied genre techniques in this novel but also finds innovative ways to use narrative technique.

Walker uses narrative technique (a method to stimulate readers' responses) to develop the novel and to convey its meaning. Essential in the evaluation of the novel, narrative technique in Walker's capable hands is a demonstration of her conscious preoccupation with the narrative flow of the novel. One technique that she incorporates is that of multiple nar-rators in the telling of the story. The point of view (the perspective from which the story is told) alternates between women and men and between those alive and those deceased. Sometimes the narrator's voice adopts the omniscient point of view, the all-knowing perspective in which the characters' actions and thoughts are carefully explained. At other times the narrator speaks from the first-person point of view, with the readers experiencing through the senses of the character only what the character desires to reveal. Walker also incorporates limited use of the central intelligence point of view, allowing readers to experience everything relating to the story from inside the mind of a single character. Walker exercises her freedom of choice in the selection of point of view and does not limit herself to one perspective in this novel.

PLOT

In the development of plot writers select certain events to reveal characters' conflicts. Most times writers outline the plot chronologically; however, Walker's *By the Light of My Father's Smile* flashes back to past events nonchronologically. The plot of this novel centers on a single motif that propels the action into play: the beating of Magdalena by her father, Señor Robinson, who uses a silver-studded belt. This one act impacts the lives of all the major characters, causing a domino effect among all family members and the boyfriend Manuelito. Because she is highly traumatized by her father's action, Magdalena makes her life's quest revenge for what she considers an invasion of her person and a rejection of her developing womanhood. Señor Robinson's wife Langley alienates herself from her husband, so distraught is she over her husband's determination to exercise patriarchal control over his daughter's sexual awakening. His passionate cries to his wife eventually allow him to love her back into his arms, but only after she purges her painful emotions through the destruction of material possessions that she holds dear. Daddy's joy to behold, Susannah wants to remain the apple of her father's eye, but Magdalena refuses to allow Susannah to forget the memory of the whipping she witnesses; thus, whenever Susannah finds herself melting under her father's overpowering charm, Magdalena sends a signal (clearing her throat) that conjures up the memory all over again. Señor Robinson goes through life without peace and acceptance from his family and without love and affection from his daughters.

Señor Robinson has to learn life's lessons in death as a Mundo. According to Mundo cosmology, "The dead are required to finish two tasks before all is over with them: one is to guide back to the path someone you left behind who is lost, because of your folly; the other is to host a ceremony so that you and others you have hurt may face eternity reconciled and complete." When he embraces Mundo cosmology, he is able to make reconciliation with the ones he has injured, causing them mental anguish and emotional distress, and face eternity a harmonious soul.

THEMES

Themes are the predominant topics of literary works, revealing larger meanings and insights about life in general. Walker's works are thematically multifocused, but the dominant themes of *By the Light of My Father's Smile* center on father-daughter relationships, love, reconciliation, sexuality, and spirituality. Walker focuses on father-daughter relationships to emphasize the importance of fathers in the lives of their daughters. Fathers are instrumental in socializing their daughters in the proper lifestyles and values. Fathers are the support system not just emotionally, but also sexually. The father-daughter relationship in this novel is first strained and then nonexistent. Walker illustrates through the character of Magdalena the vulnerability of young girls whose fathers do not provide them with a sense of compassion and belonging. Walker implies that fathers are essential in the development of daughters who are not conflict-ridden and can enter womanhood empowered and positive in the development of adult relationships.

Love is always a theme in Walker's writings. In this novel love is pervasive—love of spouse, love of children, love of siblings, and love of self. Love manifests differently in different relationships and meets different requirements in different situations. While Señor Robinson faces no difficulty in verbalizing his attachment to and his dependency on his wife Langley and his love for his daughter Susannah, he falters in expressing his love for Magdalena. His inability to demonstrate a caring attitude toward her severely handicaps her socially. She then confuses the definition of love in her relationship with her sister. Magdalena holds Susannah hostage, manipulating her into not showing Señor Robinson kindness and affection. Magdalena equates Susannah's love for her with mistreatment of their father, something that Magdalena desires. Self-love in the Robinson family suffers because they fail to show adequate affection toward each other; therefore, they cannot look inward to give themselves proper care and concern.

The theme of reconciliation in this novel is the restoration of peace and harmony to disjointed lives. When Señor Robinson proves that he possesses the human skill of empathy, it becomes crucial to the act of reconciliation with his daughter Susannah, even after death. He spends endless time hovering around her as a ghost, but he does not begin the reconciliation process until he empathizes with her. Also, when he finally listens to Manuelito and accepts the teaching of the Mundo, the door opens for him to experience full reconciliation with all of his family members. Then he is able to experience the afterlife in a constant state of harmony.

Sexuality as a theme in the novel is a celebration of Eros. For example, Susannah's attitude about sex affects the way she feels and responds sexually, that is, she is free and not confined. Her attitude about sex is healthier than Magdalena's. Furthermore, Susannah believes sex to be a source of pleasure, but Magdalena's sex life is practically nonexistent until she reunites with Manuelito. Both women identify themselves sexually as females, their biological inheritance. Susannah, however, is not locked into a traditional sex role and does not abide by dominant and submissive and independent and dependent characteristics. Instead, her behavior is androgynous (combining of male and female characteristics). At the novel's beginning she is heterosexually married, but when the relationship fizzles, she enters a same-sex relationship, indicating her flexibility in sexual matters.

Walker's theme of spirituality centers on understanding primitive belief systems rather than adhering completely to institutionalized Christianity and Judaism. The Robinsons are agnostics and do not subscribe to any spiritual belief system. Highlighted in the novel is the Mundo spiritual system, which avoids jargon about the world's end, the annihilation of evildoers, heaven and hell, and the just reaping a special reward. Through the character of Manuelito readers become aware of a system of beliefs and practices shared by the Mundo that help them cope with human existence in life and after life. Mundo cosmology acknowledges the interconnectedness of the human spirit and/or soul to all existence since time immemorial. While the Mundo do have public and private rituals, their cosmology is dependent upon the cohesiveness of the cultural group, as is evident in the fact that the culture does not disintegrate when Señor Robinson introduces a foreign religion.

CHARACTER ANALYSES

Character analyses involve exploring what characters say and what is said about them. Characters are responsible for moving the plot along, and primary characters are protagonists who are in conflict with other characters or with institutions. The major characters in this novel are Señor Robinson and Langley Robinson, Samantha/Susannah, Magdalena/June, Manuelito, Pauline, and Irene.

Señor Robinson and Langley Robinson, a married couple, are anthropologists posing as Christian missionaries in the remote Sierras of Mexico, home of the mixed African and Amerindian Mundo people. The Robinsons are in conflict with each other, although they eventually overcome the strained moments of their relationship. Señor Robinson is often overbearing and controlling, the epitome of patriarchy. He and his wife are often at odds over the upbringing of the girls. He is the stern disciplinarian and she leans more toward providing the girls opportunities to discover the world. When he insists on being uncompromising, Langley Robinson retreats into a safe zone, usually her bedroom, to regroup in her commitment to her marriage and rethink the situation. She then denies him the right of entry to the bedroom, listening to his pleas and finally acquiescing and allowing him to return. Their love is secure and their bond is strong. However, Señor Robinson is in conflict with his daughter Magdalena, a tempestuous, strong-willed child. He lacks the parenting skills to reach her at the base level because both of them are headstrong and desire to rule. Their confrontations lead to irreparable damages in their relationship. As a ghost Señor Robinson is a voyeur, witnessing the passionate lovemaking of his daughter Susannah with her Greek husband Petros and then her lesbian partner Pauline. When he is alive he is unaccepting of his daughters' sexuality and rejects the possibility that they can enjoy sex with a partner as much as he enjoys it with Langley.

Samantha/Susannah (childhood name/adult name) is the protagonist in this novel. She is a renaissance woman (an expert writer with diverse interests) who when first introduced appears to be introverted and vulnerable but emerges as a survivor. As a child she allows her sister Magdalena to stifle the love she has for her father, prohibiting her from outward expressions of affection. The result of this prohibition is alienation from her sister, which she vows to amend. The single childhood act of the whipping mars their adult life. Susannah internalizes her feelings and manifests her distress by wearing dark clothes. As she comes out of her shell her attire becomes more colorful. Susannah reconciles with Magdalena before she dies of a broken heart, and with her father in the spiritual realm after her death from old age.

Magdalena/June (childhood name/adult name), lovingly nicknamed "Mad Dog" by the Mundo because of her fearlessness and free spirit, embraces the Mundo culture and rides a black stallion named Vado with the love of her life, Manuelito, by her side. She becomes a tragic character when her father represses her sexual awakening, putting her in direct conflict with him and all whom he loves. As a defiant 15-year-old she becomes sexually intimate with her Mundo boyfriend but is discovered by her father as she emerges from the secret cave, their hideout. Señor Robinson becomes so enraged that he administers the memorable whipping with a belt that Manuelito has given her as a present. It is a punishment from which she never recovers. She and her father become estranged, and Magdalena lives the remainder of her life in the shadows. She becomes an obese academic, masking her pain with food. Her reunification with Manuelito provides the impetus for her to tackle her weight issue, but he dies before she takes the first step. Thoroughly brokenhearted, she dies, holding chocolate cake in one hand and a beer in the other.

Manuelito, her Mundo lover, is also a tragic character. He reacts to the devastation of losing Magdalena by marrying a woman who has his commitment but not his heart and fathering children with her. To cope he becomes a decorated Vietnam War veteran, but his many injuries from his tours of duty leave him barely able to move and held together with wire. Manuelito is in conflict with the military institution, but his Mundo upbringing does not allow him to harbor anger toward Señor Robinson. In the afterlife he is the guiding spirit that assists Señor Robinson in the reconciliation with his daughters.

Pauline is the love interest of Susannah and the example of the enterprising spirit. She retrieves from her mother's gardens the art of culinary competence and uses it to become financially successful. Pauline's conflict centers on overcoming the hurdle of doubt regarding her own achievements. In one area she is liberated—lesbian orgasms—and determines to remain vigilant in the celebration of Eros.

Irene is the example of man's inhumanity to man. Her dwarf physique makes her an imposition on her family, who gives her to the church following her mother's death. Because she is the product of an affair and is physically challenged, the villagers of Greece taunt her and deny her humanity. Following the deaths of her father and all his surviving sons she inherits the family's wealth, using it to travel the world and enjoy the luxuries money buys. Irene also represents knowledge, wisdom, and understanding, for in her incapacitated state she has time to devote to study, unrestricted in the requirements of home matters. Although she is small in stature, she is limitless in compassion of the heart, the giving of gifts, and imparting the knowledge that she has acquired over time. Irene's conflict is with the people in her home town in Greece, who fail to see her as a human being but rather as something grotesque, worthy only of being discarded and ignored. Nevertheless, Irene does not allow the actions of others to deter her. She lives the life that she chooses to live and partakes of the experiences that she chooses to have. She is the wise guide in the present life that Manuelito is in the afterlife.

A FORMALIST READING

The purpose of formalist criticism is to uncover the structure and meaning of literary works, a required component in the production of literary works as art forms. Formalist criticism centers on literary works only, not on extrinsic systems of evaluation such as literary history, historical contexts, sociological phenomena, or the author's life. The focus is on literary works and their shapes and effects, that is, the forms that lead to comprehension of the literary works, the discovery of unifying patterns that inform, shape, and give relevance to the whole. Literary works are independent units with interdependent components.

Formalism as a literary approach in the United States parallels the rise of New Criticism in the 1930s and 1940s. Formalist practitioners Cleanth Brooks, John Crowe Ransom (1888–1974), Allen Tate, and Robert Penn Warren (1905–89) gathered informally to discuss literature, developed a reputation as the "Fugitives," and published a literary magazine. As they critiqued their own work and the work of others, they agreed upon certain principles of analysis that became the foundation of critical analysis in universities and literary critical societies.

Formalist critics encourage fresh approaches to literary works, for these are structures of words that have specific meanings. Readers' responsibilities are to approach literary works for what they contain inside, not outside, and uncover the principles that allow literary works to reveal themselves. Careful, rigorous, close readings of texts (words, phrases, sentences, and paragraphs, from smaller units to larger units) allow total experiences of literary texts. To determine how the words of literary works form patterns is the primary step in uncovering the forms and structures of the organic whole. Texts are important in and of themselves. They have meaning based on ways the language is used to convey meanings. Formalist critics hold that literary works exist independently of readers, independently of readers' reactions to texts, and independently of the act of reading. In essence, masterful literary texts are universal and reflect immutable universal experiences, issues, and values. The study of literary texts, formalist critics believe, hones readers' sensibilities and is an integral component in the intrinsic process of edification.

Formalist critics believe that the study of poetry is ideal for the application of the formalist approach, but they also include fiction and drama. When considering fiction formalist critics often begin with point of view used by the author and how that vantage point frames the narrative. Alice Walker's *By the Light of My Father's Smile* has multiple narrators. From the beginning, Señor Robinson in his ghost form responds to Susannah's reality as he watches her as a visiting spirit, and he also reflects in flashback their lives as family members simultaneously with his visitation. The second narrator is Magdalena, who reflects back to the punishment meted out to her for becoming sexually active as a teenager. Another narrator is Petros, Susannah's Greek husband, who informs her about the Greek dwarf that is a permanent fixture in the local sanctuary. Susannah then assumes the position of narrator, concentrating on her curiosity about Irene, the dwarf. Irene becomes the next narrator, revealing her worldview and extensive knowledge. Manuelito follows Irene as narrator, providing the Mundo interpretation of "Mad Dog," the name given to Magdalena. Another narrator is Lily Paul, who struggles against family tradition and poverty to discover her own voice. The voice of the physician appears briefly as he consults with Magdalena regarding obesity issues, but his voice is with hers; he is not a sole narrator. The next voice is Pauline's, who explains how she overcomes great odds to find the door to opportunity. Then there is an omniscient voice that comments mainly about Susannah and Lily Paul. Ironically, the voice of Langley, the wife and mother, never narrates in this novel. Could it be that she is a complete person without human issues to tackle? In the afterlife, however, she sits by the side of the river, indecisive whether to cross to the other side or remain where she is.

The narrative voice that dominates is that of Señor Robinson, followed by those of Magdalena and Susannah who narrate an equal number of times—seven. Therefore, the framework of this novel centers on a father and his daughters and the proper development of parent-child relationships, specifically father-daughter relationships. All of Señor Robinson's anthropological training and his feigned Christianity do not prepare him to demonstrate the love that his daughters need to witness in him. While he is attentive to his wife Langley, he is inattentive to the culture in which he finds himself immersed. After years of studying the Mundo people, he cannot recall the lyrics of a song that is instrumental in ritualistic Mundo male initiation. This same inattentiveness extends to his daughters; he is unable to identify their need to have a father demonstrate more love than dominance. He is so consumed with being the patriarch, the leader and the controller, that he forgets to embrace his girls in the full demonstration of his human emotion.

Nonetheless, Señor Robinson is not irredeemable. Walker provides the opportunity for him to correct past wrongs in the afterlife. It is as a soul, a spirit, that he has the willingness and the desire to learn how to be a father to his daughters. The afterlife makes the vision clear and the knowledge accessible. As a ghostly voyeur he is undisturbed by his daughters' love-making; however, in life he refuses to advise them in matters of sexuality. He reserves sexual privileges only for himself with his wife Langley. He ignores the fact that his daughters are maturing and need his mentorship. He approaches Magdalena's sexual curiosity as a taboo, setting her up for life to have dysfunctional relationships or no relationships. However, in the afterlife he embraces Mundo cosmology and accepts the guidance of Magdalena's banned lover to guide him to spiritual awareness. Through this novel Walker's commentary is on the universal issue of the potentiality of fathers in general and of African American fathers in particular as positive influences in the relationships with their daughters and in their relationships with others. Through reconciliation with their daughters they acquire an angelic state of grace.

Formalist critics also encourage readers to be alert to allusions (suggested or overt references) to mythology, history, or other words of literature. This novel is vivid in its portrayal of Susannah's intimacies with Petros and Pauline. Walker celebrates Eros (Cupid), the Greek god of erotic love, presenting the impulse for gratification as a basic need for the preservation of life. Pauline is the entity with the power to aspire to or bring about fulfillment of erotic gratification. Within the text, the pursuit of erotic pleasure then brings about harmonious feelings in mind, body, and spirit. This section of Walker's novel is an allusion to Audre Lorde's "Uses of the Erotic: The Erotic as Power," an essay that explores the political issues of work and power in women's lives. Lorde sees women as having an erotic resource that operates in the realm of female spirituality. She defines the erotic as potential creative energy that women use to enhance their lives spiritually and politically. Lorde sees a need for women to tap into the potentiality of the erotic. The energy of the erotic through sharing and feeling stirs itself internally within the female but manifests itself externally. Lorde offers three specific functions of the erotic: "providing the power which comes from sharing deeply any pursuit with another person ... the open and fearless underlining of [the] capacity for joy … [and] to share the power of each other's feeling." Only women who are woman-centered, according to Lorde, actually develop the courage and determination to tap into the power of the erotic and use it to effect change in themselves and the world (Lorde, 55–58).

The purpose of Walker's depictions of female erotic intensity is to redeem African American female sexuality. While the graphic nature of the erotic scenes might be one giant leap for womankind, Walker meets Lorde's requirements for the functions of the erotic. First, Pauline and Susannah not only share a long-term relationship but also share the pursuit of economic independence and financial success. Their unity as couple as aspiration and as reality is strong, each gleaning from it human emotional needs that are both foundations and systems of support. Gratified in this sense, they then are liberated to pursue the power of the erotic without hindrance. Next, neither Pauline nor Susannah is timid in the area of the pursuit of joy, although Pauline has some insecurity issues. Both are gratified in their professional careers and, of course, gratified sexually. Pauline realizes her liberation through orgasm, knowing for sure that she is free in that area. Susannah takes steps toward her liberation as she sheds layer upon layer of stylish but dark attire. Once she completes the process, her liberation manifests itself in full color. Complete liberation, then, opens another door to experience the erotic. Last, Pauline and Susannah create the appropriate emotional state (the ability to respond emotionally) in which to share their feelings. Their consciousness, sensitivity, and awareness are intuitive reactions that permit them to make contact through feeling. Freedom at this level is yet another avenue that allows them to be open to the erotic. They attach importance to the shared elements of their relationship, which frees them to experience the depth of the erotic.

The erotic exposé in the novel is Walker's manifesto that women are naturally strong erotic beings. They need not hide behind a veil or cut themselves off from the outside world. Neither are they threats to male accomplishments, spirituality, or sexuality. Recognizing the potential for the erotic is a basic trait for the development of the whole self. Walker's novel indicates that women need to claim their freedom, and the experience of the erotic is the underlying principle of the road to freedom.

Another criterion of the formalist approach is to explore the movement of the literary work and its effect on the total shape of the work. In Alice Walker's text every section incorporates references to sorrow—whether it is the whipping that Magdalena receives at the hands of Señor Robinson, which has an effect on the totality of the Robinson household, Petro's guilt over falling in love with a white flight attendant, Irene's banishment from

Greek society, Manuelito's mistreatment by the military, or Lily Paul's disdain of family tradition. While sorrow is the common thread of the interdependent components, none of the characters is in a life-threatening situation or feels entrapped. Magdalena's death is a result of morbid obesity, not from negative influences. Moreover, none of the characters feel that they lack the power to amend their situations. Even Magdalena makes a mental note to confront her weight issue. All the characters have accessible means to life-altering alternatives if they choose to activate them. None of the characters experience a breakdown in communication, for they all have voice and articulate their intensions well. The operative force in this novel is that the characters are on quests toward resolutions of the causes of their sorrows. There is even another level to the communal thread that forms this novel. The characters' movements are in linear descending order. The common thread that forms the text again is sorrow, and the common theme that forms the text is sexuality. All the characters exhibit full sexual awareness. The text is also about crossing over, entrance into the afterlife. In order for death to take place the body must wind down, similar to the first law of thermodynamics, which hypothesizes that the earth is winding down, coming closer to death of the planet. If the characters' bodies are in constant decline or linear descending order, all the characters are then moving from life to afterlife. Their pleasure on the earth is the pursuit of eroticism through sexuality. Thus, when life ends so does sexuality. Therefore, the movement is from sexuality to spirituality—the subject of the text.

9

The Way Forward Is with a Broken Heart (2000)

The year 2000 marked the culmination of a 30-year writing cycle for Alice Walker as a novelist. She informed an assembly that gathered in Washington DC, for the book signing of her seventh work of fiction that she writes when she feels that something needs to be expressed. Walker expresses in this novel an exploration in human relationships involving all configurations of people—men and women, men and men, women and women. A banner on a church near where Walker spoke read "Love or Perish." Fittingly, the publication that Walker came to promote thematically alludes to love from beginning to end: the pursuit of it, the commitment to it, the dependence on it, the sacrifice of it, and the healing power of it.

This narrative is also a forthright memoir of her marriage to 1960s Jewish Civil Rights attorney Mel Leventhal. She shares with readers a fictionalized retrospective of events from her own life, using the craft of writing as bibliotherapy. Moreover, the women in the stories test and challenge the social order and imaginary boundaries. Walker forces readers to examine stereotypes, heterosexism, white privilege, and dysfunction in families—panoplies of issues related to life in the United States.

STRUCTURE

Alice Walker begins by dedicating *The Way Forward Is with a Broken Heart* to the American race, a borrowing from African American writer Jean Toomer (1894–1967), author of the 1923 classic *Cane,* who discussed the topic in the 1930s. A biracial American, he preferred to be identified as an American writer rather than a black one. He felt that race was of little significance and biracial offspring were the solution to pervasive racism in America. Walker helped to rescue him from literary obscurity and includes an essay on Toomer in *In Search of Our Mothers' Gardens.* She follows the dedication with a quote from American actress Mae West (1893–1980): "I wrote the story myself. It's all about a girl who lost her reputation but never missed it." In addressing the Washington DC, audience Walker made a similar comment regarding reputations and their purpose. She suggested that people lose them and be free. Some of the characters in Walker's stories are free spirits who exhibit no concern about reputations as they pursue love and work through love-related issues. The preface that follows gives a brief descriptive memoir of a love and marriage of 30 years prior that ended after 10 years. Walker discloses that the first story is her version of the love and marriage of her past, enhanced with autobiography and imagination. The remaining stories relate to the same time period and, though fictional, are wrapped in a life lived, presumably Walker's.

The fictionalized memoir includes 13 stories under seven captions: "To My Young Husband," "Orelia and John," "There Was a River," "Big Sister, Little Sister," "Growing Out," "This Is How It Happened," and "The Way Forward Is with a Broken Heart." Walker both uses the point of view of the omniscient narrator, where she articulates the story, and first-person narration in which the participating characters tell the story. As the omniscient narrator Walker imposes her will onto the story line, speaks her views, and assumes complete knowledge of all actions and thoughts. Through the stream-of-consciousness style (readers are in the minds of the characters experiencing their thoughts and world views), Walker offers an interspersion of the characters' conscious and involuntary thoughts.

SOCIOHISTORICAL CONTEXT

Coming of age in the revolutionary 1960s evoked strong emotions and vivid images of stoic protesters. The country seemed to be at war within its own borders. Not since the Civil War had the nation been so polarized. An undeclared war in Vietnam and the Civil Rights movement were the political issues that caused Americans to clash and nearly reach a point of impasse. The North and the South held fast to segregation policies; southerners, determined to maintain their influence, boasted that the North won the war but southern ideology won the nation; youth challenged age; and youth desired to overturn an old establishment stronghold for a new social order. African Americans began their challenge of the system in the heart of the South, from which emanated all the codes and laws that separated human beings and denied access to public accommodations according to skin color. Young people from the northern cities, both African American and white, joined forces with the southern protesters to crusade for equality. The movement brought together Americans who under other circumstances would never have shared each other's humanity.

Social and political revolutions were strategies enacted by antiestablishment youth to confront strict class structure and formalities. The United States had a rigid form, an apartheid system, of social stratification that imposed certain limitations on social relationships and public accommodations. The goal of protesters was to transform the reigning system, shaking to the core the foundation upon which the divisive order had been established. They wanted to dismantle the inconvenient interference and the abuse of power on local levels that prohibited civil and human decencies extended to free people. These changes interconnected with the civil rights of marginalized people and the Civil Rights movement leadership, as well as the protesters who looked more to the federal level to enforce changes because state levels were not trustworthy. Although the Civil Rights movement was primarily African American focused, citizens from various social and economic classes rallied behind the cause. Single-minded unification placed individuals together working side by side, some developing bonds that went beyond the parameters of merely movement work, but led to romantic involvement. The development of such relationships was the greatest fear of those behind the established order, who knew that group integration allowed some to see beyond color and into character.

Interracial relationships were the great taboo in the United States, but individuals involved in the movement challenged the restriction just as strongly as they challenged denial of civil rights. Many states had anti-interracial-marriage laws, applying especially to African American and white couples. When Alice Walker and Melvyn Leventhal resided in Mississippi and worked in the movement, their marriage there was illegal. Fortunately, the Supreme Court of the United States intervened in the actions of several states and struck down the laws forbidding interracial marriage. Young people coming of age during the movement found it easier to act on their attraction to members of another group. The preponderance of hatred and animosity toward this type of coupling did nothing to lessen it, although as a norm the numbers of interracial couples were small. Many of these relationships grew out of movement work where young professional college educated people found themselves attracted to others of similar interests but who happened to be of a skin color different from their own. As a result of the movement racially mixed coupling is more common and has undergone a growing acceptance, although even today some groups still want to ban it.

Gay and lesbian relationships began to emerge from a cloud of secrecy and appear openly during the period of civil rights struggle, affording more same-sex couples opportunities to take the risks of disclosing their sexual orientation. The heterosexual-homosexual rift prevented an open display of same-sex love, but the Civil Rights movement allowed other groups to challenge the system for their rights as well. Gays and lesbians in open couple relationships demonstrated similar commitment, responsibility, and sacrifice to these relationships as heterosexual couples. Young gays and lesbians coming of age at this time found the hostility toward them waning slowly over time, which made them more willing to be openly gay and lesbian rather than shroud their orientation in secrecy. They discovered that citizens in cities such as San Francisco, Los Angeles, and New York were more tolerant of their living arrangements than people in other U.S. cities. Moreover, the movement itself helped emboldened them to live life as they chose to live it.

Thus, protests, marches, freedom rides, sit-ins, and love-ins marked the turbulent movement period. The movement brought together individuals who had previously been separated from each other under societal structuring. Relationships of all kinds developed as a result of movement encounters, which also fueled women's rights and gay and lesbian rights. Walker writes about some of these relationship issues involving women in the aftermath of the movement, as well as across generations. In classic Walker fashion, the stories demonstrate how to triumph and survive whole over devastating obstacles.

GENRE AND NARRATIVE TECHNIQUE

Memoir is one genre incorporated into this collection centering on Walker's marriage to the Jewish civil rights attorney she met in

Mississippi in the heart of the civil right struggle. The genre of autobiographical fiction employed divulges Walker's deeply personal discovery of bisexuality. It also reveals her personal feelings about either the marriage that she yearns for or the friendship that she desires to maintain with her former husband, whose physical absence from her life she feels profoundly. She writes about bliss in their marriage in the middle of a racist climate, and an equally happy period in Brooklyn. However, the stress of living interracially took a toll on them. Bibliotherapy is apparent in this novel for two reasons. First, Walker believes in journal writing, and vignettes from reality are common in her journals and in this narrative. Second, Walker views writing as healing. The first story, "To My Young Husband," and the last story, "The Way Forward Is with a Broken Heart," appear to be part of a chain of events that she continues to work through therapeutically via the writing craft.

Walker develops the stories using narrative, monologues, and epistolary forms. For example, at times readers hear a single discourse, only Walker's voice or the voice of Dianne, when readers are made privy to her diary. Some of the stories contain a stream-of-consciousness technique in that Walker's characters go through phases of conscious thought, unconscious associations, sensory perceptions, repressed verbalizations, and memory. Walker uses this technique to provide character depth, but it is not used exclusively throughout the whole novel. The first and last stories are epistolary memoirs that evolve into monologues. Introspectively, she examines the positive outlook of the John F. Kennedy (1917–63) administration and the idealistic future Walker and her former husband believed it offered. Unable to change the world, she would rather view her and her former husband's attempt positively, as that of two young people on a destined course that needs its own recognition, acknowledgement, and affirmation. She proceeds forward, though brokenhearted, whether over a union with a man who is incommunicado or with a movement and a nation that failed to live up to its ideals, still anticipating change through love and art.

PLOT AND CHARACTER ANALYSES

The function of plot in these short stories is to explore the development of their meanings as they illustrate a basic idea. Walker's narratives emphasize the meanings of the stories more than the roles the characters play. The oral storytelling technique merges with the end message to produce art.

The obvious, although unnamed, characters in "To My Young Husband" are Alice Walker and Melvyn Leventhal. Walker, initially resentful of him for working in her movement, finds herself attracted to him in an environment of political and sexual rebellion. They endure the hostility of the period, sharing romance and love and reading the classics to each other. A deceased interracial couple to whom Walker alludes, Dianne and Harold, find ways to cope with the Mississippi system through their undying love for each other. Siblings Rosa and Barbara of "Kindred Spirits" face Aunt Lily, a woman of stubborn reserve, on a trip to Florida to bring closure to the issue of missing their grandfather's funeral.

Orelia and John of "Olive Oil," "Cuddling," and "Charms" develop a trusting relationship after she comes to grips with her past and the effects of her brother Raymond's betrayal on her adult life. Her infatuation with Everett Jordan, a local politician, and a woman she meets at a music festival force her into a reality check and an analysis of her relationship preferences. John also becomes involved with Belinda, a divorced mother of two and a colleague with whom he has an affair, but prefers Orelia's company and returns to her in the end.

Marcella, Angel (the lover), and Sally (the best friend) in "There Was a River" find themselves cast aside by Marcella, who realizes that she benefits from the relationship with the best friend more than she does with the lover.

Big Sister and Little Sister assess familial bonds with Uncle Loaf and Auntie Putt-Putt and indicators of affection or the lack of them displayed by the elderly couple in "Uncle Loaf and Auntie Putt-Putt" and "Blaze." The sad stories told by the elderly aunt hold Big Sister in an emotional prison from which she needs to liberate herself. Big Sister and Little Sister examine their commitment to each other as siblings, evincing their sisterhood when the two venture to locate Uncle Loaf's old house, encountering several obstacles along the way. Little Sister remains supportive of Big Sister, finding a way through the thicket that represents real life barriers. Little Sister is the "other woman" in a marriage and needs to determine her comfortableness with being scheduled in the relationship arrangement. Discussing the racial and sexual attitudes inherited from their ancestors, the sisters realize the disadvantage of holding onto them and the advantage of discarding such unwholesome attitudes and inheritances. In "Blaze" the narrator grapples with the humiliation felt after being told that she needs to refer to her white childhood friend as "Miss" Blaze, that a first-name address alone is unsuitable. This experience teaches her that white women are incapable of supporting real friendship or sisterhood.

In "Growing Out" and "Conscious Birth," Anne (an African American woman previously interracially married) and Jason are a couple, but she has had a previous lesbian relationship. The auto mechanic Jerri (a lesbian), is Anne's friend, and Suni (a white woman previously married to Jason, but who now dates women and has a biracial child) and Anne have a strong attraction that Anne finds disturbing. Anne replaces Jason in her life with the younger Adam, but she and Suni remain friends.

In "This Is How It Happened" Marissa introduces the narrator to the lifestyle of a gay bar that is the hang out for all manner of women. The short story "The Brotherhood of the Saved" introduces Hannah, a lesbian, who attempts to rescue her relationship with her mother, keeping it out of the clutches of fundamentalist religious bigots who urge her mother to ostracize her daughter. Hannah takes her mother, Miss Mary, and Auntie Fannie, of an older generation, to see the cinematic feature *Deep Throat*, arousing their curiosity about the forbidden topic of sex and even getting them to exchange commentary. She makes progress with Miss Mary and Auntie Fannie, but her mother remains evasive.

THEME

The major theme throughout these stories is love relationships. Walker writes about attachment issues and the meaning of being appended to other people, establishing bonds that are not easily broken. She focuses on matters of dependency involving building trust and reliance on partners. Also, caring for and helping one's partner are obligatory responsibilities to which the partners adhere. At the core of these relationships is the desire for intimacy between partners and long-term interactions. She analyzes the rightness and wrongness of relationships, that is, the coupling either is beneficial or causes misery or insane reactions. Walker also explores the varied emotional levels of relationships, ranging from anger or anxiety to euphoric bliss. She covers many of the minefields women navigate to have meaningful love relationships.

Walker's worldview or overall message throughout all the stories is that people enter into relationships to give love and receive love; she considers that all people love regardless of sexual orientation. She discloses the inner workings, complexities, and ramifications of love. The stories investigate the possible reasons people love. Walker explores the legitimacy of strong attraction at first sight, or the sense of being smitten. She also delves into the endurance of love, its length, growing together, and separation after growth ceases. The stories examine the need for personal space, body language, and verbal and nonverbal communication. The stories that focus on family relationships show the importance of stability in relationship patterns because they have an effect on future interactions. Families are often close companions who share mutual ancestral information that contributes to deep personal convictions that lead to healthy hearts and healthy minds. All the relationships ultimately show that commitment and sacrifice are formulas for cohesive, satisfying experiences.

In addition, she delves into familial love relationships and what the love of fathers, mothers, or sisters means in the lives of those who love them. She looks at the ways parental and sibling interaction influences adult relationships and expectations. She explores the trust factor and the "good daughter" and "good sister" factors, how these lend themselves to family loyalty or family disappointment. She looks at the need for consistent affectionate care, and also at what not having that might possibly mean. She tests the essential truth in these relationships, whether it pleases or displeases to be brutally honest. Walker also explores platonic love in relationships. She looks at the development of close relationships between individuals who are support systems for others and make themselves available to help to sort out distractions that hinder reconciliation toward the ideal.

Another theme in this volume is healing, that is, making the difficult choices required to bring balance to relationships. To achieve this balance Walker focuses on choice as an option—the choice to leave or remain, and choice as a major factor in the well-being of women. Relationship choices often challenge society's overriding opinions and exceed established boundaries. In these stories the women refeel, rethink, and restructure their lives to empower themselves to have control of their lives; they acquire the knowledge necessary to limit or eradicate the effects that damaging experiences have on them. They heal well because they love individuals and learn to work through love issues, and some of them love men and women in succession or simultaneously. Whatever undesirable conditions or contentious forces cloud their lives, they emerge of sound mind and with healthy attitudes, as whole human beings.

The South is a recurring theme in the works of Alice Walker. The first story reminds readers of the oppressive South and its inhumane treatment of people determined to overturn its debilitating hierarchal social structure. Melvyn Leventhal was not only a knight in shining armor for Walker, who felt protected by him as he faced and challenged devout racists in Mississippi, but also a rescuer from the deep recesses of hopelessness for the African American people of Mississippi.

A QUEER THEORY READING

Queer theory is an outgrowth of gay/lesbian studies, which itself evolved from feminist studies and feminist theory. The argument of feminist theory centers on gender, positing that biological factors have less to do with gender identity than socialization. Thus, feminist theory separates the social from the biological, indicating that the social has mutability but the biological is unchangeable. In view of this idea, feminists theorize that gender is not the all-important factor in a people's identities. They conclude that gender identity is a shifting self. As a result, other ideas about identity surface. Gay/lesbian studies examine social constructs that define sexuality as act and as identity, sexuality as normal and as abnormal, and sexuality as moral and as immoral. The theory then expands to challenge the idea of "normal" sexuality. The goal of feminist studies and gay/lesbian studies is to change or end the binary categories of normal and abnormal. Queer theory indicates that all categories of sexuality, normal and abnormal, linked to sexual identity are social constructs.

Judith Butler argues in her book *Gender Trouble* (1990, 1999) that fixed gender identities are fictitious, and gender is "fluid" and shifts and changes, depending on the context and depending on the time. She also posits the theory that through the destruction of the traditional binary constructions (male/female, masculine/feminine, normal/abnormal), all configurations of gender-related sexual identities are free to emerge. Heterosexual attraction is a causal relationship established on sex-gender-desire, pathologizing anything that falls outside of that realm. Butler believes that gender exists at the "level of discourse" and that celebration of radical diversity and pleasure is more appropriate.

Alice Walker's *The Way Forward Is with a Broken Heart* adheres to the concepts of queer theory, specifically Judith Butler's idea that identity-based politics is an escape route for female emancipation. Walker deconstructs the systems of social power that establish the norms, for example, the sex-gender-desire construct that is standard in the patriarchal system. The short story "This Is How It Happened" has a strong connection to *Gender Trouble.* The narrator states that she and her partner Tripper separated after a dozen years, and although her love for him remains, it is familial love. His lovemaking had become habitual and scheduled, no longer the gratification of spontaneity. Therefore, this separation is a turning away from the traditional binary relationship. Gone is the binary sex (male/female), gone is the binary gender (masculine/feminine), and gone is the desire. She no longer feels that they can achieve sufficient growth that would be satisfying to both of them. These thoughts belong to the narrator; therefore, she exercises empowerment.

Walker then introduces an identity that exceeds the traditional binary construction. She explains her infatuation for Marissa, a friend of some years. The narrator makes no clarification of the word *infatuation*, implying neither admiration nor love. However, the comment that follows is an implicit indicator of the narrator's proclivities at that time and her propensity for queer language. She informs readers that her friend is "a dyke, pure and strange," emphasizing Butler's idea of "variable construction of identity," that is, not the traditional male/masculine or female/feminine. Stressing Marissa's beauty, figure, and coloring, the narrator affirms that whenever she sees Marissa, she is filled with awe. This passage refers to the traditional male gaze or stare, the power men have over women's physicality, but now becomes womanpower, one woman subjecting another woman to the scrutiny of the stare. Later the narrator divulges that the mutual image of infatuation is the required catalyst they both needed to separate from their partners, to explore other gender variations. In addition, the narrator offers descriptions of Marissa that traditionally fall into oppositional categories of the male/masculine as opposed to female/feminine; however, Marissa's identity according to tradition is now deconstructed, giving her the attributes of both traditional sexuality and identity. More specifically, the narrator clarifies that Marissa is attractive but also wires houses as an electrician and repairs automobiles; is financially self-sufficient; is strong, independent, and free; speaks in soft tones; and masks a wild side. In essence, the narrator makes Marissa complimentarily sexy without making her detrimentally victimizing.

Walker continues to appropriate masculine power in her character descriptions, placing women in both oppositional positions (heterosexually male/female and homosexually female/female). For instance, the narrator's marital partner is "a decent, honorable man" who does not dance, and she turns away from men who hinder women's development. Moreover, the narrator attaches to this explanation a clarification that she "never seriously considered women" as partners, and she does not know that she has an option. This passage supports Butler's view of "fluid" sexual identity, a nonconstant that allows flexibility in sexuality. However, readers learn that Marissa chooses a dictatorial partner, the opposite of the narrator's choice in a man. Marissa's partner Libby is identical to her father, "[d]omineering, bossy, a real pain in the neck" without a sex drive, but after drinking excessively will demand sex and take it forcefully if necessary. In addition, Libby's father sees his daughter's partner as an object of sexual attraction. Marissa and Libby negotiate gender identification in their relationship, in keeping with Butler's theory that gender exists at the level of discourse (negotiation of roles assumed), but something more happens on this level. The passage references oppression of one woman over another in this relationship. Walker the writer enhances gender blending in a situation that is less than optimistic.

The reader learns that the narrator moves on to another male-female relationship with Chung, compatible in height to the narrator but inept at toaster repair, acquiescing to Marissa, who declares the toaster unfixable. Once again, no traditional gender specifics exist; if anything, the roles are reversed. Chung is not proficient at appliance repair, but Marissa has a good eye for it. Both Chung and Marissa retrieve beers from the refrigerator but at different times, and are thus not drinking buddies. Marissa's friendship is with the narrator, who drives and accompanies her to a "dykey joint" that she finds intimidating. However, she recognizes within herself her attraction for "femme-looking" women in low-cut, colorful sexy attire, as well as "butches" in fitted jeans, leather jackets, and neck scarves. Marissa and the narrator share what Butler refers to as a "celebration of pleasure" that does not progress to a partnership or lovers' relationship. The narrator has issues with Butler's term "gender performance." Marissa is thoroughly at ease and free with her identity "self," asserting core naturalness. While the narrator loves and admires Marissa, she feels that Marissa's naturalness is something that she can only acquire through edification, and the possibility of a lover relationship with Marissa causes her discomfort. According to queer theory, identities are not the manifestations of a core self but are the result of performance. That is to say, identity is free energy, free floating as Marissa exhibits or performs, disconnected from anything that might be perceived as innate. Queer theory postulates that this idea is an essential truth, whether the identities are gendered or nongendered. Identity, at the whim of the individual, reinvents itself, as the narrator participates in male-female and female-female performance.

The narrator points out that women at the dance dress in diversified styles, but her curiosity stems from the presence of three or four males at a "dykey joint" (they are most likely biological females). She needs answers to the questions her mind asks about their identity, wondering whether they are perhaps bouncers, male siblings there to protect their sisters, lovers of the women, straights, bisexuals, or gays. Marissa's response is an emphatic "What men?" The narrator fails to recognize all the women in "celebration of radical diversity," the inclusion of all identities celebrating life.

The narrator refers to Marissa as a "queen" at the dance because of her dancing ability. Walker here uses queer language traditionally applied as a gay male descriptive. Nevertheless, its use also references Marissa's dominant performance, as well as her dancing strength. A fantastic dancer, Marissa is wild on the dance floor. Dancers who do not exhibit equal freedom on the dance floor bore her; she prefers those who rival her in her wildness. Dancing alone is also her forte, inviting in those who watch her exhibitionism. Marissa is the character encapsulation of identity as free, nonconfining, and not biologically fixed. Her character represents the key ideas of queer theory, "celebration of radical diversity," "celebration of difference," and "celebration of pleasure."

The story's conclusion is open ended. The narrator is mesmerized by a woman holding a baby and selling apparel. She offers the woman a seat at her table, but the woman declines it until she completes some sales. The narrator finds herself holding the baby until the woman joins them. She describes the woman's physical appearance and her attire, concluding with "[t]he woman a being I'd never seen before." The passage reflects queer theory in that the narrator is transitioning or reinventing her identity, releasing herself from traditional prescriptions of sexuality and gender.

10

Now Is the Time to Open Your Heart: A Novel
(2004)

In Alice Walker's first novel of the new millennium, her philosophy and spirituality coalesce into an organic whole. The probability is great that Alice Walker depicts her own worldview in the character of Kate, using the character to illuminate her philosophical and spiritual stances regarding the world's deficiencies and how to heal them. The novel, moreover, details events from Walker's life experiences and characterizes some of the associates who shared her personal journey in search of the meaning of life and existence. Therefore, she borrows from real life the references to ancestors, books, botany, deities, healers, icons, music, nature, relationships, and sex.

Anything that Walker pens is a must-read because of her literary stature. The distinguishing aspect of this novel is the vivid characterization of baby boomer Kate Nelson Talkingtree. This unforgettable woman of deep truth, honesty, and sensitivity chronicles from a woman's perspective the fears and weaknesses and even strengths involved in confronting advancing age and a midlife crisis. Walker's masterful depiction of the character is a realistic portrayal of a woman in search of the deepest truth of the self and the meaning of life. The character's trust and belief in the spiritual force is a testament to a woman's approach to resolving the personal issues that plague her.

STRUCTURE

The dedication is to Anunu and Enoba, a shaman and her assistant, two women characters in the novel who advise Kate on her journeys of discovery. True to her tradition of expounding thematically on powerful connections to the earth and the wisdom of the ancients, Walker continues the trend in this novel. On the Hawaiian Islands Anunu is the botanical identification of a medicinal plant, and in southeast Nigeria, West Africa, Enoba is the name of a local tribe. Hawaii is a key setting in the novel, and Walker's African references are to the African continent as the origin of life and to the need for restoration of its people to the circle of humanity. The novel begins with an acknowledgment of the immaterial essences that are constant companions to those with the questing spirit—the first indication of the path the novel takes. She follows with two interrelated quotes. The first, from Marlo Morgan, assigns purpose to every universe inhabitant, and the second, from Winnie Mandela, touts the freedom to dream. Next, Walker provides a prefatory genealogical background for the novel's fictional protagonist, who shares the name of Walker's murdered paternal grandmother (maiden name Nelson). As a tribute to her memory, the novel is an imaginary odyssey through the psychic sentiments this nineteenth-century foremother might have developed had she lived. Writing this novel made Walker realize how much she longed for the presence of the grandmother that she never knew.

Walker's creative impulses in this novel cause it to deviate from the broadest sense of the term to read more like autobiography and memoir in the guise of fiction. Written in the third person, the novel is an introspection into events that happened in the author's personal life, as well as the people and places associated with those occurrences. The first four chapters introduce the main character, Kate, engulfed in interpersonal conflict, disillusioned with her Buddhist practices and puzzled by a recurring dream. Subsequent chapters alternate between Kate and her love interest, Yolo, as they venture on parallel journeys of discovery, overcoming obstacles and peeling back layers of personality to uncover themselves truthfully. Walker titles the first four chapters according to the subject under development; however, the remaining chapters are titled similarly to an untitled poem, by the words that appear in the first line. Walker's explanatory paragraph in the afterword informs the reader about the South American hallucinogenic beverage that is the model for the magical drink Kate consumes in the novel to make contact with the spiritual grandmother. She ends the novel by thanking those in her life who were instrumental in guiding her in the knowledge and understanding of the supreme secret.

SOCIOHISTORICAL CONTEXT

A postmodern (the era after World War II) social, cultural, and spiritual movement commonly referred to as New Age undergirds Alice Walker's first novel of the twenty-first century. This movement has its genesis in the freethinkers of the intellectual and cultural movement identified as the Enlightenment that developed in the seventeenth century, reached its apex in the eighteenth century, and continued its influence into the nineteenth and twentieth centuries. Participants in the Enlightenment movement celebrated rationalism, the scientific method, perfection of self and society, and deism.

In addition to a confidence in human reasoning, Enlightenment thought included a rational religious thought known as deism. Followers of Enlightenment thought accepted God as the ruler of the world through established universal laws that were perfected upon creation but rejected the interference of God in an already perfected universe. They accepted natural religion as an outgrowth of reason and the study of nature, but rejected revealed religion emanating from a particular person, group of people, or mere faith alone. Moreover, they accepted the common principles that were indicative of all religions throughout eternity but rejected any revelations deemed for a particular individual or group. They sanctioned morality as practiced universally but rejected moral principles that were not innate or appeared unsound through reasoning. They also believed the Bible to be an instructional guide through life; however, they discounted it as historically accurate or divinely inspired. They deemed superstitious the divinity of Jesus Christ, as well as the Trinity, miracles, and reconciliation of sin. Ultimately, people progress toward perfection, they believed, through natural observation and human rationality. Many deists were agnostics, atheists, Freemasons, and similarly categorized. Some deists, however, professed Christianity and assimilated deism and Enlightenment thought into their everyday Christian practices and beliefs.

Similar to the Enlightenment movement, the New Age movement is both philosophical and spiritual in its approaches and practices. Unlike the practitioners of the Enlightenment movement, followers of New Age thought do not subscribe to any established creed, doctrine, dogma, or principles outlined in any authoritative text representative of the compilation of sacred writings. They have no centralized location or headquarters and no individual clergy, intercessor, or spiritual authority at the helm. Instead, New Age thought embodies the primitive, Christian, Eastern, and esoteric fundamentals adhered to by a network of practitioners. Conservatives, liberals, progressives, humanists, and secularists incorporate New Age fundamentals into their daily lives. For some it is their only spiritual outreach; for others it is New Age thought combined with the organized or institutionalized religion that they practice. Followers receive instruction through classes, conferences, lectures, publications, seminars, technological sources, workshops, experienced converts, and indigenous practitioners.

New Age thought emerged as a popular movement in England in the 1960s, stemming from public interest in astrology, Buddhism, channeling, Gnosticism, Hinduism, neopaganism, Taoism, and Theosophy. During the 1970s and 1980s the movement surged internationally, partly because of continued interest in ancient spiritual principles and partly because of dissatisfaction with the strictness of rationality and science and the inability of organized Christianity's clergy to meet the complete spiritual needs of some of its followers. From the 1990s and into the new millennium the movement continued to grow, its followers choosing what to practice from an eclectic menu of spiritual systems. Celebrities, moreover, helped to garner public interest in New Age thought. For example, Hollywood actress Shirley MacLaine publicly acknowledged her interest in channeling and published several books about her experiences and past existences. Comedienne Rosanne Barr and popular music icon Madonna professed their practice of Kabbalah, placing Kabbalistic mysticism in the public domain and stimulating curiosity about this ancient spiritual wisdom not only among other entertainers but also among average citizens. Alice Walker, too, articulated her interest in primitivism and feminine divinity, charting the way for an inquisitive public to make similar explorations. The movement's popularity continues to swell with new practitioners seeking instruction in New Age philosophy.

The Enlightenment movement of the seventeenth and eighteenth centuries and the contemporary New Age movement share some similar spiritual aspects. Monotheism is central in both schools of thought, with those Enlightenment followers who were not atheists subscribing to one God of the universe and New Age practitioners believing in a God source, a universal oneness, a divine energy source that for some is feminine. Female divinity, called Gaia or Mother Earth, often manifests in the earth in the form of natural surroundings or trees. Like Enlightenment advocates of the past, New Age followers are freethinkers in search of new interpretations of the self, and they strive toward perfection of the self. Primarily through meditation and, in the case of some, indigenous hallucinogens they retreat within themselves to connect with divine energy and to search for divine truth and higher consciousness. Through this mechanism followers seek internal peace and balance and undergo healing of the self. This personal transformation results in elevation of the body, mind, and spirit, an instrumental state of consciousness that helps to achieve healing of the planet. They believe that in heightened transformation they also impact society positively, taking art, politics, science, and spirituality to higher and improved dimensions. Nature is central in their quest for knowledge, wisdom, and understanding, for in it is found the natural law of the divine.

They also believe that the world is a segment of a universal whole that operates in perfect harmony. The harmony of the universe is indestructible and infinite. Love, too, is essential in New Age thought. The participant purges the self of anger, fear, hatred, and prejudice only through love. When the individual learns to love self, then love of others is easily attainable; one of Alice Walker's favorite expressions is "It's all about love." Human life recycles itself in New Age philosophy, that is, life reincarnates in a series of repeated existences to learn from new experiences. For some, numerous reincarnations are vicious cycles that are to be avoided because of the pain and suffering involved in the life cycle. When practitioners of New Age thought rely on and develop through empiricism and rationalism (the internal intelligence that is a gift from the divine source) and achieve a blessed state of full comprehension and heightened spiritual consciousness, awareness, and clarity, individuals are then enlightened.

According to practitioners of New Age philosophy, the world recently (in the nineteenth century for some, twentieth century for others) entered a new age, the Age of Aquarius, symbolized by the water bearer, indicating cleansing of the earth and a coming together in oneness. The previous age was the Piscean Age, symbolized by the fish. During this age significant numbers of earth's people turned from animal sacrifice and accepted Christian principles. The energy cycle of this age was agape, a love feast for humankind. A recurring controlling pattern of Walker's _Now Is the Time to Open Your Heart_ is the emphasis on cleansing and love.

The heroine of the novel seeks New Age enlightenment through several avenues. One path is Buddha, known as Siddhartha Gautama before his transformation. Born into wealth and opulence, he was captive to luxury and plenty. Stolen ventures beyond his pleasure palaces exposed him to the pain and suffering outside his comfortable edifices. Ultimately leaving his wife and young son, he went in search of the wisdom that would help him teach humankind how to alleviate the ill of suffering. The solution to life's conundrum came to him as he sat meditating under a fig tree. Upon rising he became the Buddha (Enlightened One) and provided instruction in the Four Noble Truths of Buddhism: life is full of suffering; suffering is craving, leading to a cycle of rebirth (samsara); craving/suffering can be annihilated; and the Noble Eightfold Path is the way to escape craving/suffering. The Noble Eightfold Path includes right views, intentions, speech, conduct, livelihood, effort, mindfulness, and concentration. Adherence to the Noble Eightfold Path brings about nirvana (bliss). The Buddha's 45 years of dedication to teaching others and practicing the Noble Eightfold Path earned him *maha-parinirvana* (great total extinction). Buddhism is an Eastern spiritual system that some followers incorporate into New Age thought.

On the main character's home altar in the novel are several deities, one of whom is the Virgen de Guadalupe. An interesting supernatural occurrence surrounds the emergence of this deity. Juan Diego, an indigenous Mexican Aztec, experienced apparitions, the appearances taking place over four days, from December 9 to December 12, 1531. Diego believed the visions to be the mother of Jesus who instructed him to inform Friar Juan de Zumárraga, Spanish bishop assigned to the region, to construct a temple. Having no faith in Diego's words, the bishop dismissed Diego's account and sent him away. Diego witnessed a second appearance and heard the lady repeat the original instruction. He hastened to the bishop and again issued the request quite demonstrably. This time the bishop told Diego to request proof from the lady of her existence. He also had Diego followed, for the bishop was suspicious of Diego's intent. Upon his presence in the sight of the lady a third time he appeared to vanish, so that the bishop's spies lost view of him. The lady promised Diego that she would provide proof the following day.

The next day Diego went in search of a priest to console his ailing uncle, Juan Bernardino, only to encounter the lady a fourth time. She sent him to the top of a hill, where he discovered fragrant roses blooming during the frosty winter month. Instructing him to pick the flowers and put them inside his cape, she touched them, informing Diego that the flowers were the proof that the bishop required. Straightaway Diego rushed to see the bishop, opening his covering, which had the image of the lady impressed on it. While Diego was with the bishop, the lady was with his uncle, whom she healed of his infirmity. The lady's image on the cape is intact and on display in a shrine in Mexico City where tourists and locals come to view it daily. The Virgen de Guadalupe is a feminine deity that Latin Catholics, as well as some practitioners of New Age philosophy, consult for intervention in their daily lives.

Also on Kate's home altar is the Buddhist bodhisattva goddess of compassion and mercy Quan Yin, a true enlightened deity. With the ability to manifest in the earthly realm in numerous forms, Quan Yin primarily appears in feminine essence, possessing unwavering commitment to bring the living to enlightenment. Foregoing her own nirvana, she hears the petitions of those struggling with life issues, particularly assisting women who desire to have children or offering alternative spiritual outlets for women who do not desire to become wives. Alice Walker treats both of these subjects in the novel. Often carrying pearls of illumination and pouring healing water, Quan Yin embodies the divine mother potential of Buddha as healer, educating earth dwellers in indigenous medicinal herbs and holistic health. Her skills also include dream interpretation, a technique that Kate masters in the novel. Using her ingenuity and competence, Quan Yin's overall objective is to bring into fruition universal consciousness.

PLOT AND CHARACTER ANALYSES

Now Is the Time to Open Your Heart has more narrative detail than complicated plot. Walker does not burden the reader with heavy external conflict between a protagonist and antagonist. Nevertheless, Walker structures this narrative of subtle tension with such clarity that its meaning surfaces with ease. Two complex characters in the novel are at crisis points, which effect change in their attitudes. The story is one of interpersonal conflict centered on Kate Nelson Talkingtree and Yolo Day, who interact with characters who have their own interpersonal disharmony. The two major characters resolve their issues by taking parallel quests, traveling parallel waterways, and receiving instruction in parallel circles. The first four chapters center on Kate; the remaining chapters form parallel structure, swinging like a pendulum from Yolo to Kate and back again.

The protagonist in the novel is Kate, a 57-year-old successful writer and affluent suburbanite on a collision course with life and love. As if these agitations were not enough, her mind is also tormented by dreams of empty freezers and snake images and a recurrent dream of dry rivers. Encouraged by her friends to find a real river to explore, she bids her lover and her home goodbye and begins her quest with a group of other women seekers white-water rafting on the turbulent Colorado River. In the first section, Kate has taken a new name, ceases her fascination with Buddhism, has disquieting dreams, reminisces about the Black Freedom movement, dismantles her home altar, and vows to change her restless spirit.

The twists and turns of the Colorado River and its elevated rapids make Kate ill, but the challenge of the river represents the uneasiness of her life, and she must become ill in order to become better. This experience on the river is the beginning of Kate's understanding of internal and external life. Through consistent regurgitation Kate's body begins to cleanse itself, each emptying of her innards representing the casting off of past burdens, such as domestic abuse in her first marriage and the accidental death of her mother. Her resolution to return home and live as a virgin proves fruitless, thereby creating the need for a second quest.

Kate's retreat to the rainforest unites her with a heterogeneous group of medicine seekers and with Armando, the Yoda of the Amazon, knowledgeable in the transcendental spirituality of the Amerindians from time immemorial. The Amazon rain forest is a greater challenge, requiring the need for even more regurgitation, and it is also the place where Kate comes into complete understanding of internal and external life. Through his requirements of silence, meditation, and inner-world contact the shaman Armando guides Kate to in-depth objectivity and enlightenment through the careful dispensing of Grandmother *yagé*, a frothy medicinal herb beverage that the ancient indigenous South American people used to cleanse the physical body so that contact with the spirit of origins and endings could not be impeded. The beverage also creates hallucinogenic dreams and helps Kate along her inward journey of self-discovery, and Bobinsana, another medicinal beverage, helps her have lucid dreams.

With other seekers of enlightenment Kate develops deeper compassion for humankind by listening to her peer travelers and their heartrending tales of life conflicts. Her greatest needs are to regenerate her spirit, explore other avenues to greater enlightenment, find renewed inspiration in the rescue of the globe from indifferent human behavior, and come to terms with her true life's purpose. Concluding that she no longer requires the Grandmother medicine, she advances to a higher lever of sensitivity, helping others to make the necessary transitions and becoming a healer in her own right.

Kate's live-in younger lover, Yolo, is a complex character but not the antagonist; he is more like a parallel protagonist. Changing his name from Henry to Yolo, a Poewin Indian name symbolizing "a place in the river where wild rushes grow," he feels his name is more suitable to his personality; he thus has in common with Kate the changing of names. Kate had been the aggressor in their romantic encounter, pursuing him until he conformed to her desires. A charismatic, handsome, monogamous, sincere individual who embraces feminism, Yolo is an independent, self-sufficient successful artist. He enjoys the middle-class lifestyle of freedom, mobility, options, and choice. His flaws are unworthy of serious attention, but Walker's creative impulse makes him a little less than perfect. He, too, has physical and spiritual life issues that require resolution, such as his addiction to tobacco and his disintegrating relationship with Kate.

In Kate's empty house Yolo finds himself wandering about like a winding, twisting river. Kate's house is clean, clear, and open; his house not far from hers is a repository for every collectible knickknack he manages to take home. She has given him hints that decluttering his life is appropriate, each year giving him a copy of _Clear Your Clutter with Feng Shui_ for Kwanza. Each year he has ignored the suggestion. However, now Kate's absence distracts his inner peace, causing him to contemplate change.

Yolo's quest begins here too, for in Kate's absence he realizes the importance of her presence in his life. He dreams as she had dreamed, and upon waking he has a spiritual awakening, realizing that he is now part of her journey and will be forever. Also in her absence Yolo intuitively empathizes with Kate's compassionate yearnings and adopts a tone of self-analysis to preserve their relationship. His quest is a vacation in Hawaii, one in which he hopes to do the beach routine and read voraciously. A dead man interrupts Yolo's peace, connecting him to mesmerizing living men who alter the course of his life's path. He comes to a full understanding of universal truths in a place distant from his home with Kate, where the indigenous people instruct him at the Sangha (gathering of men in a circle) to respect the ancestral mores and guide him into a deeper understanding of life. His charge is to resist smoking and eating toxic foods.

GENRE AND NARRATIVE TECHNIQUE

As storyteller Alice Walker experiments with the novel tradition to produce a new effect, contriving a narrative that involves experimentation in forms and reflects more her life's roots and personal experiences than complex inventive prose. The interesting story line, though, is a revelation about Walker's character, especially her philosophical and spiritual concerns. Walker's devotion to ancient theology and goddess worship entraps readers in the events and relationships that are the foundation of the narrative. Even without knowledge of Walker's background, the story in and of itself is realistic, vivid, imaginative, energetic, and moving, though not too eventful, in its characterization, dialogue, and description. *Now Is the Time to Open Your* Heart, a third-person account of the disillusionment of a middle-aged woman, a devout Buddhist, with her life's purpose and most recent love interest, concentrates the action on the search for the meaning and significance of life. Overcoming her despair, fluctuating feelings over her younger lover, and searching for inner peace are the incidents that move the novel along.

Walker creates a loosely episodic story that centers on the adventures of Kate as she faces the challenges of the rough Colorado River and the expansive Brazilian Amazon. However, it is also somewhat a novel of character in that the revealed knowledge of the protagonist's introspection provides glimpses into the positive traits attributed to her. The adventures are interconnected through the heightened development of the protagonist's character as the details of her life unfold. The reader learns of Kate's marriages, children, lovers, friends, and associates and their connection to the crisis point at which she finds herself. White-water rafting down the Colorado River helps her to iron out some of the disquieting issues plaguing her but does not give her total resolution. Not until she delves into indigenous spiritual soul-searching practices in the forests bordering the Amazon River does the experience prove therapeutic and beneficial. She emerges from the experience sound of mind, body, and spirit, ready to face the rest of her life and exchange expressions of commitment—not legal marriage—with her lover. Thus, the cohesiveness of the narrative is more dependent on the circumstances surrounding Kate as the primary character and less dependent on action.

The narrative as a novel of sensibility also represents the characters' great concerns with and emotive reactions to the world's ills and distresses. A group of women gathers on the banks of the Colorado and a heterogeneous group gathers at the side of the Amazon to purge themselves of personal assaults they have done to others or others have done to them. They need an outlet for their pent-up emotions, an explanation for their reduction in coping skills in an ordinary but troubled world, and a new path for them to take that offers serenity and long-lasting peace. As an instructional manual, the narrative includes subtle references for greater understanding of the ancient Hawaiian people, such as *Shark Dialogues,* or the New Age lifestyle, such as *Way of the Shaman* (Davenport; Harner). To highlight the art of imparting knowledge and skill, Kate becomes a protégée of experienced shamans Anunu and Armando. Under their wise protection and didactic guidance Kate advances in theory and practice in the spiritual and medicinal methodologies of the ancients. The result is acuity in observation, listening, and interpretation; oneness with Mother Nature in her earthy, vegetative, and animalistic variants; and a sensitized consciousness in communion with the Grandmother spirit, so that the student Kate ascends to the level of becoming shamanlike, a *curandera* capable of intermediary action on behalf of others in search of enlightenment.

The novel is also a quest narrative, in the sense that the protagonist searches for something valuable that is mandatory, in this case Kate's sense of well-being and relevance in the world. The Colorado trip's purpose is to provide a contemplative space where she can become one with nature, clear her mind, sort through her demons, and rationalize the direction and structure of her life. This quest proves effective, though not completely, leading to the need for more notable adventure. Finding her identity, seeking her fortune, the wealth of her soul, and facing her fate require Kate to leave home once again. The South American tropical rain forest bordering the Amazon River is the locale for Kate's second quest. She discovers the tranquility of a tree-laden environment, the metaphysical world of the Grandmother spirit, the ability to counsel in the matter of human psychosis, and the nature of her own relationship to humankind. Kate ends her quest having acquired enlightenment, resolved the perplexities of her life, and accepted the fact that the aging process is an inherent part of the living process, a fundamental fact of life.

Finally, Walker's storyline has elements of the novel of the soil, illustrating the character and temperament of indigenous Hawaiians. Kate's lover Yolo travels to the island of paradise only to find himself entwined in a local tragedy; his vacation is transformed into cultural enlightenment. Solicited by native Hawaiian Jerry to watch over the body that washes up on the beach, Yolo learns that the deceased young man is the son of his ex-lover Alma, also known as Leilani, a native Hawaiian of mixed ancestry. This event becomes the catalyst for Yolo's involvement with the Mahus, as he accepts their invitation to sit with the men in the circle to receive instruction in the history, culture, and charge of the Hawaiians. Mesmerized by the Hawaiian revelations taught to him by Jerry and the Mahus, Yolo becomes sensitized to the motherland—to the land and sea, to the extraordinary healing qualities of the variety of flora, to the rule of women, for example, Queen Lili'uokalani, the last reigning Hawaiian queen, and to Hawaiian nationality and spirituality. The Hawaiians instill into Yolo their basic principles; their geography is significant to their history and presence.

THEMES

Critical scholars always concern themselves with themes of literary works, the primary step in the full appreciation of literary productions. Themes are the controlling topics of discourse of artistic representations. *Now Is the Time to Open Your Heart* is thematically complex, but there are specific generalizations about life that dominate this novel. These are themes with which Walker is most identified and which permeate all of her creative and nonfiction works. This literary work focuses on the major themes of ancestor reverence, cleansing, and meditation, and the minor themes of environmentalism, dreams, spirituality, and instruction.

Ancestor reverence is prevalent in the novel. Photographic images of Kate's parents, friend Sarah Jane, and freedom fighter Ernesto "Che" Guevara have a place on Kate's home altar. Hawaiian Queen Lili'uokalani and South African Saartjie Bartmann (spellings vary), labeled the Hottentot Venus, are women honored with mention in the novel. Walker admires the revolutionary questing spirit and gives those who possess it a place in her writings.

Argentina-born Guevara was the partner of Fidel Castro in the Cuban revolution. Using the military tactics of guerrilla warfare he struggled against imperialism in Cuba, but his failed attempt in Bolivia brought about his demise at the hands of Bolivian soldiers under the auspices of United States CIA operatives. Many consider Guevara the ideal revolutionary martyr.

Upon King Kal kaua's death in 1891, Queen Lili'uokalani succeeded her brother to the throne of Hawaii until the overthrow of the Hawaiian monarchy in 1893. A republic government accused the queen first of treason and then misprision of treason (failing to disclose an act of treason), forcing her to renounce any claim to the throne and placing her under permanent house arrest. Confined to her quarters she stitched a quilt, a living history of her ordeal, evidence that she left to progeny to pursue her quest for justice.

Baptized and given a Christian name, Saartjie Bartmann, born around 1789, was a member of the Khoi Khoi tribe of Cape Town, South Africa, often referred to by the derogatory term *Hottentot*. Sensing a profit motive in her developed derrière and genitalia, natural among Khoisan women, William Dunlop kidnapped her in 1810, took her to London, and put her on exhibition in Piccadilly as a scientific curiosity and freak of nature. Later sold to a French businessman, she became a victim of alcoholism and prostitution. Upon her death in 1816 she was dissected in the name of science, her preserved body parts and genitalia put in jars and placed on public display along with her skeleton in the Musée de l'Homme in Paris. With the dissolution of apartheid in South Africa, Nelson Mandela in 1994 petitioned French President François Mitterrand to return her body parts to Cape Town. In February 2002 the French government in special parliamentary action paved the way for her return as a goodwill gesture, and she was received by South African Ambassador Dr. Zola Skweyiya amid the background singing of a children's choir in May 2002, finally home again (Associated Press). Walker in remembrance acknowledges the endurance of Saartjie Bartmann under colonial exploitation.

Cleansing also is a central theme in the novel. By means of nausea, regurgitation, and diarrhea Kate alters her state of consciousness to understand past lives and past existences, ridding her mind of the burdensome memory of her first marriage and accepting the loss of her mother. The water motif, an effective conduit for bringing about cleansing on several levels, is emphasized from the novel's beginning to its end. Water imagery ebbs through the novel in the same way that the rivers snake through the canyon and the rain forest. The protagonist needs a life cleansing, given her midlife crisis. Her entrance into the Colorado River and Amazon River by either boat or immersion is an act of cleansing, bringing about change in her inner self. Water flushes toxins from the land, the body, and even from itself in the form of deposits. By the novel's end Kate is completely cleansed and becomes more intuitive and transcendental. Cleansing, like water, becomes a life essential, purifying her soul, leaving her refreshed, and becoming the gateway to her spiritual enlightenment.

Meditation, too, as a major theme dominates the narrative. Encouraged by Armando, the characters quiet their minds, shedding of worldly considerations, and put their bodies at rest so that they are in states of extreme concentration and relaxation. This heightened consciousness allows them to visualize that which is unseen in the physical world, invoke the divine, and converse with immaterial essence or perceived beings. The meditative character also aids the seekers in developing calmer dispositions, a sense of equanimity, and becoming ambassadors of compassion and goodwill toward humankind. Through meditation their mental faculties improve, their health improves, and their insight into the nature of reality improves. They go on the retreat to be healed, but through meditation they emerge as healers.

Other themes include environmentalism, dreams, spirituality, and instruction. Walker focuses on nature and the preservation of it, especially trees, earth, and water. There is also emphasis on the tiniest creatures of nature, whose role in the life chain cannot be ignored. The interpretation of dreams is significant. In Walker's novel dreams always have meaning; there is no recreational dreaming. The characters' dreams must be justified and the relevance to their lives examined and explicated. References to the Lord Buddha relate to the theme of spirituality, as well as contact with the Grandmother spirit's energy through inner exploration. Instruction as a theme comes through in the many examples of Anunu and Enoba and Armando and Cosmi imparting knowledge and demonstrating their skills in the ancient medicinal practices. They pass on the known facts, illuminating the secrets of the spiritual world.

The novel's remaining characters are true-to-life foils (minor characters). Their representative life stresses and struggles are believable contrasts to the chaos of Kate and Yolo. The middle-aged southern European professor is the dharma who lectures on the "cool" revolution of the Lord Buddha. It is his lecture that precipitates Kate's wandering mind and lack of concentration. A local shaman, an African-Amerindian woman named Anunu, and a white woman named Enoba, her assistant, work together to nurture Kate into a state of progressive healing. Another character that gets casual mention is Lolly, who resembles Kate's cousin. With her Kate enters into a ceremonial marriage but later comes to terms with the fact that Lolly is a gold digger who sees Kate as a cash cow.

The three-week Colorado retreat, marking the beginning step in Kate's transformation, includes nine women who channel their energies into solid womanpower. With oarswomen navigating the rushing waters of the Grand Canyon, the women master together the sport of white-water rafting. Avoa, Kate's African-Eurasian confidante, Cheryl, Lauren, Margery, Sally, and Sue (who knows botanical identification of plants and their medicinal purposes) converse about topics that only women find interesting—to fear or not to fear old age, to dye or not to dye hair, to straighten or not to straighten hair, plastic surgery, liposuction, bisexuality, and men's anatomy.

Two men and five women comprise the seven medicine seekers in the Amazon rain forest, the final stage of Kate's new attitude. Like Geoffrey Chaucer's pilgrims, they have personal stories to tell. Armando Juarez is spirit leader, a 40-something grandfather who, as shaman, sings healing songs called *icaros* to each individual seeker. His apprentice shaman

Cosmi prepares and serves the herbal beverages that help to usher in the Grandmother spirit. The older man, Hugh Brentforth V, is from Utah and needs to learn the kind of devotion that he witnesses in the annual pilgrimage of the indigenous American who trespasses on his land to pay respect to the deceased at an Indian burial ground on his property. Brentforth's ancestors homesteaded the massive acreage and took it from its inhabitants when the government wanted to settle that corner of the country with different people. Rick Richards, the younger man with dyed reddish hair, a slender Italian from New York whose father anglicized their name, has guilt feelings about the family business. His family's wealth stems from their attachment to a crime syndicate that sold illegal drugs to African Americans in impoverished communities. The women vary in ages; Lalika, a 30-something African American from Mississippi, murdered her rapist, who also attempted to rape her friend Gloria. The two women escaped the crime scene, only to be caught and imprisoned where they were raped repeatedly by the jailers. Lalika sheds layers of pain, hoping to learn forgiveness. Missy is an incest victim from birth, the perpetrator her mother's father, Timmy Wimmins, who played the role of father and husband to Missy. After struggling to cope through pharmaceuticals and illegal drugs, she comes on the retreat to learn to achieve peace.

In Hawaii Yolo meets Jerry Izkamakawiwo'ole, whose chance introduction pulls him into a local family tragedy. Because Yolo appears to be a "bradda," Jerry asks him to sit with the body while he goes to get family members. Yolo later finds himself coincidentally at the church where the funeral is being held for the deceased Marshall. Jerry draws him into the circle of friends and relatives, which becomes Yolo's initiation into ancient Hawaiian practices. The brother of the deceased, Poi, is part of the circle. Leilani/Alma, named for Aunty Alma, a well-known Hawaiian kahuna (healer), is mother of the deceased and Yolo's former girlfriend from the days when he lived in New England. He met her when Saul, her boyfriend at the time, insisted that she demonstrate her natural hula abilities to guests at a party. Yolo later meets her in a chance encounter and reintroduces himself. Aunty Pearlua, a cross-dressing Mahu, is the keeper of the knowledge of the old ways. Having overwhelming respect for women, chosen Mahus live as women to honor women's place in the home and community. Like an African griot, Aunty Pearlua articulates the knowledge of old to the younger generations. Two young Australian aborigines are also among the members of the circle to reaffirm their dwindling sense of identity.

A NEW AGE READING

A controversial cinematic production, *What the #$*! Do We Know!?*, starring actress Marlee Matlin, has generated debate in academia and among nonacademic moviegoers alike. The movie presents a hypothesis that reality is formed through consciousness and quantum mechanics/physics. In New Age theory everything old is new again. The philosophers of the Enlightenment debated the relevance of science, mathematics, and spirituality in an ever changing universe. Cartesian philosophy is resurrected for twenty-first century examination. Those in search of the link between the conscious and unconscious world are in no short supply. The probe continues into the probability of existence at the subatomic level.

New Age spirituality encompasses the universality of nature and the human spirit. Those who practice New Age philosophy interest themselves in consciousness raising in order to comprehend their unconscious perceptions. They select their vehicle of understanding from a plethora of fundamental beliefs held by New Age followers. The dictates of organized and institutionalized religion and political authority hold no dominance over their pursuit of otherworld knowledge. While followers of New Age philosophy embrace rationalism and empiricism, they determine the boundaries in which these belief systems will advance them to the next level. The advancement is individualistic, practitioners entering higher realms of consciousness at singular paces in their own time, place, and space. Experiences also vary individually based on practitioners' willingness to embrace and accept certain phenomena. Since practitioners envision the wholeness of the universe and earth as an entity of the wholeness, the divine energy is patient in the instruction of New Age followers, waiting for them to take the next step in the development of their consciousness. There is no schedule and no rush, but rather freedom to determine when, where, and how they want to transcend their present reality and evolve into new awareness.

New Age spirituality may be referred to as mind-body-spirit phenomenon, self-spirituality, or new spirituality. To understand New Age philosophy, knowledge of ancient world traditions is mandatory. New Age followers revisit the spiritual belief systems of ancient Africa and Asia and pre-Socratic and pre-Columbian times, when comprehension of the natural world emerged through rationalism, not through fallacious appeals to authority, religion, or tradition. People of these eras used their minds to envision the nature of the world and divinity within nature and within themselves. They understood that air, earth, and water were with them always and through investigation conceived various ways that they connected to these elements. Their ability to think freely about nature and their surroundings profoundly affected the attitudes and beliefs of individuals centuries into the future, who would return to early spiritual systems for comprehension of the world in which they find themselves. Alice Walker's protagonist Kate practices old world traditions and New Age philosophy using meditation, ancestor worship, reincarnation, medicinal and hallucinogenic plants, and ecological responsibility to transform her psychically and to acquire a greater understanding of her role in the universe.

Meditation, a key initiative in New Age principles, requires complete absence from distraction as a prerequisite to soliciting the presence of divine energy. Practitioners use their minds to put themselves into heightened states of relaxation in order to achieve inner peace. To elicit divine presence followers (preferably but not necessarily) rely on quiet, natural surroundings, relaxed positions, images or words of concentration, and receptive attitudes. Retreating within to unite with divine energy results in explicit self-knowledge and communion with the God source. The practitioner emerges from the state of contemplative meditation with full knowledge of the experiences encountered and remembrance of all instruction received.

Kate embraces meditation as a vehicle to understanding her inner world, talking with the female deity, and comprehending the physical world around her. Along with other practitioners, she meditates in a spacious hall in a natural setting of redwood trees. The Buddhist teachers encourage the meditators to do slow walking meditations, the kind of meditative performance that Kate finds agreeable. During one of these experiences she feels the need to change her name to something that references trees, something like Kate Nelson-Fir, but eventually settles on Kate Nelson Talkingtree. The meditative spirit also suggests to participants when the time comes to move to the next level; thus, Kate reaches fulfillment with Buddhism and feels the need to experience another level of meditation. Kate's next meditative journey is with the group of women tackling the art of white-water rafting down the Colorado River. During the time that they are not on the river, Kate does walking meditations along the river's bank. While this experience is fulfilling, it does not complete her. She opts to journey to the Amazon to receive instruction from the indigenous shaman of South America. This experience is different in that it involves both meditation and the consumption of herbs.

Ancestor worship involves respect and reverence for deceased relatives, who are not only members of the spiritual world but also mediators into the lives of the living. Ancestors are influential in charting the correct course of action for their living relatives, often communicating with the living through dreams and visions. In the living relatives' dreams the ancestors appear healed from the afflictions that caused their demise from the physical world; these improved conditions enable them to be of assistance to the living. They are the connection between the past and the present, the material and the immaterial. Those who are alive make contact with the ancestors through contemplation, prayer, propitiation, and supplication.

Kate keeps on her home altar photographs of her deceased parents, as well as friends and strangers whom Kate believes are worthy of honor. Through her dreams she contacts the spirit of her mother, who appears healed from the condition that she suffered in the process of dying. As an ancestor her mother helps her to overcome the issues that burden her, allowing Kate to continue to exist in the physical world without obstacles in her path. Kate also uses writing as therapy. The long journey to the Amazon allows her time to initiate the storytelling process on borrowed pieces of paper. The story Kate creates later helps her to work through issues surrounding her mother's death and to discern secrets that her mother did not reveal to her while alive. Thus, Kate breaks through the unseen world to channel information from her mother that was never expressed in life.

Reincarnation, sometimes referred to as the transmigration of souls, is a widely accepted belief in New Age theory. It is also an essential component of African religious cosmology, Hinduism, a variant of Buddhism, and other theological practices. It is a privilege of humans who have lived before. In some instances disembodied spirits choose their parentage and choose their life experiences. It means that following decomposition of the human body—a significant period of time after physical death—the human spirit passes into another body. In some circles reembodiment of humans is not limited to human body access but is also available in animal form or plant form. Adherents to some theologies do not subscribe to the rebirth cycle. They believe that it should be avoided at all costs, for it is torture to repeat earthly experiences.

In Walker's novel Kate has had many explorations involving the human soul, traveling deep into the past. While the character does not articulate the reincarnation path, her practices indicate that she might be a believer.

Medicinal and hallucinogenic plants are commonly used among indigenous people and by some who embrace New Age theories for the purpose of mind expansion. Plants that are grown throughout the world—especially among indigenous people who use them to heighten religious experiences—are the sources of the concoctions used to affect consciousness. These herbal drinks have been in use since before recorded history, passed down from generation to generation. In indigenous cultures their uses are monitored and often reserved for special ritualistic ceremonies. South American Amerindians are one cultural group that incorporates hallucinogens into their religious ceremonies. Many New Age practitioners prefer medicinal herbs for physical ailments to synthetic pharmaceuticals.

One of the medicinal herbs that Kate uses to calm her queasy stomach in the novel is desert thistle weed. Another wild plant that Kate samples is mushrooms, which she uses to help her through periods of overwhelming grief. The hallucinogen passed around to the seekers of nature's promise is the Grandmother medicine, a horrible tasting frothy liquid. Each person on the journey is to consume one-half gallon of the beverage. Its purpose is first to cleanse the body through diarrhea and regurgitation and next to begin the enlightenment process. The experiences that occur from inducement of the Grandmother medicine are called *yagé* journeys. Armando and Cosmi also use *agua florida*, another beverage that aids in the enlightenment process. Yet another medicinal beverage called Bobinsana, an earth-colored liquid, helps to bring about lucid dreams. Kate ingests the plant peyote in the novel during one of the meditative journeys, resulting in intuitive acuity (American law prohibits the ingestion of peyote). Also, the novel references the term *ethnobotanists*. These are people who travel to folk cultures researching the relationship between people and their plants.

New Age believers adopt the concept of ecological responsibility. Often referred to as tree huggers they espouse recycling, decluttering, and purifying. Planet Earth and its land, water, and air are their concern, that is, they want people to honor the planet by keeping everything clean. They campaign constantly, encouraging people to avoid using such things as polystyrene containers. They are also against disposing of materials that are not biodegradable in landfills. Those who subscribe to the New Age belief system do not want people to use things that give off toxic waste and fumes and to stop using so much packaging. They promote a healthy lifestyle and want to see more trees planted, as well as other natural vegetation.

   Walker's novel begins and ends with Kate surrounded by trees. She has an affinity for them. The pastoral setting is crucial to her existence. Throughout the entire novel she moves from one natural setting to the next. She meditates around redwood trees. The Colorado River is an inviting escape to the Grand Canyon to enjoy a serene setting. She surrounds herself with some of the oldest vegetation on earth in the South American Amazon. Nature is everywhere in the novel, and Kate wears nature as if it were a robe.

Bibliography

WORKS BY ALICE WALKER

Novels

By the Light of My Father's Smile. New York: Random, 1998.
The Color Purple. New York: Harcourt, 1982.
Meridian. New York: Harcourt, 1976.
Now Is the Time to Open Your Heart: A Novel. New York: Random, 2004.
Possessing the Secret of Joy. New York: Harcourt, 1992.
The Temple of My Familiar. San Diego: Harcourt, 1989.
The Third Life of Grange Copeland. New York: Harcourt, 1970.
The Way Forward Is with a Broken Heart. New York: Random, 2000.

Stories

Alice Walker: The Complete Stories. London: Orion, 1994.
In Love and Trouble: Stories of Black Women. New York: Harcourt, 1973.
You Can't Keep a Good Woman Down: Stories. New York: Harcourt, 1981.

Poetry

Absolute Trust in the Goodness of the Earth: New Poems. New York: Random, 2003.
Five Poems. Detroit: Broadside, 1972.
Good Night Willie Lee, I'll See You in the Morning. New York: Dial, 1979.

Her Blue Body Everything We Know: Earthling Poems, 1965–1990. San Diego: Harcourt, 1991.
Horses Make the Landscape Look More Beautiful. San Diego: Harcourt, 1984.
Once: Poems. New York: Harcourt, 1968.
A Poem Traveled Down My Arm: Poems and Drawings. New York: Random, 2003.
Revolutionary Petunias and Other Poems. New York: Harcourt, 1973.

Nonfiction

Letters of Love and Hope: The Story of the Cuban Five. London: Ocean P., 2005.
Warrior Marks: Female Genital Mutilation and the Sexual Blinding of Women. New York: Harcourt, 1993.

Autobiographical Writings

Alice Walker Banned: The Banned Works. San Francisco: Aunt Lute, 1996.
Anything We Love Can Be Saved: A Writer's Activism. New York: Random House, 1997.
The Same River Twice: Honoring the Difficult: A Meditation on Life, Spirit, Art, and the Making of the Film The Color Purple, Ten Years Later. New York: Scribner, 1996.
Sent by Earth: A Message from the Grandmother Spirit after the Bombing of the World Trade Center and the Pentagon. New York: Seven Stories P., 2001.

Essays: Collections

I Love Myself When I Am Laughing . . . and Then Again When I *Am Looking Mean and Impressive: A Zora Neale Hurston Reader.* Old Westbury, NY: Feminist, 1979.
In Search of Our Mothers' Gardens: Womanist Prose. New York: Harcourt, 1983.
Living by the Word: Selected Writings, 1973–1987. San Diego: Harcourt, 1988.

Essays and Articles

"After 20 Years, Meditation Still Conquers Inner Space." *New York Times,* 23 Oct. 2000, The Arts: 1–2.
Afterword: "Looking for Zora." *I Love Myself When I Am Laughing . . . and Then Again When I Am Looking Mean and Impressive: A Zora Neale Hurston Reader.* Ed. Alice Walker. New York: Feminist, 1979. 297–313.
"A Legacy of Betrayal: Confronting the Evil Tradition of Female Genital Mutilation." *Ms.,* Nov./Dec. 1993: 55–57.
"Alice Walker." *Essence,* July 1988: 71+.
"Alice Walker: Old South, New World." *Atlanta Magazine,* May 2001: 126.
"America Should Have Closed Down on the First Day a Black Woman Observed That Supermarket Collard Greens Tasted Like Water." *Ms.,* Jan. 1985: 53+.

"Am I Blue?" *Ms.*, July 1986: 29–30.

"Am I Blue? Thoughts on Animal Feelings, Human Rights, and Justice for All." *Utne Reader*, Jan./Feb. 1989: 98–99+.

"Beyond the Peacock: The Reconstruction of Flannery O'Conner." *Ms.*, Dec. 1975: 77–79, 102–6.

"Birth." *Ms.*, May 1989: 58–60.

"By the Light of My Father's Smile." *Ms.*, Sep./Oct. 1998: 47–48.

"By the Light of My Father's Smile." *We*, Nov./Dec. 1998: 86–90.

"China." *Ms.*, Mar. 1985: 51–52+.

"Cuddling." *Essence*, July 1985: 74–76+.

Dedication: "On Refusing to Be Humbled by Second Place in a Contest You Did Not Design: A Tradition by Now." *I Love Myself When I Am Laughing . . . and Then Again When I Am Looking Mean and Impressive: A Zora Neale Hurston Reader.* Ed. Alice Walker. New York: Feminist, 1979. 1–5.

"Disinformation Advertising." *Ms.*, Mar./Apr. 1991: 95.

"Don't Bury My Heart." *Nation*, 4–11 Sep. 1989: 226.

"Even As I Hold You." *Essence*, Sep. 1990: 110.

"Every Morning." *Ladies' Home Journal*, May 1985: 103.

"Father: For What You Were." *Essence*, May 1985: 93–94+.

"Finding Celie's Voice." *Ms.*, Dec. 1985: 71–72+.

"Finding Langston." *Essence*, Dec. 2000: 141–42.

"Foreword." *In Her Hands: Craftswomen Changing the World.* By Paola Gianturco and Toby Tuttle. London: Power House, 2005.

Foreword: "Zora Neale Hurston: A Cautionary Tale and a Partisan View." *Zora Neale Hurston: A Literary Biography.* By Robert E. Hemenway. Urbana: U of Illinois P, 1978. xi-xviii.

"For My Sister Molly Who in the Fifties." *Alice Walker: "Everyday Use."* Ed. Barbara T. Christian. New Brunswick, NJ: Rutgers UP, 1994.

"Giving the Party: Aunt Jemima, Mammy, and the Goddess Within." *Ms.*, May/June 1994: 22–25.

"How Long Shall They Torture Our Mothers?" *Ms.*, May/June 1991: 22–25.

"I Must Whistle Like a Woman Undaunted." *Essence*, Oct. 1984: 90–91.

"In the Closet of the Soul." *Ms.*, Nov. 1986: 32–35.

"In Search of Our Mothers' Gardens." *Alice Walker: "Everyday Use."* Ed. Barbara T. Christian. New Brunswick, NJ: Rutgers UP, 1994. 39–49.

"In Search of Our Mothers' Gardens." *In Search of Our Mothers' Gardens: Womanist Prose.* By Alice Walker. New York: Harcourt, 1983. 231–43.

"In Search of Our Mothers' Gardens." *Ms.*, Sep./Oct. 1997: 11–15.

"In Search of Our Mothers' Gardens." *Within the Circle: An Anthology of African American Literary Criticism from the Harlem Renaissance to the Present.* Ed. Angelyn Mitchell. Durham, NC: Duke UP, 1994. 401–9.

"In Search of Our Mother's Gardens: Honoring the Creativity of the Black Woman." *Jackson State Review* 6.1 (1974): 44–53.

"Kindred Spirits." *Esquire,* Aug. 1985: 106–7+.

"Looking for Zora." *Ms.,* March 1975: 74–79, 85–89.

"Looking for Zora." *Between Women: Biographers, Novelists, Critics, Teachers, and Artists Write about Their Work on Women.* Eds. Carol Ascher, et al. Boston: Beacon, 1984. 431–47.

"Malcolm." *Essence,* May 1990: 205.

"Marriage vs. Freedom." *Essence,* May 1989: 81–82+.

"My Father's Country Is the Poor." *New York Times,* 21 Mar. 1977. www.newyork-times.com.

"Ndebele." *Ms.,* Nov./Dec. 1990: 45.

"New Face." *Essence,* Nov. 1983: 122.

"The Ocean Told Me to Tell You This." *Utne Reader,* May/June 2001: 42–44.

"Olive Oil." *Ms.,* Aug. 1985: 34–36+.

"The Only Reason You Want to Go to Heaven Is That You Have Been Driven Out of Your Mind." *Humanist,* Sep./Oct. 1997: 29–33.

"Oppressed Hair Puts a Ceiling on the Brain." *Ms.,* June 1988: 52–53.

"The Place Where I Was Born." *Essence,* June 1991: 58–59.

"Poem at Thirty-Nine." *Ms.,* June 1983: 101.

"Remembering Mr. Sweet." *New York Times Book Review,* 8 May 1988: 33.

"The Shifting Text." *London Times Literary Supplement,* 23 Apr. 1964, 355.

"Six Notes on *All's Well That Ends Well*." *Shakespeare Quarterly* 33.3 (1982): 339–42.

"Staying Home in Mississippi." *New York Times,* 26 August 1973. www.newyork-times.com.

"The Temple of My Familiar." *Mother Jones,* Apr. 1989: 53–54.

"The Text of *Measure for Measure*." *Review of English Studies: A Quarterly Journal of English Literature and the English Language* 34.133 (1983): 1–20.

"To Hell with Dying!" *Reader's Digest,* Oct. 1983: 110–14.

"Turning into Love: Some Thoughts on Surviving and Meeting Langston Hughes." *Callaloo: A Journal of African American and African Arts and Letters* 12.4 (1989): 663–66.

"The Two of Us." *Essence,* May 1995: 172–73+.

"Ungovernable Women: A Conversation between Alice Walker and Clarrissa Pinkola Estés, Speaking of Their Ancestors, Raising Children and Writing, and What Matters about the Broken Heart." *Bloomsbury Review* 21.6 (2001): 17–19.

"The Universe Responds: Or, How I Learned We Can Have Peace on Earth." *At Home on the Earth: Becoming Native to Our Place: A Multicultural Anthology.* Ed. David Landis Barnhill. Berkeley: U of California P, 1999. 307–12.

"What Can the White Man ... Say to the Black Woman?" *The Nation,* 22 May 1989: 691–92.

"When a Tree Falls ...." *Ms.,* Jan. 1984: 48–49+.

"When the Other Dancer Is the Self." *Ms.,* May 1983: 70+.

"You Have All Seen." *Ms.,* Mar./Apr. 1997: 53–59.

Juvenile Literature

Everyday Use. New Brunswick, NJ: Rutgers UP, 1994.
Finding the Green Stone. San Diego: Harcourt, 1991.
Langston Hughes, American Poet. New York: Crowell, 1974.
There Is a Flower at the Tip of My Nose Smelling Me. New York: HarperCollins, 2006.
To Hell with Dying. San Diego: Harcourt, 1988.

Films

The Color Purple (Directed by Stephen Spielberg), 1985.
Warrior Marks (with Pratibha Parmar), 1993.

Reviews

"A Daring Subject Boldly Shared." Rev. of *Loving Her* by Ann Shockley. *Ms.,* Apr. 1976: 120–24.
"A Writer Because of, Not in Spite of, Her Children." Rev. of *Second Class Citizen* by Buchi Emecheta. New York: George Braziller, 1976.
"A Writer Because of, Not in Spite of, Her Children." Rev. of *Second Class Citizen* by Buchi Emecheta. *Ms.,* Jan. 1976: 2, 4, 106.
Rev. of *Good Morning Revolution: Uncollected Writings of Social Protest by Langston Hughes* by Faith Berry. *Black Scholar* July-Aug 1976: 53–55.

Other Writings

"Letter to President Bill Clinton." 13 March 1996. www.cubasolidarity.net/awalker.html.
et al. "The Life of a Black Man." *Nation,* 15 Nov. 1999: 7.

WORKS ABOUT ALICE WALKER

Biographies

Dictionary of Literary Biography: Afro-American Fiction Writers after 1955. Vol. 33. Detroit: Gale, 1984.
Lauret, Maria. *Alice Walker.* New York: St. Martin's, 1999.
White, Evelyn C. *Alice Walker: A Life.* New York: Norton, 2004.
Winchell, Donna Haisty. *Alice Walker.* New York: Twayne, 1992.

Bibliographies

Banks, Erma Davis, and Keith Byerman. *Alice Walker: An Annotated Bibliography: 1968–1986.* New York: Garland, 1989.

Bloxham, Laura J. "Alice (Malsenior) Walker (1944-)." *Contemporary Fiction Writers of the South: A Bio-Bibliographical Sourcebook.* Eds. Joseph M. Flora and Robert Bain. Westport, CT: Greenwood, 1993. 457–67.

Byerman, Keith, and Erma Banks. "Alice Walker: A Selected Bibliography, 1968–1988." *Callaloo: A Journal of African American and African Arts and Letters* 12.2 (1989): 343–45.

Kirschner, Susan. "Alice Walker's Nonfictional Prose: A Checklist, 1966–1984." *Black American Literature Forum* 18.4 (1984): 162–63.

Pratt, Louis H., and Darnell D. Pratt. *Alice Malsenior Walker, Annotated Bibliography: 1968–1986.* Westport, CT: Meckler, 1988.

Roden, Molly. "Alice Walker (1944–)." *Contemporary African American Novelists: A Bio-Bibliographical Critical Sourcebook.* Ed. Emmanuel S. Nelson. Westport, CT: Greenwood, 1999. 458–68.

Williams, Ora. *American Black Women in the Arts and Social Sciences: A Bibliographic Survey.* Metuchen, NJ: Scarecrow, 1978.

Interviews

Bonnetti, Kay. *Alice Walker.* Interview. Audiocasette. San Francisco: American Audio Prose Library, 1981.

O'Brien, John. "Interview with Alice Walker." *Alice Walker: "Everyday Use."* Ed. Barbara T. Christian. New Brunswick, NJ: Rutgers UP, 1994. 55–81.

O'Brien, John. *Interviews with Black Writers.* New York: Liveright, 1973.

Roemer, Astrid H., and Wanda Boeke, trans. "Astrid H. Roemer Meets Alice Walker in Amsterdam." *Callaloo: A Journal of African American and African Arts and Letters* 18.2 (1995): 212–13.

Steinem, Gloria. "Do You Know This Woman? She Knows You—A Profile of Alice Walker." *Ms.,* June 1982.

Tate, Claudia. "Alice Walker." *Black Women Writers at Work.* Ed. Claudia Tate. New York: Continuum, 1983. 175–87.

Wilson, Sharon. "A Conversation with Alice Walker." *Kalliope: Journal of Women's Art* 6.2 (1984): 37–45.

Zinn, Howard. "Howard Zinn Talks with Alice Walker." *Brick* 53 (1996): 14–21.

REVIEWS

Anything We Love Can Be Saved

Anderson, Michael. *New York Times Book Review,* 25 May 1997: 17.

Cumming, Charles. *New Statesman,* 15 Aug. 1997: 48 [London, England].

Jones, Mary Paumier. *Library Journal,* 1 May 1997: 104.

Nolan, Margaret. *School Library Journal,* Aug. 1997: 191.

Pettis, Joyce. *African American Review* 33.4 (1999): 715–16.

Seaman, Donna. *Booklist,* 1 Mar. 1997: 1067.

By the Light of My Father's Smile

Adil, Alev. *Times Literary Supplement,* 6 Nov. 1998: 24.
Byrd, Rudolph P. *African American Review* 33.4 (1999): 719–22.
Flexman, Ellen. *Library Journal,* Aug. 1998: 136.
Palmer, Trudy. *Christian Science Monitor,* 1 Oct. 1998: B6.
Pemberton, Gayle. *Women's Review of Books* Dec. 1998: 20.
Prose, Francine. *New York Times Book Review* 4 Oct. 1998: 18.
Seaman, Donna. *Booklist,* 1–15 June 1998: 1671.

The Color Purple

Bartelme, Elizabeth. *Commonweal,* 11 Feb. 1983: 93–94.
Kelley, Ernece B. *CLA Journal* 27 (1983): 91–96.
Mootry-Ikerionwu, Maria K. *CLA Journal* 27 (1984): 345–48.
Pinckney, Darryl. *New York Review of Books,* 29 Jan. 1987: 17–20.

Her Blue Body Everything We Know: Earthling Poems

DeCandido, GraceAnne A. *Library Journal,* 15 Apr. 1991: 97.
Oktenberg, Adrian T. *Women's Review of Books,* Dec. 1991: 24.

Horses Make a Landscape Look More Beautiful

Gernes, Sonia. *America,* 2 Feb. 1985: 93–94.

In Search of Our Mothers' Gardens

Allen, Bruce. *Smithsonian,* Jan. 1984: 133–34.
Brown, Beth. *CLA Journal* 27 (1984): 348–52.
Clark, Beverly Lyon. *Modern Fiction Studies* 30 (1984): 334.
Davidon, Ann Morrissett. *Progressive,* Feb. 1984: 42–43.
Mort, Jo-Ann. *Commonweal,* 1 June 1984: 345–46.
Munro, C. Lynn. *Black American Literature Forum* 18 (1984): 161.
Rhodes, Jewell Parker. *America,* 25 Feb. 1984: 137–38.
Smith, Valerie. *Sewanee Review* 93 (1985): xxxi–xxxii+.
Vigderman, Patricia. *Nation,* 17 Dec. 1983: 635+.

Living by the Word

Byrd, Rudolph P. *MELUS: Journal of the Society for the Study of the Multi-Ethnic Literature of the United States* 15 (1988): 109–15.
Perrin, Noel. *New York Times Book Review,* 5 June 1988: 42–43.
Ziegenhals, Gretchen E. *Christian Century,* 16 Nov. 1988: 1036–37.

Meridian

New York Times, 23 May 1976. www.newyorktimes.com.

Now Is the Time to Open Your Heart: A Novel

Burkhardt, Joanna M. *Library Journal*, 1 Dec. 2004: 182.
Bush, Vanessa. *Booklist*, 15 Oct. 2003: 358.
Elam, Patricia. *The New Crisis*, 111.5 (2004): 51.
Flexman, Ellen. *Library Journal*, 15 Nov. 2003: 100.
Kirkus Reviews, 15 Dec. 2003: 1422.
McHenry, Susan. *Black Issues Book Review*, May–June 2004: 44.
Waldman, Debby. *People*, 3 May 2004: 45.
Zaleski, Jeff. *Publisher's Weekly*, 17 Nov. 2003: 38.

Possessing the Secret of Joy

Benn, Melissa. *New Statesman and Society*, 9 Oct. 1992: 36.
Chadwell, Faye A. *Library Journal*, 15 May 1992: 122.
Erickson, Peter. *Kenyon Review* 15 (1993): 197–207.
Giddings, Paula. *Essence*, July 1992: 58–60+.
Hospital, Janette Turner. *New York Times Book Review*, 28 June 1992: 11–12.
Ndombele, Simon. *CLA Journal* 37 (1994): 473–76.
Sage, Lorna. *Times Literary Supplement*, 9 Oct. 1992: 22.
Shapiro, Laura. *Newsweek*, 8 June 1992: 56–57.
Wilentz, Gay. *Women's Review of Books*, Feb. 1993: 15.

The Same River Twice: Honoring the Difficult: A Meditation on Life, Spirit, Art, and the Making of the Film The Color Purple, Ten Years Later

Burns, Ann. *Library Journal*, Dec. 1995: 110.
Seaman, Donna. *Booklist*, 15 Nov. 1995: 514.
Walton, David. *New York Times Book Review*, 14 Jan. 1996: 18.

The Temple of My Familiar

Bingham, Sallie. *American Book Review*, May/June 1990: 10.
Birch, Dinah. *London Review of Books*, 21 Dec. 1989: 19.
Coetzee, J.M. *New York Times Book Review*, 30 Apr. 1989: 7.
Davenport, Doris. *Women's Review of Books*, Sep. 1989: 13.
Gates, David. *Newsweek*, 24 Apr. 1989: 74–75.
Gray, Paul. *Time*, 1 May 1989: 69.
Gurnah, Abdulrazak. *Times Literary Supplement*, 22 Sep. 1989: 1023.

Koenig, Rhoda. *New York*, 8 May 1989: 76–77.
Le Guin, Ursula K. *San Francisco Review of Books*, Summer 1989: 12.
Maynard, Joyce. *Mademoiselle*, July 1989: 70+.
Rubin, Merle. *Christian Science Monitor*, 4 May 1989: 13.
Tate, J. O. *National Review*, 30 June 1989: 48.
Wheelwright, Julie. *New Statesman and Society*, 22 Sep 1989: 34.
Wolcott, James. *New Republic*, 29 May 1989: 28–30.
Zinn, Christopher. *America*, 12–19 Aug. 1989: 90.

To Hell with Dying

Wesley, Valerie Wilson. *New York Times Book Review*, 14 Aug. 1988: 28.

Warrior Marks

King, Lovalerie. *African American Review* 31 (1997): 542–45.
McCoy, Frank. *Black Enterprise*, May 1994: 103.
Lambda Book Report, Sep.–Oct. 1994: 37.

The Way Forward Is with a Broken Heart

Bader, Eleanor J. *Library Journal*, 1 Sep. 2000: 254.
Bashir, Samiya A. *Ms.*, Oct./Nov. 2000: 90.
Birne, Eleanor. *Times Literary Supplement*, 16 Feb. 2001: 23.
Osborne, Linda Barrett. *New York Times Book Review*, 10 Dec. 2000: 32.
Rubin, Merle. *Christian Science Monitor*, 9 Nov. 2000: 18–19.

You Can't Keep a Good Woman Down

New York Times, 24 May 1981.

CRITICISM OF THE NOVELS

The Color Purple

Abbandonato, Linda. "A View from Elsewhere: Subversive Sexuality and the
    Rewriting of the Heroine's Story in *The Color Purple*." *Publications of the
    Modern Language Association* 106.5 (1991): 1106–15.
Allan, Tuzyline Jita. "Womanism Revisited: Women and the (Ab)Use of Power
    in *The Color Purple*." *Feminist Nightmares: Women at Odds: Feminism and the
    Problem of Sisterhood*. Eds. Susan Ostrov Weisser, et al. New York: New York
    UP, 1994. 88–105.
Alps, Sandra. "Concepts of Self-Hood in *Their Eyes Were Watching God* and *The
    Color Purple*." *Pacific Review* 1 (1986): 106–12.

Babb, Valerie. *"The Color Purple:* Writing to Undo What Writing Has Done." *Phylon: A Review of Race and Culture* 47.2 (1986): 107–16.

Babb, Valerie. "Women and Words: Articulating the Self in *Their Eyes Were Watching God* and *The Color Purple.*" *Alice Walker and Zora Neale Hurston: The Common Bond.* Ed. Lillie P. Howard. Westport, CT: Greenwood, 1993. 83–93.

Berlant, Lauren. "Race, Gender, and Nation in *The Color Purple.*" *Critical Inquiry* 11.1 (1988): 831–59.

Bobo, Jacqueline. *"The Color Purple:* Black Women as Cultural Readers." *Female Spectators: Looking at Film and Television.* Ed. E. Deidre Pribram. London: Verso, 1988. 90–109.

Bobo, Jacqueline. "Sifting through the Controversy: Reading *The Color Purple.*" *Callaloo: A Journal of African American and African Arts and Letters* 12.2 (1989): 332–42.

Brown-Clark, Sally. "In the Community of Black Women in *The Color Purple.*" *Women in History, Literature and the Arts: A Festschrift for Hildegard Schnuttgen in Honor of Her Thirty Years of Outstanding Service at Youngstown State University.* Ed. Lorrayne Y. Baird-Lange. Youngstown, OH: Youngstown State U, 1989. 295–305.

Butler, Cheryl B. *"The Color Purple* Controversy: Black Woman Spectatorship." *Wide Angle: A Film Quarterly of Theory, Criticism, and Practice* 13.3–1 (1991): 62–69.

Chambers, Kimberly R. "Right on Time: History and Religion in Alice Walker's *The Color Purple.*" *College Language Association Journal* 31.1 (1987): 44–62.

Cheung, King-Kok. "'Don't Tell': Imposed Silences in *The Color Purple* and *The Woman Warrior.*" *Emerging Voices.* Ed. Janet Madden Simpson. Fort Worth: Holt, 1990. 400–21.

Cheung, King-Kok. "'Don't Tell': Imposed Silences in *The Color Purple* and *The Woman Warrior.*" *Publications of the Modern Language Association* 103.2 (1988): 162–71.

Christophe, Marc A. *"The Color Purple:* An Existential Novel." *College Language Association Journal* 36.3 (1993): 280–90.

Coleman, Viralene J. "Miss Celie's Song." *Publications of the Arkansas Philological Association* 11.1 (1985): 27–34.

Collins, Gina Michelle. *"The Color Purple:* What Feminism Can Learn from a Southern Tradition." *Southern Literature and Literary Theory.* Ed. Jefferson Humphries. Athens: U of Georgia P, 1990. 75–87.

Cutter, Martha J. "Philomela Speaks: Alice Walker's Revisioning of Rape Archetypes in *The Color Purple.*" *MELUS: Journal of the Society for the Study of the Multi-Ethnic Literature of the United States* 25.3–4 (2000): 161–80.

Davis, Jane. *"The Color Purple:* A Spiritual Descendant of Hurston's *Their Eyes Were Watching God.*" *Griot: Official Journal of the Southern Conference on Afro American Studies* 6.2 (1987): 79–96.

Davis, Lisa. "An Invitation to Understanding among Poor Women of the Americas: *The Color Purple* and *Hasta no verte Jesus mio.*" *Reinventing the Americas: Comparative Studies of Literature of the United States and Spanish America.*

Eds. Bell Gale Chevigny and Gari Laguardia. New York: Cambridge UP, 1986. 224–41.

Dawson, Emma J. Waters. "Redemption through Redemption of the Self in *Their Eyes Were Watching God* and *The Color Purple.*" *Alice Walker and Zora Neale Hurston: The Common Bond.* Ed. Lillie P. Howard. Westport, CT: Greenwood, 1993. 69–82.

Digby, Joan. "From Walker to Spielberg: Transformations of *The Color Purple.*" *Novel Images: Literature in Performance.* Ed. Peter Reynolds. London: Routledge, 1993. 157–74.

Dole, Carol M. "The Return of the Father in Spielberg's *The Color Purple.*" *Literature Film Quarterly* 21.1 (1996): 12–16.

Dozier, Judy. "Who You Calling a Lady?: Resisting Sexual Definition in *The Color Purple.*" *Official Journal of the Southern Conference on Afro-American Studies, Inc.* 21.2 (2002): 8–16.

Duckworth, Victoria. "The Redemptive Impulse: Wise Blood and *The Color Purple.*" *Flannery O'Connor Bulletin* 15 (1986): 51–56.

Early, Gerald. "*The Color Purple* as Everybody's Protest Art." *Antioch Review* 50.1–2 (1992): 399–412.

Elliott, Emory. "History and Will in *Dog Soldiers, Sabbatical,* and *The Color Purple.*" *Arizona Quarterly: A Journal of American Literature, Culture, and Theory* 43.3 (1987): 197–217.

Ellis, R. J. "Out from Under the Cucumber: *The Color Purple*'s Discursive Critique of Postmodern Deferral." *Liminal Postmodernisms: The Postmodern, the (Post-)Colonial, and the (Post-)Feminist.* Eds. Theo D'haen, et al. Amsterdam: Rodopi, 1994. 275–99. [Netherlands]

El Saffar, Ruth. "Alice Walker's *The Color Purple.*" *International Fiction Review* 12.1 (1985): 11–17. [Canada]

Elsley, Judy. "Laughter as Feminine Power in *The Color Purple* and *A Question of Silence.*" *New Perspectives on Women and Comedy.* Ed. Regina Barreca. Philadelphia: Gordon, 1992. 193–99.

Elsley, Judy. "'Nothing Can Be Sole or Whole That Has Not Been Rent': Fragmentation in the Quilt and *The Color Purple.*" *Weber Studies: An Interdisciplinary Humanities Journal* 9.2 (1992): 71–81.

Fannin, Alice. "A Sense of Wonder: The Pattern for Psychic Survival in *Their Eyes Were Watching God* and *The Color Purple.*" *Zora Neale Hurston Forum* 1.1 (1986): 1–11.

Fifer, Elizabeth. "Alice Walker: The Dialect and Letters of *The Color Purple.*" *Contemporary American Women Writers: Narrative Strategies.* Eds. Catherine Rainwater, et al. Lexington: UP of Kentucky, 1985. 155–71.

Fitzsimmons, Kate. "Go Ask Alice: Alice Walker Talks about *The Color Purple* 10 Years Later." *San Francisco Review of Books,* Mar./Apr. 1996: 20–23.

Harris, Trudier. "From Victimization to Free Enterprise: Alice Walker's *The Color Purple.*" *Studies in American Fiction* 14.1 (1986): 1–17.

Harris, Trudier. "On *The Color Purple*, Stereotypes, and Silence." *Black American Literature Forum* 18.4 (1984): 155–61.

Hayes, Elizabeth T. "'Like Seeing You Buried': Persephone in *The Bluest Eye, Their Eyes Were Watching God*, and *The Color Purple*." *Images of Persephone: Feminist Readings in Western Literature*. Ed. Elizabeth T. Hayes. Gainesville: UP of Florida, 1994. 170–94.

Heglar, Charles J. "Named and Namelessness: Alice Walker's Pattern of Surnames in *The Color Purple*." *ANQ: A Quarterly Journal of Short Articles, Notes, and Reviews* 13.1 (2000): 39–41.

Henderson, Mae G. "*The Color Purple*: Revisions and Redefinitions." *Sage: A Scholarly Journal on Black Women* 2.1 (1985): 14–18.

Hiers, John T. "Creation Theology in Alice Walker's *The Color Purple*." *Notes on Contemporary Literature* 14.4 (1984): 2–3.

Hite, Molly. "Romance, Marginality, Matrilineage: Alice Walker's *The Color Purple* and Zora Neale Hurston's *Their Eyes Were Watching God*." *Novel: A Forum on Fiction* 22.3 (1989): 257–73.

Jackson, Kathy Dunn. "The Epistolary Text: A Voice of Affirmation and Liberation in *So Long a Letter* and *The Color Purple*." *Griot* 12.2 (1993): 13–20.

Jamison-Hall, Angelene. "She's Just Too Womanish for Them: Alice Walker and *The Color Purple*." *Censored Books: Critical Viewpoints*. Eds. Nicholas J. Karolides, et al. Metuchen, NJ: Scarecrow, 1993. 191–200.

Jenkins, Candice M. "Queering Black Patriarchy: The Salvific Wish and Masculine Possibility in Alice Walker's *The Color Purple*." *Modern Fiction Studies* 48.4 (2002): 969–1000.

Johnson, Cheryl Lynn. "A Womanist Way of Speaking: An Analysis of Language in Alice Walker's *The Color Purple*, Toni Morrison's *Tar Baby*, and Gloria Naylor's *Women of Brewster Place*." *The Critical Response to Gloria Naylor*. Eds. Sharon Felton, et al. Westport, CT: Greenwood, 1997. 23–26.

Karanja, Ayana. "Zora Neale Hurston and Alice Walker: A Transcendent Relationship—*Jonah's Gourd Vine* and *The Color Purple*." *Alice Walker and Zora Neale Hurston: The Common Bond*. Ed. Lillie P. Howard. Westport, CT: Greenwood, 1993. 121–37.

Kelly, Lori Duin. "Theology and Androgyny: The Role of Religion in *The Color Purple*." *Notes on Contemporary Literature* 18.2 (1988): 7–8.

Kim, Minjung. "The Subversiveness of the Letters from Africa: Alice Walker's *The Color Purple*." *Feminist Studies in English Literature* 8.2 (2001): 105–29.

Kunishiro, Tadao. "'So Much of Life in Its Meshes!': Alice Walker's *The Color Purple* and Zora Neale Hurston's *Their Eyes Were Watching God*." *Marjorie Kinnan Rawlings Journal of Florida Literature* 7 (1996): 67–83.

Leder, Priscilla. "Alice Walker's American Quilt: *The Color Purple* and American Literary Tradition." *Journal of the American Studies Association of Texas* 20 (1989): 79–93.

Lenhart, Georgann. "Inspired Purple?" *Notes on Contemporary Literature* 14.3 (1984): 2–3.

Lewis, Catherine E. "Sewing, Quilting, Knitting: Handicraft and Freedom in *The Color Purple* and *A Woman's Story.*" *Literature Film Quarterly* 29.3 (2001): 236–45.

Lewis, T. W., III. "Moral Mapping and Spiritual Guidance in *The Color Purple.*" *Soundings: An Interdisciplinary Journal* 73.2–3 (1990): 183–91.

Light, Alison. "Fear of the Happy Ending: *The Color Purple,* Reading and Racism." *Plotting Change: Contemporary Women's Fiction.* Ed. Linda Anderson. London: Edward Arnold, 1990. 84–96.

Marvin, Thomas F. "'Preachin' the Blues': Bessie Smith's Secular Religion and Alice Walker's *The Color Purple.*" *African American Review* 28.3 (1994): 411–21.

McKenzie, Tammie. "*The Color Purple*'s Celie: A Journey of Selfhood." *Conference of College Teachers of English Studies* 51 (1986): 50–58.

Montelaro, Janet J. *Producing a Womanist Text: The Maternal as Signifier in Alice Walker's The Color Purple.* Victoria, BC: U of Victoria, 1996.

Morgan, Winifred. "Alice Walker: *The Color Purple* as Allegory." *Southern Writers at Century's End.* Ed. James A. Perkins. Lexington, KY: UP of Kentucky, 1997. 177–84.

Powers, Peter Kerry. "'Pa Is Not Our Pa': Sacred History and Political Imagination in *The Color Purple.*" *South Atlantic Review* 60.2 (1995): 69–72.

Premo, Cassie. "Lessons for Life in *Meridian* and *The Color Purple.*" *North Carolina Humanities* (1993): 35–45.

Proudfit, Charles. "A Century of Change: A Look at Contemporary Psychoanalytic Ego Psychology from the Perspectives of George Vaillant's *The Wisdom of the Ego* and Alice Walker's *The Color Purple.*" *Journal of Evolutionary Psychology* 19.1–2 (1998): 61–69.

Proudfit, Charles L. "Celie's Search for Identity: A Psychoanalytic Developmental Reading of Alice Walker's *The Color Purple.*" *Contemporary Literature* 32.1 (1991): 12–37.

Quashie, Kevin E. "The Other Dancer as Self: Girlfriend Selfhood in Toni Morrison's *Sula* and Alice Walker's *The Color Purple.*" *Meridians: Feminism, Race, Transnationalism* 2.1 (2001): 187–217.

Ridley, Chauncey A. "Animism and Testimony in Alice Walker's *The Color Purple.*" *MAWA Review* 4.2 (1989): 32–36.

Robinson, Daniel. "Problems in Form: Alice Walker's *The Color Purple.*" *Notes on Contemporary Literature* 16.1 (1986): 2.

Ross, Daniel W. "Celie in the Looking Glass: The Desire for Selfhood in *The Color Purple.*" *Modern Fiction Studies* 34.1 (1988): 69–81.

Ross, Daniel W. "The Making of Celie in Alice Walker's *The Color Purple.*" *Teaching American Ethnic Literatures: Nineteen Essays.* Eds. John R. Maitino and David R. Peck. Albuquerque: U of New Mexico P. 1996. 159–74.

Saunders, James Robert. "Womanism as the Key to Understanding Zora Neale Hurston's *Their Eyes Were Watching God* and Alice Walker's *The Color Purple*." *Hollins Critic* 25.4 (1988): 1–11.

Scholl, Diane Gabrielsen. "With Ears to Hear and Eyes to See: Alice Walker's Parable *The Color Purple*." *Christianity and Literature* 40.3 (1991): 255–66.

Seidel, Kathryn Lee. "The Lilith Figure in Toni Morrison's *Sula* and Alice Walker's *The Color Purple*." *Weber Studies: An Interdisciplinary Humanities Journal* 10.2 (1993): 85–94.

Selzer, Linda. "Race and Domesticity in *The Color Purple*." *African American Review* 29.1 (1995): 67–82.

Sevillano, Lilia Maria. "The Treatment of Women in Toni Morrison's *Song of Solomon* and Alice Walker's *The Color Purple:* A Feminist Reading." Likha 16.1 (1995–96): 89–101.

Shattuo, Jane. "Having a Good Cry over *The Color Purple:* The Problem of Affect and Imperialism in Feminist Theory." Melodrama: Stage Picture Screen. Eds. Jacky Bratton, et al. London, England: BFI, 1994. 147–56.

Smith-Wright, Geraldine. "Revision as Collaboration: Zora Neale Hurston's *Their Eyes Were Watching God* as Source for Alice Walker's *The Color Purple*." *Sage: A Scholarly Journal on Black Women* 4.2 (1987): 20–25.

Tapia, Elena. "Symmetry as Conceptual Metaphor in Walker's *The Color Purple*." *International Journal of English Studies* 3.1 (2003): 29–44.

Tavormina, M. Teresa. "Dressing the Spirit: Clothworking and Language in *The Color Purple*." *Journal of Narrative Technique* 16.3 (1986): 220–30.

Thomas, Jackie. "Reverend Samuel: The Missionary Minister in *The Color Purple*." *Griot: Official Journal of the Southern Conference on Afro American Studies* 16.2 (1997): 15–18.

Tucker, Lindsey. "Alice Walker's *The Color Purple:* Emergent Woman, Emergent Text." *Black American Literature Forum* 22.1 (1988): 81–95.

Turner, Daniel E. "Cherokee and Afro-American Interbreeding in *The Color Purple*." *Notes on Contemporary Literature* 21.5 (1991): 10–11.

Wall, Wendy. "Lettered Bodies and Corporeal Texts in *The Color Purple*." *Studies in American Fiction* 16.1 (1988): 83–97.

Walsh, Margaret. "The Enchanted World of *The Color Purple*." *Southern Quarterly: A Journal of the Arts in the South* 25.2 (1987): 89–101.

Warhol, Robyn R. "How Narration AProduces Gender: Femininity as Affect and Effect in Alice Walker's *The Color Purple*." *Narrative* 9.2 (2001): 182–87.

Waters-Dawson, Emma. "From Victim to Victor: Walker's Women in *The Color Purple*." *The Aching Hearth: Family Violence in Life and Literature*. Eds. Sara Munson Deats, et al. New York: Plenum, 1991. 255–68.

Weisenburger, Steven C. "Errant Narrative and *The Color Purple*." *Journal of Narrative Technique* 19.3 (1989): 257–75.

Williams, Carolyn. "'Trying to Do without God': The Revision of Epistolary Address in *The Color Purple*." *Writing the Female Voice: Essays on Epistolary*

Literature. Ed. Elizabeth Goldsmith. Boston: Northeastern UP, 1989. 273–85.

Meridian

Ahokas, Pirjo. "Hybridized Black Female Identity in Alice Walker's *Meridian.*" *America Today: Highways and Labyrinths.* Ed. Gigliola Nocera. Siracusa, Italy: Grafiá, 2003. 481–88.

Ahokas, Pirjo. "Constructing Hybrid Ethnic Female Identities: Alice Walker's *Meridian* and Louise Erdrich's *Love Medicine.*" *Literature on the Move: Comparing Diasporic Ethnicities in Europe and the Americas.* Ed. Dominique Marcais, et al. Heidelberg, Germany: Carl Winter U, 2002. 199–207.

Anderson, Jace. "Re-Writing Race: Subverting Language in Anne Moody's *Coming of Age in Mississippi* and Alice Walker's *Meridian.*" *Autobiography Studies* 8.1 (1993): 33–50.

Barker, Deborah E. "Visual Markers: Art and Mass Media in Alice Walker's *Meridian.*" *African American Review* 31.3 (1997): 163–79.

Barnett, Pamela E. "'Miscegenation,' Rape, and 'Race' in Alice Walker's *Meridian.*" *Southern Quarterly: A Journal of the Arts in the South* 39.3 (2001): 65–81.

Brown, Joseph A. "'All Saints Should Walk Away': The Mystical Pilgrimage of Meridian." *Callaloo: A Journal of African American and African Arts and Letters* 12.2 (1989): 310–20.

Byrd, Rudolph P. "Shared Orientation and Narrative Acts in *Cane, Their Eyes Were Watching God,* and *Meridian.*" *MELUS: Journal of the Society for the Study of the Multi-Ethnic Literature of the United States* 17.4 (1991–1992): 41–56.

Collins, Janelle. "'Like a Collage': Personal and Political Subjectivity in Alice Walker's *Meridian.*" *College Language Association Journal* 44.2 (2000): 161–88.

Daly, Brenda O. "Teaching Alice Walker's *Meridian*: Civil Rights according to Mothers." *Narrating Mothers: Theorizing Maternal Subjectivities.* Eds. Brenda O. Daly, et al. Knoxville: U of Tennessee P, 1991. 239–57.

Danielson, Susan. "Alice Walker's *Meridian,* Feminism, and the 'Movement'." *Women's Studies: An Interdisciplinary Journal* 16.3–4 (1989): 317–30.

DeLancey, Frenzella E. "Squaring the Afrocentric Circle: Womanism and Humanism in Alice Walker's *Meridian.*" *Literary Griot: International Journal of Black Expressive Cultural Studies* 5.1 (1993): 1–16.

DeLancey, Frenzella Elaine. "Squaring the Afrocentric Circle: Womanism and Humanism in Alice Walker's *Meridian.*" *MAWA Review* 7.2 (1992): 84–101.

Downey, Anne M. "'A Broken and Bloody Hoop': The Intertexuality of *Black Elk Speaks* and Alice Walker's *Meridian.*" *MELUS: Journal of the Society for the Study of the Multi-Ethnic Literature of the United States* 19.3 (1994): 37–45.

Hall, Christine. "Art, Action and the Ancestors: Alice Walker's *Meridian* in Its Context." *Black Women's Writing.* Ed. Gina Wisker. New York: St. Martin's, 1993. 96–110.

Hendrickson, Robert M. "Remembering the Dream: Alice Walker, *Meridian* and the Civil Rights Movement." *MELUS: Journal of the Society for the Study of the Multi-Ethnic Literature of the United States* 24.3 (1999): 111–28.

Hollenberg, Donna Krolik. "Teaching Alice Walker's *Meridian:* From Self-Defense to Mutual Discovery." *MELUS: Journal of the Society for the Study of the Multiethnic Literature of the United States* 17.4 (1991–1992): 81–89.

Jones, Suzanne W. "Dismantling Stereotypes: Interracial Friendships in *Meridian* and *A Mother and Two Daughters*." *The Female Tradition in Southern Literature.* Ed. Carol S. Manning. Urbana: U of Illinois P, 1993. 140–57.

McDowell, Deborah E. "The Self in Bloom: Alice Walker's *Meridian*." *College Language Association Journal* 24.3 (1981): 262–75.

McGowan, Martha J. "Atonement and Release in Alice Walker's *Meridian*." *Critique: Studies in Contemporary Fiction* 23.2 (1981): 25–36.

Nadel, Alan. "Reading the Body: Alice Walker's *Meridian* and the Archeology of Self." *Modern Fiction Studies* 34.1 (1988): 55–68.

Pifer, Lynn. "Coming to Voice in Alice Walker's *Meridian:* Speaking Out for the Revolution." *African American Review* 26.1 (1992): 77–88.

Porter, Nancy. "Women's Interracial Friendships and Visions of Community in *Meridian, The Salt Eaters, Civil Wars,* and *Dessa Rose*." *Tradition and the Talents of Women.* Ed. Florence Howe. Urbana: U of Illinois P, 1991. 251–67.

Premo, Cassie. "Lessons for Life in *Meridian* and *The Color Purple*." *North Carolina Humanities* (1993): 35–45.

Ray, Arunima. "The Quest for 'Home' and 'Wholeness' in *Sula* and *Meridian:* Afro-American Identity in Toni Morrison and Alice Walker." *Indian Journal of American Studies* 23.2 (1993): 59–65. [India]

Warren, Nagueyalti. "Resistant Mothers in Alice Walker's *Meridian* and Tina McElroy *Ansa's Ugly Ways*." *Southern Mothers: Fact and Fictions in Southern Women's Writing.* Ed. Nagueyalti Warren. Baton Rouge: Louisiana State UP, 1999. 182–203.

Weston, Ruth D. "Inversion of Patriarchal Mantle Images in Alice Walker's *Meridian*." *Southern Quarterly: A Journal of the Arts in the South* 25.2 (1987): 102–7.

Possessing the Secret of Joy

Applegate, Nancy. "Feminine Sexuality in Alice Walker's *Possessing the Secret of Joy*." *Notes on Contemporary Literature* 24.4 (1994): 11.

Buckman, Alyson R. "The Body as a Site of Colonization: Alice Walker's *Possessing the Secret of Joy*." *Journal of American Culture* 18.2 (1995): 89–94.

Dieke, Ikenna. "From Fractured Ego to Transcendent Self: A Reading of Alice Walker's *Possessing the Secret of Joy*." *Literary Griot: International Journal of Black Expressive Cultural Studies* 11.1 (1999): 18–68.

Gourdine, Angeletta K. M. "Postmodern Ethnography and the Womanist Mission: Postcolonial Sensibilities in *Possessing the Secret of Joy*." *African American Review* 30.2 (1996): 237–44.

Howard, Lillie P. "Benediction: A Few Words about *The Temple of My Familiar, Variously Experienced,* and *Possessing the Secret of Joy.*" *Alice Walker and Zora Neale Hurston: The Common Bond.* Ed. Lillie P. Howard. Westport, CT: Greenwood, 1993. 139–46.

Moore, Geneva Cobb. "Archetypal Symbolism in Alice Walker's *Possessing the Secret of Joy.*" *Southern Literary Journal* 33.1 (2000): 111–21.

Pollock, Kimberly Joyce. "A Continuum of Pain: A Woman's Legacy in Alice Walker's *Possessing the Secret of Joy.*" *Women of Color: Mother-Daughter Relationships in 20th Century Literature.* Ed. Elizabeth Brown-Guillory. Austin: U of Texas P, 1996. 38–56.

Sample, Maxine. "Psychic Journeys and the Fragmented Self: Navigating Bessie Head's *A Question of Power* and Alice Walker's *Possessing the Secret of Joy:* Proceedings of the First Conference of the Cape American Studies Association, 4 July 1996." *Fissions and Fusions.* Eds. Lesley Marx, et al. Bellville, South Africa: University of the Western Cape, 1997. 64–71.

Sample, Maxine. "Walker's *Possessing the Secret of Joy.*" *Eplicator* 58.3 (2000): 169–72.

Souris, Stephen. "Multiperspectival Consensus: Alice Walker's *Possessing the Secret of Joy,* the Multiple Narrator Novel, and the Practice of 'Female Circumcision'." *College Language Association Journal* 10.4 (1997): 105–31.

Toombs, Veronica M. "Deconstructing Violence against Women: William Faulkner's *Sanctuary* and Alice Walker's *Possessing the Secret of Joy:* Selected Papers: 1995 Conference: Society for the Interdisciplinary Study of Social Imagery, March 9–11, 1995." *The Image of Violence in Literature, the Media, and Society.* Eds. Will Wright, et al. Pueblo, CO: Society for the Interdisciplinary Study of Social Imagery, 1995. 212–17.

The Temple of My Familiar

Braendlin, Bonnie. "Alice Walker's *The Temple of My Familiar* as a Pastiche." *American Literature: A Journal of Literary History, Criticism, and Bibliography* 68.1 (1996): 17–67.

Dieke, Ikenna. "Toward a Monastic Idealism: The Thematics of Alice Walker's *The Temple of My Familiar.*" *African American Review* 26.3 (1992): 507–14.

Durso, Patricia Keefe. "Private Narrative as Public (Ex)Change: 'Intimate Intervention' in Alice Walker's *The Temple of My Familiar.*" *In Process: A Journal of African American and African Diasporan Literature and Culture* 2 (2000): 137–54.

Howard, Lillie P. "Benediction: A Few Words about *The Temple of My Familiar, Variously Experienced,* and *Possessing the Secret of Joy.*" *Alice Walker and Zora Neale Hurston: The Common Bond.* Ed. Lillie P. Howard. Westport, CT: Greenwood, 1993. 139–46.

Jablon, Madelyn. "Rememory, Dream History, and Revision in Toni Morrison's *Beloved* and Alice Walker's *The Temple of My Familiar.*" *College Language Association Journal* 37.2 (1993): 136–44.

Sol, Adam. "Questions of Mastery in Alice Walker's *The Temple of My Familiar.*"
     Studies in Contemporary Fiction 43.3 (2002): 393–404.
Walter, Roland. "The Dialectics between the Act of Writing and the Act of Reading
     in Alice Walker's *The Temple of My Familiar,* Gloria Naylor's *Mama Day* and
     Toni Morrison's *Jazz.*" *Southern Quarterly: A Journal of the Arts in the South*
     35.3 (1997): 55–66.
Wisker, Gina. "'Disremembered and Unaccounted For': Reading Toni Morrison's
     Beloved and Alice Walker's *The Temple of My Familiar.*" *Black Women's
     Writing.* Ed. Gina Wisker. New York: St. Martin's, 1993. 78–95.

The Third Life of Grange Copeland

Butler, Robert. "Visions of Southern Life and Religion in O'Connor's *Wise Blood*
     and Walker's *The Third Life of Grange Copeland.*" *College Language Association
     Journal* 36.4 (1993): 349–70.
Butler, Robert James. "Alice Walker's Vision of the South in *The Third Life of Grange
     Copeland.*" *African American Review* 27.2 (1993): 195–204.
Butler, Robert James. "Making a Way Out of No Way: The Open Journey in Alice
     Walker's *The Third Life of Grange Copeland.*" *Black American Literature Forum*
     22.1 (1988): 65–79.
Cochran, Kate. "'When the Lessons Hurt': *The Third Life of Grange Copeland* as
     Joban Allegory." *Southern Literary Journal* 34.1 (2001): 79–100.
Cornwell, JoAnne. "Searching for Zora in Alice's Garden: Rites of Passage in
     Hurston's *Their Eyes Were Watching God* and Walker's *The Third Life of
     Grange Copeland.*" *Alice Walker and Zora Neale Hurston: The Common Bond.*
     Ed. Lillie P. Howard. Westport, CT: Greenwood, 1993. 97–107.
Ensslen, Klaus. "Collective Experience and Individual Responsibility: Alice
     Walker's *The Third Life of Grange Copeland.*" *The Afro-American Novel since
     1960.* Eds. Peter Bruck, et al. Amsterdam: Gruner, 1982. 189–218.
Ensslen, Klaus. "History and Fiction in Alice Walker's *The Third Life of Grange
     Copeland* and Ernest Gaines' *The Autobiography of Miss Jane Pittman.*" *History
     and Tradition in Afro-American Culture.* Ed. Gunter H. Lenz. Frankfurt:
     Campus, 1984. 147–63.
Gaston, Karen C. "Women in the Lives of *Grange Copeland.*" *College Language
     Association Journal* 24.3 (1981): 276–86.
Harris, Trudier. "Violence in *The Third Life of Grange Copeland.*" *College Language
     Association Journal* 19 (1975): 238–47.
Hogue, W. Lawrence. "History, the Feminist Discourse, and Alice Walker's *The
     Third Life of Grange Copeland.*" *MELUS: The Journal of the Society for the Study
     of the Multiethnic Literature of the United States* 12.2 (1985): 45–62.
Jackson, Tommie L. "Orphanage in Simone Schwarz-Bart's *The Bridge of Beyond*
     and Alice Walker's *The Third Life of Grange Copeland.*" *Griot: Official Journal
     of the Southern Conference on Afro-American Studies* 15.2 (1996): 7–13.

Mason, Theodore O., Jr. "Alice Walker's *The Third Life of Grange Copeland:* The Dynamics of Enclosure." *Callaloo: A Journal of African American and African Arts and Letters* 12.2 (1989): 297–309.

Thomas, H. Nigel. "Alice Walker's Grange Copeland as a Trickster Figure." *Obsidian II: Black Literature in Review* 6.1 (1991): 60–72.

The Way Forward Is with a Broken Heart

Levin, Tobe, and Freifrau von Gleichen. "Alice Walker, Activist: Matron of FORWARD." *Black Imagination and the Middle Passage.* Eds. Maria Diedrich, Henry Louis Gates, and Carl Pedersen. New York: Oxford UP, 1999.

CRITICISM OF THE STORIES

"Advancing Luna—and Ida B. Wells"

McKay, Nellie Y. "Alice Walker's 'Advancing Luna—and Ida B. Wells': A Struggle toward Sisterhood." *Rape and Representation.* Eds. Lynn A. Higgins, et al. New York: Columbia UP, 1991. 248–60.

"The Child Who Favored Daughter"

Harris, Trudier. "Tiptoeing through Taboo: Incest in 'The Child Who Favored Daughter'." *Modern Fiction Studies* 28.3 (1982): 495–505.

Lester, Neal A. "'Not My Mother, Not My Sister, but It's Me, O Lord, Standing . . .': Alice Walker's 'The Child Who Favored Daughter' as Neo-Slave Narrative." *Studies in Short Fiction* 34.3 (1997): 289–305.

"The Diary of an African Nun"

Fontenot, Chester J. "Alice Walker: 'The Diary of an African Nun' and Dubois' Double Consciousness." *Journal of Afro-American Issues* 5 (1977): 192–96.

Fontenot, Chester J. "Alice Walker: 'The Diary of an African Nun' and Du Bois' Double Consciousness." *Sturdy Black Bridges: Vision of Black Women in Literature.* Eds. Roseann P. Bell, et al. Garden City, NY: Doubleday, 1979. 150–56.

"Everyday Use"

Baker, Houston A., Jr., and Charlotte Pierce-Baker. "Patches: Quilts and Community in Alice Walker's 'Everyday Use'." *Southern Review* 21.3 (1985): 706–20.

Baker, Houston A., Jr., and Charlotte Pierce-Baker. "Patches: Quilts and Community in Alice Walker's 'Everyday Use'." *Alice Walker: "Everyday Use."* New Brunswick, NJ: Rutgers UP, 1994. 149–65.

Bauer, Margaret D. "Alice Walker: Another Southern Writer Criticizing Codes Not Put to 'Everyday Use'." *Studies in Short Fiction* 29.2 (1992): 143–51.

Byrne, Mary Ellen. "Welty's 'A Worn Path' and Walker's 'Everyday Use': Companion Pieces." *Teaching English in Two-Year Colleges* 16.2 (1989): 129–33.

Christian, Barbara T. "Alice Walker: The Black Woman Artist as Wayward." *Alice Walker: "Everyday Use."* Ed. Barbara T. Christian. New Brunswick, NJ: Rutgers UP, 1994.

Christian, Barbara T., ed. *Alice Walker: "Everyday Use."* New Brunswick, NJ: Rutgers UP, 1994.

Cowart, David. "Heritage and Deracination in Walker's 'Everyday Use'." *Studies in Short Fiction* 33.2 (1996): 171–81.

Davis, Thadious M. "Alice Walker's Celebration of Self in Southern Generations." *Alice Walker: "Everyday Use."* New Brunswick, NJ: Rutgers UP, 1994. 105–21.

Gruesser, John. "Walker's 'Everyday Use'." *Explicator* 61.3 (2003): 183–85.

Kane, Patricia. "The Prodigal Daughter in Alice Walker's 'Everyday Use'." *Notes on Contemporary Literature* 15.2 (1985): 7.

Kelley, Margot Anne. "Sisters' Choices: Quilting Aesthetics in Contemporary African-American Women's Fiction." *Alice Walker: "Everyday Use."* New Brunswick, NJ: Rutgers UP, 1994. 167–94.

Noe, Marcia. "Teaching Alice Walker's 'Everyday Use': Employing Race, Class, and Gender, with an Annotated Bibliography." *Eureka Studies in Teaching Short Fiction* 5.1 (2004): 123–36.

Showalter, Elaine. "Common Threads." *Alice Walker: "Everyday Use."* Ed. Barbara T. Christian. New Brunswick, NJ: Rutgers UP, 1994. 195–224.

Tate, Claudia C. "*Everyday Use.*" *African American Review* 30 (1996): 308–9.

Tuten, Nancy. "Alice Walker's 'Everyday Use'." *Explicator* 51.2 (1993): 125–28.

Wilson, Charles E., Jr. "'Everyday Use' and *Incidents in the Life of a Slave Girl*: Escaping Antebellum Confinement." *Southern Mothers: Fact and Fictions in Southern Women's Writing.* Eds. Nagueyalti Warren, et al. Baton Rouge: Louisiana State UP, 1999. 169–81.

Whitsitt, Sam. "In Spite of It All: A Reading of Alice Walker's 'Everyday Use'." *African American Review* 34.3 (2000): 443–59.

"The Flowers"

Loeb, Monica. "Walker's 'The Flowers'." *Explicator* 55.1 (1996): 60–62.

In Love and Trouble, Stories of Black Women

Hubbard, Dolan. "Society and Self in Alice Walker's *In Love and Trouble.*" *American Women Short Story Writers: A Collection of Critical Essays.* Ed. Julie Brown. New York: Garland, 1995. 209–33.

"Nineteen Fifty-Five"

Crosland, Andy. "Alice Walker's 'Nineteen Fifty-Five': Fiction and Fact." *English Language Notes* 31.2 (1996): 59–63.

Douglas, Jackie. "'Nineteen Fifty-Five': A Second Opinion." *Journal of College Writing* 4.1 (2001): 103–6.

Mickelsen, David J. "'You Ain't Never Caught a Rabbit': Covering and Signifyin' in Alice Walker's 'Nineteen Fifty-Five'." *Southern Quarterly: A Journal of the Arts in the South* 42.3 (2004): 5–20.

"The Revenge of Hannah Kemhuff"

Navarro, Mary L., and Mary H. Sims. "Settling the Dust: Tracking Zora through Alice Walker's 'The Revenge of Hannah Kemhuff'." *Alice Walker and Zora Neale Hurston: The Common Bond.* Ed. Lillie P. Howard. Westport, CT: Greenwood, 1993. 21–29.

"Strong Horse Tea"

Winchell, Mark Royden. "Fetching the Doctor: Shamanistic House Calls in Alice Walker's "Strong Horse Tea." *Mississippi Folklore Register* 15.2 (1981): 97–101.

"To Hell with Dying"

Hollister, Michael. "Tradition in Alice Walker's 'To Hell with Dying'." *Studies in Short Fiction* 26.1 (1989): 90–91.

SECONDARY SOURCES

Books

Awkward, Michael. *Inspiriting Influences: Tradition, Revision, and Afro-American Women's Novels.* New York: Columbia UP, 1991.

Bell, Bernard. *The Afro-American Novel and Its Tradition.* Amherst, MA: U of Massachussets P, 1987.

Bloom, Harold, ed. *Alice Walker.* New York: Chelsea, 1989.

Butler, Judith. *Gender Trouble: Feminism and the Subversion of Identity.* New York: Routledge, 1990.

Butler-Evans, Elliott. *Race, Gender, and Desire: Narrative Strategies in the Fiction of Toni Cade Bambara, Toni Morrison, and Alice Walker.* Philadelphia: Temple UP, 1989.

Christian, Barbara T., ed. *Alice Walker: "Everyday Use."* New Brunswick, NJ: Rutgers UP, 1994.

Cooper, Anna Julia. *A Voice from the South, By a Black Woman of the South.* 1892. Ed. Henry Louis Gates Jr. New York: Oxford UP, 1988.

Crafts, Hannah. *The Bondwoman's Narrative.* Ed. Henry Louis Gates Jr. and Hollis Robbins Warner. New York: Oxford UP, 2002.

Davenport, Kiana. *Shark Dialogues.* New York: Plume, 1995.

Davis, Charles T., and Henry Louis Gates Jr. *The Slave's Narrative.* New York: Oxford UP, 1985.

Dieke, Ikenna, ed. *Critical Essays on Alice Walker.* Westport, CT: Greenwood, 1999.

Gates, Henry Louis Jr., ed. *Reading Black, Reading Feminist: A Critical Anthology.* New York: Meridian, 1990.

Gates, Henry Louis Jr., and Hollis Robbins, ed. *In Search of Hannah Crafts: The Bondwoman's Narrative.* New York: BasicCivitas, 2004.

Giddings, Paula. *When and Where I Enter: The Impact of Black Women on Race and Sex in America.* New York: Morrow, 1984.

Gourdine, Angeletta. *The Difference Place Makes: Gender, Sexuality and Diaspora Identity.* Columbus: Ohio State UP, 2003.

Graham, Maryemma, ed. *The Cambridge Companion to the African American Novel.* Cambridge, England: Cambridge UP, 2004.

Harner, Michael. *The Way of the Shaman.* New York: Harper, 1980.

Hite, Molly. *The Other Side of the Story: Structures and Strategies of Contemporary Feminist Narratives.* Ithaca: Cornell UP, 1989.

hooks, bell. *Feminist Theory from Margin to Center.* Boston: South End, 1984.

Howard, Lillie P., ed. *Alice Walker and Zora Neale Hurston: The Common Bond.* Westport, CT: Greenwood, 1993.

Hudson-Weems, Clenora. *Africana Womanism: Reclaiming Ourselves.* 2nd ed. Troy, MI: Bedford, 1994.

Hull, Gloria T., Patricia Bell Scott, and Barbara Smith, ed. *All the Women Are White, All the Blacks Are Men, but Some of Us Are Brave: Black Women's Studies.* New York: Feminist, 1992.

Johnson, Yvonne. *The Voices of African American Women: The Use of Narrative and Authorial Voice in the Works of Harriet Jacobs, Zora Neale Hurston, and Alice Walker.* New York: Lang, 1998.

Lightfoot-Klein, Hanny. *Prisoners of Ritual: An Odyssey into Female Genital Circumcision in Africa.* New York: Harrington Park, 1989.

Logan, Rayford W., and Irving S. Cohen. *The American Negro: Old World Background and New World Experience.* New York: Houghton, 1967.

Lorde, Audre. *Sister Outsider: Essays and Speeches.* New York: Crossing, 1984.

Neihardt, John G. *Black Elk Speaks.* 1932. Lincoln: U of Nebraska P, 1972.

Nelson, Emmanuel S. *African American Autobiographers: A Sourcebook.* Westport, CT: Greenwood, 2002.

Quarles, Benjamin. *The Negro in the Making of America.* 3rd ed. New York: Touchstone, 1987.

Shelton, Austin J., ed. *"The 'Old' Life." The African Assertion: A Critical Anthology of African Literature.* New York: Odyssey, 1968.

Showalter, Elaine. *A Literature of Their Own: British Women Novelists from Bronte to Lessing.* Princeton: Princeton UP, 1977.

van Sertima, Ivan. *They Came Before Columbus: The African Presence in Ancient America.* New York: Random, 1976.

Wall, Cheryl A., ed. *Changing Our Own Words: Essays on Criticism, Theory, and Writing by Black Women*. New Brunswick: Rutgers UP, 1989.

Wexler, Sanford. *The Civil Rights Movement: An Eyewitness History*. New York: Facts of File, 1993.

White, Vernessa C. *Afro-American and East German Fiction*. New York: Lang, 1983.

Book Articles

Adisa, Opal Palmer. "A Writer/Healer: Literature, a Blueprint for Healing." *Healing Culture: Art and Rligion as Curative Practices in the Caribbean and Its Diaspora*. Ed. Olmos Fernández, et al. New York: Palgrave, 2001. 179–93.

Allan, Tuzyline-Jita. "A Voice of One's Own: Implications of Impersonality in the Essays of Virginia Woolf and Alice Walker." *The Politics of the Essay: Feminist Perspectives*. Eds. Ruth Ellen Boetcher Joeres, et al. Bloomington: Indiana UP, 1993. 131–47.

Appiah, Kwame Anthony, and Henry Louis Gates Jr., ed. "Mexico." *Africana: The Encyclopedia of the African and African American Experience*. New York: Basic, 1999. 1293–98.

Baker, Houston A. Jr. "There Is No More Beautiful Way: Theory and Poetics of Afro-American Women's Writing." *Afro-American Literary Study in the 1990s*. Ed. Houston A. Baker Jr. and Patricial Redmond. Chicago: U of Chicago P, 1989. 135–63.

Barnes, Paula C. "Alice Walker (1944–)." *African American Autobiographers: A Sourcebook*. Ed. Emmanuel S. Nelson. Westport, CT: Greenwood, 2002. 360–64.

Bauer, Margaret D. "When a Convent Seems the Only Viable Choice: Questionable Callings in Stories by Alice Dunbar-Nelson, Alice Walker, and Louise Erdrich." *Critical Essays on Alice Walker*. Ed. Ikenna Dieke. Westport, CT: Greenwood, 1999.

Bochman, Andrew A. "The Inscription of Violence and Historical Recovery." *The Image of Violence in Literature, the Media, and Society*. Eds. Will Wright and Steven Kaplan. Pueblo, CO: Society for the Interdisciplinary Study of Social Imagery, 1995. 302–6.

Brock, Sabine, and Anne Koenen. "Alice Walker in Search of Zora Neale Hurston: Rediscovering a Black Female Tradition." History and Tradition in Afro-American Culture. Ed. Gunter H. Lenz. Frankfurt: Campus, 1981. 167–80. [Germany]

Byerman, Keith. "Gender and Justice: Alice Walker and the Sexual Politics of Civil Rights." *The World Is Our Culture: Society and Culture in Contemporary Southern Writing*. Eds. Jeffrey J. Folks and Nancy Summers Folks. Lexington: UP of Kentucky, 2000.

Christian, Barbara. "Alice Walker: The Black Woman Artist as Wayward." *Black Women Writers 1950–1980: A Critical Evaluation*. Ed. Mari Evans. Garden City, NY: Anchor, 1984. 457–77.

Christian, Barbara T. "Alice Walker." *The History of Southern Women's Literature.* Ed. Carolyn Perry, et al. Baton Rouge: Louisiana State UP, 2002. 563–69.

Christian, Barbara T. "Alice Walker: The Black Woman Artist as Wayward." *Alice Walker: "Everyday Use."* Ed. Barbara T. Christian. New Brunswick, NJ: Rutgers UP, 1994. 123–47.

Coleman, Jeffrey Lamar. "Revolutionary Stanzas: The Civil and Human Rights Poetry of Alice Walker." *Critical Essays on Alice Walker.* Ed. Ikenna Dieke. Westport, CT: Greenwood, 1999.

Courington, Chella. "Virginia Woolf and Alice Walker: Family as Metaphor in the Personal Essay." *Virginia Woolf: Emerging Perspectives.* Ed. Mark Hussey and Vara Neverow. New York: Pace UP, 1994. 239–45.

Dieke, Ikenna. "Alice Walker: Poesy and the Earthling Psyche." *Critical Essays on Alice Walker.* Ed. Ikenna Dieke. Westport, CT: Greenwood, 1999.

Fernald, Anne. "A Room, A Child, A Mind of One's Own: Virginia Woolf, Alice Walker and Feminist Personal Criticism." *Virginia Woolf: Emerging Perspectives.* Eds. Mark Hussey and Vara Neverow. New York: Pace UP, 1994. 245–51.

Gates, Henry Louis, Jr. "Color Me Zora: Alice Walker's (Re)Writing of the Speakerly Text." *Intertextuality and Contemporary American Fiction.* Eds. Patrick O'Donnell and Robert Con Davis. Baltimore: Johns Hopkins UP, 1989. 144–67.

Grewal, Inderpal. "Warrior Marks: Global Womanism's Neo-Colonial Discourse in a Multicultural Context." *Keyframes: Popular Cinema and Cultural Studies.* Ed. Matthew Tinkcom, et al. London, England: Routledge, 2001. 52–71.

Grimes, Dorothy. "Mariama Ba's *So Long a Letter* and Alice Walker's *In Search of Our Mothers' Gardens:* A Senegalese and an African American Perspective on 'Womanism'." *Global Perspectives on Teaching Literature: Shared Visions and Distinctive Visions.* Eds. Sandra Ward Lott, et al. Urbana, IL: National Council of Teachers of English, 1993. 65–76.

Harley, Sharon. "The Middle Class." *Black Women in America: An Historical Encyclopedia.* Ed. Darlene Clark Hine, Elsa Barkley Brown, and Rosalyn Terborg-Penn. Vol. 2. New York: Carlson, 1993. 2 vols. 786–89.

Harris, Trudier. "Three Black Women Writers and Humanism: A Folk Perspective." *Black American Literature and Humanism.* Ed. R. Baxter Miller. Lexington: UP of Kentucky, 1981. 50–74.

Harris, Trudier. "Our People, Our People." *Alice Walker and Zora Neale Hurston: The Common Bond.* Ed. Lillie P. Howard. Westport, CT: Greenwood, 1993. 31–42.

Hedges, Elaine. "The Needle or the Pen: The Literary Rediscovery of Women's Textile Work." *Tradition and the Talents of Women.* Ed. Florence Howe. Urbana: U of Illinois P, 1991. 338–64.

Henke, Suzette A. "Women's Life-Writing and the Minority Voice: Maya Angelou, Maxine Hong Kingston, and Alice Walker." *Traditions, Voices, and Dreams: The American Novel since the 1960s.* Eds. Melvin J. Friedman and Ben Siegel. Newark: U of Delaware P, 1995. 210–33.

Hughes, Langston. "The Negro Artist and the Racial Mountain." *The Nation* 23 June 1923. Reprinted in Henry Louis Gates Jr. and Nellie Y. McKay, ed. *The Norton Anthology of African American Literature.* 2nd ed. New York: Norton, 2004. 1311–14.

Kanneh, Kadiatu. "'Africa' and Cultural Translation: Reading Difference." *Cultural Readings of Imperialism: Edward Said and the Gravity of History.* Eds. Pearson Keith Ansell, et al. New York: St. Martin's, 1997. 267–89.

Karrer, Wolfgang. "Nostalgia, Amnesia, and Grandmothers: The Uses of Memory in Albert Murray, Sabine Ulibarri, Paula Gunn Allen, and Alice Walker." *Memory, Narrative, and Identity: New Essays in Ethnic American Literatures.* Eds. Amritjit Singh, et al. Boston: Northeastern UP, 1994. 128–44.

Kenyon, Olga. "Alice Walker and Buchi Emecheta Rewrite the Myth of Motherhood." *Forked Tongues? Comparing Twentieth-Century British and American Literature.* Eds. Ann Massa and Alistair Stead. London: Longman, 1994. 336–54.

Kester, Gunilla. T. "The Blues, Healing, and Cultural Representation in Contemporary African American Women's Literature." *Women Healers and Physicians: Climbing a Long Hill.* Ed. Lilian R. Furst. Lexington: UP of Kentucky, 1997. 114–27.

Kieti, Nwikali. "Homesick and Eurocentric? Alice Walker's Africa." *Of Dreams Deferred, Dead or Alive: African Perspectives on African-American Writers.* Ed. Ade Femi Ojo. Westport, CT: Greenwood, 1996. 157–69.

King, Lovalerie. "African American Womanism: From Zora Neale Hurston to Alice Walker." *The Cambridge Companion to the African American Novel.* Ed. Maryemma Graham. Cambridge, England: Cambridge UP, 2004. 233–52.

Kubitschek, Missy Dehn. "Subjugated Knowledge: Toward a Feminist Exploration of Rape in Afro-American Fiction." *Black Feminist Criticism and Critical Theory.* Eds. Joe Weixlmann and Houston A. Baker Jr. Greenwood, FL: Penkevill, 1988. 43–56.

Larson, Angela. "An Adamantine Emotion." *The Image of Violence in Literature, the Media, and Society.* Eds. Will Wright and Steven Kaplan. Pueblo, CO: Society for the Interdisciplinary Study of Social Imagery, 1995. 443–47.

Lauret, Maria. "'I've Got a Right To Sing the Blues': Alice Walker's Aesthetic." *Dixie Debates: Perspectives on Southern Culture.* Eds. Richard H. King and Helen Taylor. New York: New York UP, 1996. 51–66.

Manvi, Meera. "The Second Reconstruction and the Southern Writer: Alice Walker and William Kelley." *Literature and Politics in Twentieth Century America.* Eds. J.L. Plakkoottam and Prashant K. Sinha. Hyderabad: American Studies Research Centre, 1993. 92–98. [India]

Marshall, Paule. "Characterizations of Black Women in the American Novel." *In the Memory and Spirit of Frances, Zora, and Lorraine: Essays and Interviews on Black Women and Writing.* Ed. Juliette Bowles. Washington, DC: Institute for the Arts & the Humanities, 1979. 76–79.

McDowell, Deborah E. "New Directions for Black Feminist Criticism." *The New Feminist Criticism: Essays on Women, Literature, and Theory.* Ed. Elaine Showalter. New York: Pantheon, 1985. 186–99.

Murphy, Patrick D. "Voicing Another Nature." *A Dialogue of Voices: Feminist Literary Theory and Bakhtin.* Eds. Karen Hohne and Helen Wussow. Minneapolis: U of Minnesota P, 1994. 59–82.

O'Connor, Mary. "Subject, Voice, and Women in Some Contemporary Black American Women's Writing." *Feminism, Bakhtin, and the Dialogic.* Eds. Dale M. Bauer and Susan Jaret McKinstry. Albany: State U of New York P, 1991. 199–217.

Palumbo-Liu, David. "The Politics of Memory: Remembering History in Alice Walker and Joy Kogawa." *Memory and Cultural Politics: New Approaches to American Ethnic Literatures.* Eds. Joseph T. Skerrett Jr. and Robert E. Hogan. Boston: Northeastern UP, 1996. 211–26.

Payant, Katherine B. "Female Friendship in Contemporary Bildungsroman." *Communication and Women's Friendships: Parallels and Intersections in Literature and Life.* Eds. Janet Doubler Ward and JoAnna Stephens Mink. Bowling Green, OH: Popular, 1993. 151–63.

Pullin, Faith. "Landscapes of Reality: The Fiction of Contemporary Afro-American Women." *Black Fiction: New Studies in the Afro-American Novel since 1945.* Ed. Robert A. Lee. New York: Barnes and Noble, 1980. 173–203.

Reddy, Maureen T. "Maternal Reading: Lazarre and Walker." *Narrating Mothers: Theorizing Maternal Subjectivites.* Eds. Brenda O. Daly and Maureen T. Reddy. Knoxville: U of Tennessee P, 1991. 222–38.

Restuccia, Frances L. "Literary Representations of Battered Women: Spectacular Domestic Punishment." *Bodies of Writing, Bodies in Performance.* Eds. Carol Siegel, et al. New York: New York UP, 1996. 42–71.

Saunders, Sylvia. "African Tales and Myths." *Humanities in the Ancient and Pre-Modern World: An Africana Emphasis.* Ed. Wendell P. Jackson, Frances Alston, Linda M. Carter, and Lillian Dunmars Roland. Needham Heights, MA: Pearson, 1999.

Schomburg, Connie R. "Southern Women Writers in a Changing Landscape." *The History of Southern Women's Literature.* Ed. Carolyn Perry, et al. Baton Rouge: Louisiana State UP, 2002. 478–90.

Schwenk, Katrin. "Lynching and Rape: Border Cases in African American History and Fiction." *The Black Columbiad: Defining Moments in African American Literature and Culture.* Eds. Werner Sollors and Maria Diedrich. Cambridge: Harvard UP, 1994. 312–24.

Smith, Barbara. "Toward a Black Feminist Criticism." *The New Feminist Criticism: Essays on Women, Literature, and Theory.* Ed. Elaine Showalter. New York: Pantheon, 1985. 168–85.

Smith, Barbara. "The Truth That Never Hurts: Black Lesbians in Fiction in the 1980s." *Feminisms: An Anthology of Literary Theory and Criticism.*

Eds. Robyn R. Warhol and Diane Price Herndl. New Brunswick, NJ: Rutgers UP, 1997. 784–806.

Spillers, Hortense J. "'The Permanent Obliquity of an In(pha)llibly Straight': In the Time of the Daughters and the Fathers." *Changing Our Own Words: Essays on Criticism, Theory, and Writing by Black Women.* Ed. Cheryl A. Wall. New Brunswick, NJ: Rutgers UP, 1989.

Stanford, Ann Folwell. "Dynamics of Change: Men and Co-Feeling in the Fiction of Zora Neale Hurston and Alice Walker." *Alice Walker and Zora Neale Hurston: The Common Bond.* Ed. Lillie P. Howard. Westport, CT: Greenwood, 1993. 109–19.

Thielmann, Pia. "Alice Walker and the 'Man Question'." *Critical Essays on Alice Walker.* Ed. Ikenna Dieke. Westport, CT: Greenwood, 1999.

Torsney, Cheryl B. "Everyday Use: My Sojourn at Parchman Farm." *The Intimate Critique: Autobiographical Literary Criticism.* Ed. Diane P. Freedman, et al. Durham, NC: Duke UP, 1993. 67–74.

Ulman, H. Lewis. "Seeing, Believing, Being, and Acting: Ethics and Self-Representation in Ecocriticism and Nature Writing." *Reading the Earth: New Directions in the Study of Literature and Environment.* Eds. Michael P. Branch, et al. Moscow: U of Idaho P, 1998. 225–33.

Wade-Gayles, Gloria. "Black, Southern, Womanist: The Genius of Alice Walker." *Southern Women Writers: The New Generation.* Ed. Tonette Bond Inge. Tuscaloosa: U of Alabama P, 1990. 301–23.

Washington, Mary Helen. "An Essay on Alice Walker." *Alice Walker: 'Everyday Use'.* Ed. Barbara T. Christian. 1994.

Washington, Mary Helen. "An Essay on Alice Walker." *Sturdy Black Bridges: Vision of Black Women in Literature.* Eds. Roseann P. Bell, et al. Garden City, NY: Doubleday, 1979. 133–49.

Washington, Mary Helen. "An Essay on Alice Walker." *Sturdy Black Bridges: Visions of Black Women in Literature.* Ed. Roseann P. Bell, Bettye J. Parker, and Beverly Guy-Sheftall. New York: Anchor, 1979. 133–49.

Washington, Mary Helen. "I Sign My Mother's Name: Alice Walker, Dorothy West, Paule Marshall." *Mothering the Mind: Twelve Studies of Writers and Their Silent Partners.* Eds. Ruth Perry and Martine Watson Brownley. New York: Holmes, 1984. 142–63.

Weston, Ruth D. "Who Touches This Touches a Woman: The Naked Self in Alice Walker." *Critical Essays on Alice Walker.* Ed. Ikenna Dieke. Westport, CT: Greenwood, 1999.

Williams, Delores S. "Black Women's Literature and the Task of Feminist Theology." *Immaculate and Powerful: The Female in Sacred Image and Social Reality.* Eds. Clarrissa W. Atkinson, et al. Boston: Beacon, 1985. 88–110.

Williams, Sherley Anne. "Some Implications of Womanist Theory." *Reading Black, Reading Feminist: A Critical Anthology.* Ed. Henry Louis Gates Jr. New York: Meridian, 1990. 68–75.

Wilson, Mary Ann. "'That Which the Soul Lives By': Spirituality in the Works of Zora Neale Hurston and Alice Walker." *Alice Walker and Zora Neale Hurston: The Common Bond.* Ed. Lillie P. Howard. Westport, CT: Greenwood, 1993. 57–67.

Worsham, Fabian Clements. "The Poetics of Matrilineage: Mothers and Daughters in the Poetry of African American Women: 1965–1985." *Women of Color: Mother-Daughter Relationships in 20th Century Literature.* Ed. Elizabeth Brown Guillory. Austin: U of Texas P, 1996. 177–81.

Journal, Magazine, and Newspaper Articles

"Alice Walker: A Special Section." *Callaloo: A Journal of African American and African Arts and Letters* 12.2 (1989): 295–345.

Barksdale, Richard K. "Castration Symbolism in Recent Black American Fiction." *College Language Association Journal* 29.4 (1986): 400–13.

Bass, Margaret Kent. "Alice's Secret." *College Language Association Journal* 28.1 (1994): 1–10.

Bauer, Margaret D. "Alice Walker: Another Southern Writer Criticizing Codes Not Put to 'Everyday Use'." *Studies in Short Fiction* 29.2 (1992): 143–51.

Buncombe, Marie H. "Androgyny as Metaphor in Alice Walker's Novels." *College Language Association Journal* 30.4 (1987): 419–27.

Byerman, Keith. "Desire and Alice Walker: The Quest for a Womanist Narrative." *Callaloo: A Journal of African American and African Arts and Letters* 12.2 (1989): 321–31.

Campbell, Jennifer. "Teaching Class: A Pedagogy and Politics for Working-Class Writing." *College Literature* 23.2 (1996): 116–30.

Carby, Hazel V. "'On the Threshold of Woman's Era': Lynching, Empire, and Sexuality in Black Feminist Theory." *Critical Inquiry* 12.1 (1985): 262–77.

Carter, Nancy Corson. "Claiming the Bittersweet Matrix: Alice Walker, Sandra Cisneros, and Adrienne Rich." *Critique: Studies in Contemporary Fiction* 35.4 (1994): 195–204.

Christian, Barbara. "The Race for Theory." *Cultural Critique* 6 (1987): 51–63.

Davis, Thadious. "Alice Walker's Celebration of Self in Southern Generations." *Southern Quarterly: A Journal of the Arts in the South* 21.4 (1983): 39–53.

Davis, Thadious. "Poetry as Preface to Fiction: Alice Walker's Recurrent Apprenticeship." *Mississippi Quarterly: The Journal of Southern Culture* 11.2 (1991): 133–42.

Duck, Leigh Anne. "Rethinking Community: Post-Plantation Literatures in Postmodernity." *Mississippi Quarterly: The Journal of Southern Cultures* 56.4 (2003): 511–19.

Erickson, Peter. "'Cast Out Alone / To Heal / And Re-Create / Ourselves': Family-Based Identity in the Work of Alice Walker." *College Language Association Journal* 23 (1979): 71–94.

Estes, David C. "Alice Walker's 'Strong Horse Tea': Folk Cures for the Dispossessed."
 Southern Folklore 50.3 (1993): 213–29.

Estes-Hicks, Onita. "The Way We Were: Precious Memories of the Black Segregated
 South." *African American Review* 27.1 (1993): 9–18.

Fike, Matthew. "Jean Toomer and Okot p'Bitek in Alice Walker's 'In Search of Our
 Mothers' Gardens'." *MELUS: Journal of the Society for the Study of the Multi-
 Ethnic Literature of the United States* 25.3–4 (2000): 141–60.

Fishman, Charles. "Naming Names: Three Recent Novels by Women Writers."
 Names: A Journal of Onomastics 32.1 (1984): 33–44.

Freeman, Alma S. "Zora Neale Hurston and Alice Walker: A Spiritual Kinship."
 Sage: A Scholarly Journal on Black Women 2.1 (1985): 37–40.

Friedman, Sandra, and Alec Irwin. "Christian Feminism, Eros, and Power in
 Right Relation." *Cross Currents: The Journal of the Association for Religion and
 Intellectual Life* 10.3 (1990): 387–405.

Froula, Christine. "The Daughter's Seduction: Sexual Violence and Literary
 History." *Signs: Journal of Women in Culture and Society* 11.4 (1986): 621–44.

Gardiner, Judith Kegan. "Empathic Ways of Reading: Narcissism, Cultural
 Politics, and Russ's Female Man." *Feminist Studies* 20.1 (1994): 87–111.

George, Olakunle. "Alice Walker's Africa: Globalization and the Province of
 Fiction." *Comparative Literature* 53.4 (2001): 354–72.

Gerhardt, Christine. "The Greening of African-American Landscapes: Where
 Ecocriticism Meets Post-Colonial Theory." *Mississippi Quarterly: The Journal
 of Southern Cultures* 55.4 (2002): 515–33.

Grewal, Inderpal, and Caren Kaplan. "Warrior Marks: Global Womanism's Neo-
 Colonial Discourse in a Multicultural Context." *Camera Obscura: A Journal
 of Feminism, Culture, and Media Studies* 39 (1996): 4–33.

Grimes, Dorothy G. "'Womanist Prose' and the Quest for Community in American
 Culture." *Journal of American Culture* 15.2 (1992): 19–24.

Gussow, Mel. "Once Again, Alice Walker Is Ready to Embrace Her Freedom to
 Change." *New York Times* 26 Dec. 2000, E1.

Harris, Trudier. "Folklore in the Fiction of Alice Walker: A Perpetuation of
 Historical and Literary Traditions." *Black American Literature Forum* 11
 (1977): 3–8.

Homans, Margaret. "'Her Very Own Howl': The Ambiguities of Representation in
 Recent Women's Fiction." *Signs: Journal of Women in Culture and Society* 9.2
 (1983): 186–205.

Houser, Catherine. "Missing in Action: Alienation in the Fiction of Award-
 Winning Women Writers." *Mid-American Review* 14.2 (1994): 33–39.

Hubert, Linda. "To Alice Walker: Carson McCullers' Legacy of Love." *Pembroke
 Magazine* 20 (1988): 89–95.

Iannone, Carol. "A Turning of the Critical Tide?" *Commentary*, Nov. 1989: 57–59.

Irwin, Edward E. "Freedoms as Value in Three Popular Southern Novels." *Proteus:
 A Journal of Ideas* 6.1 (1989): 37–41.

Johnson, Maria V. "'You Just Can't Keep a Good Woman Down': Alice Walker Sings the Blues." *African American Review* 30.2 (1996): 221–36.

Keating, Gail. "Alice Walker: In Praise of Maternal Heritage." *Literary Griot: International Journal of Black Expressive Cultural Studies* 6.1 (1991): 26–37.

Kim, Min-Jung. "'Creative Mistranslation?': Adaptation as Violence." *Feminist Studies in English Literature* 9.2 (2002): 49–76.

Korenman, Joan S. "African-American Women Writers, Black Nationalism, and the Matrilineal Heritage." *College Language Association Journal* 38.2 (1994): 143–61.

Krauth, Leland. "Mark Twain, Alice Walker, and the Aesthetics of Joy." *Proteus: A Journal of Ideas* 1.2 (1984): 9–14.

Kuhlmann, Deborah J. "Alice Walker's Secret of Joy: The Role of the Artist." *Griot: Official Journal of the Southern Conference on Afro American Studies* 14.2 (1995): 21–27.

Kuhne, Dave. "Alice Walker's African Connection." *Conference of College Teachers of English Studies* 63 (1998): 69–76.

Lenhart, Georgann. "Inspired Purple?" *Notes on Contemporary Literature* 14.3 (1984): 2–3.

Lupton, Mary Jane. "Clothes and Closure in Three Novels by Black Women." *Black American Literature Forum* 20.4 (1986): 409–21.

Mainino, Wirba Ibrahim. "The Problem of Language in Modern Feminist Fiction by BlackWomen: Alice Walker and Calixthe Beyala." *New Literatures Review* 37 (2000): 59–74.

Manzulli, Mia. "Edith Wharton's Gardens as a Legacy to Alice Walker." *Edith Wharton Review* 11.2 (1994): 9–12.

McDowell, Deborah E. "'The Changing Same': Generational Connections and Black Women Novelists." *New Literary History: A Journal of Theory and Interpretation* 18.2 (1987): 281–302.

McDowell, Margaret B. "The Black Woman as Artist and Critic: Four Versions." *Kentucky Review* 7.1 (1987): 19–41.

Menke, Pamela Glenn. "'Hard Glass Mirrors' and Soul Memory: Vision Imagery and Gender in Ellison, Baldwin, Morrison, and Walker." *West Virginia University Philological Papers* 38 (1992): 163–70.

Mitgang, Herbert. "Alice Walker Recalls the Civil Rights Battle." *New York Times* 16 Apr. 1983 <http://www.nytimes.com/books/98/10/04/specials/walker-civil.html.>

Nowik, Nan. "Mixing Art and Politics: The Writings of Adrienne Rich, Marge Piercy, and Alice Walker." *Centennial Review* 30.2 (1986): 208–18.

Petry, Alice Hall. "Alice Walker: The Achievement of the Short Fiction." *Modern Language Studies* 19.1 (1989): 12–27.

Phillips, Rebecca. "The Thousand and First Face of the Hero." *Bulletin of the West Virginia Association of College English Teachers* 13.2 (1991): 91–102.

Pratt, Louis H. "Alice Walker's Men: Profiles in the Quest for Love and Personal Values." *Studies in Popular Culture* 12.1 (1989): 12–57.

Preble, Niemi Oralia. "Magical Realism and the Great Goddess in Two Novels by Alejo Carpentier and Alice Walker." *Comparatist: Journal of the Southern Comparative Literature Association* 16 (1992): 101–14.

Royster, Philip M. "In Search of Our Fathers' Arms: Alice Walker's Persona of the Alienated Darling." *Black American Literature Forum* 20.4 (1986): 347–70.

Sadoff, Dianne F. "Black Matrilineage: The Case of Alice Walker and Zora Neale Hurston." *Signs: Journal of Women in Culture and Society* 11.1 (1985): 4–26.

Segrest, Mab. "Rebirths of a U.S. Nation: Race and Gendering of the Nation State." *Mississippi Quarterly: The Journal of Southern Cultures* 57.1 (2003–2004): 26–40.

Smith, Felipe. "Alice Walker's Redemptive Art." *African American Review* 26.3 (1992): 437–51.

Smith, Pamela A. "Green Lap, Brown Embrace, Blue Body: The Ecospirituality of Alice Walker." *Cross Currents: The Journal of the Association for Religion and Intellectual Life* 48.4 (1998–1999): 471–87.

Stade, George. "Womanist Fiction and Male Characters." *Partisan Review* 52.3 (1985): 264–70.

Tharp, Julie. "Ideology and Eros: An Approach to Writing by Women of Color." *West Virginia University Philological Papers* 38 (1992): 236–45.

Turner, Darwin. "A Spectrum of Blackness." *Parnassus: Poetry in Review* 4.2 (1976): 202–18.

Vanessa, E. "Walker's Way Her New Collection Binds Memoir and Fiction, Capturing the South She Left." *Boston Globe* 11 Oct. 2000, C1.

Walker, Robbie Jean. "Implications for Survival: Coping Strategies of the Women in Alice Walker's Novels." *College Language Association Journal* 30.1 (1987): 401–18.

Walker, Robbie Jean. "Implications for Survival: Coping Strategies of the Women in Alice Walker's Novels." *Explorations in Ethnic Studies: Journal of the National Association for Ethnic Studies* 10.1 (1987): 9–21.

Ward, Cynthia. "Reading African Women Readers." *Research in African Literatures* 27.3 (1996): 78–86.

Warren, Nagueyalti, and Sally Wolff. "'Like the Pupil of an Eye': Sexual Blinding of Women in Alice Walker's Works." *Southern Literary Journal* 31.1 (1998): 1–16.

Washington, J. Charles. "Positive Black Male Images in Alice Walker's Fiction." *Obsidian II: Black Literature in Review* 3.1 (1988): 23–48.

Washington, Mary Helen. "Black Women Image Makers." *Black World* 23.10 (1974): 10–18.

Waxman, Barbara Frey. "Dancing out of Form, Dancing into Self: Genre and Metaphor in Marshall, Shange, and Walker." *MELUS: Journal of the Society for the Study of the Multi-Ethnic Literature of the United States* 19.3 (1994): 91–106.

Weston, Ruth D. "Who Touches This Touches a Woman: The Naked Self in Alice Walker." *Weber Studies: An Interdisciplinary Humanities Journal* 9.2 (1992): 49–60.

White, Evelyn C. "Alice Walker's Compassionate Crusade." *Sojourner: The Women's Forum* 19.7 (1994): 1H–2H.

Willis, Susan. "Alice Walker's Women." *New Orleans Review* 12.1 (1985): 33–41.

Winchell, Mark Royden. "Fetching the Doctor: Shamanistic House Calls in Alice Walker's 'Strong Horse Tea'." *Mississippi Folklore Register* 15.2 (1981): 97–101.

Yeo, Jae-Hyuk. "Alice Walker: Community, Quilting and Sewing." *Studies in Modern Fiction* 8.2 (2001): 111–35.

Zeiger, William. "The Circular Journey and the Natural Authority of Form." *Rhetoric Review* 8.2 (1990): 208–19.

Video

A Conversation with Alice Walker. Dir. Matteo Bellinelli. Narr. Edwina Moore. Videocasette. San Francisco: California Newsreel, 1992.

My Life As Myself. Alice Walker. Videocasette. Boulder, CO: Sounds True Audio, 1996.

Index

About the Author

GERRI BATES is Associate Professor of English, African American Literature, and Women's Literature at Bowie State University in Bowie, Maryland. She is a founding member of the Middle Atlantic Writers Association and author of numerous articles on African American literature.

.

Critical Companions to Popular Contemporary Writers
First Series—*also available on CD-ROM*